Advance Praise for *Mastering Alliance Strategy*

"*Mastering Alliance Strategy* is a must-read for anyone in corporate or business unit management who is contemplating a strategic alliance or who wants to improve or exit a current alliance."
— Jon T. Elsasser, senior vice president, corporate development, The Timken Company

"I am fascinated! This is one of those rare books delivering valuable learning for both newcomers and experienced alliance pioneers such as Lufthansa, a cobuilder of Star Alliance. The book covers the whole alliance life cycle, providing winning strategies, timeless principles, simple tools, and compelling real-life examples."
— Thomas Sattelberger, executive vice president, product and service, Lufthansa German Airlines

"In today's network organizations, you need to manage without command and control. Written clearly, realistically, and full of insights, this is must reading on both sides of the Pacific."
— Hiroyuki Itami, professor, Hitotsubashi University, Japan

"The authors have the deep knowledge and capability to help large corporations get alliance strategy and execution right. This book brings all the insights, processes, and tools together in one place, and provides a road map for exceptional implementation."
— Patrick Canavan, senior vice president for global governance, Motorola

"Provides a wealth of concrete and practical insight and advice on how to get the best possible results from strategic alliances. It is based on fascinating examples and draws on the work of leading experts on managing strategic alliances."
— Yves Doz, professor, INSEAD; coauthor, *Alliance Advantage*

"We can't do it alone; for most businesses we must have allies. This book brings experience, insight, and wisdom to elevate the management of strategic alliances into a major source of value for all businesses."
— Thomas C. MacAvoy, Darden School, University of Virginia; vice chairman (retired), Corning Inc.; coauthor, *Alliance Competence*

"This is not just another book on business combinations. The concept of 'alliance strategy' is invaluable in making us focus on the whole strategy, not just on a single transaction. It is a must-read in today's world of industry consolidation and global commerce."
— Nita Seelinger, president, DuPont Food Industry Solutions

"Unique in depth and breadth of coverage, this book is at once practical and rigorous. It brings together some of the best ideas from the invaluable *Alliance Analyst* and will benefit anyone seeking to understand alliance strategy."
—Ranjay Gulati, professor, Kellogg School of Management, Northwestern University

"Alliances are now a fact of life for business, an important piece of current operations as well as future strategy. Ben Gomes-Casseres has long been a knowledgeable guide to the challenging world of partnering, helping many companies get value from their alliances."
—Rosabeth Moss Kanter, professor, Harvard Business School; best-selling author of *Evolve!: Succeeding in the Digital Culture of Tomorrow*

"As in other sectors of the economy, alliances will be crucial to the success of hospitals too. The authors expertly cover the salient elements for hospital senior leadership to understand, direct, and navigate this relatively new strategy in their organizations."
—William A. Himmelsbach, executive officer, VHA Metro LLC; senior vice president, VHA Inc.

"Years of focus on the evolution of business alliances have given the authors deep insight on this powerful global development. Readers will appreciate the growing complexity of these alliances and the value to be gained from their serious study."
—William S. Edgerly, chairman emeritus, State Street Corporation

"This book provides an important and very useful perspective on alliance strategy. No other book that I have read provides such a comprehensive and practical approach to this important topic."
—Lynda Applegate, professor, Harvard Business School

"A must-read for any executive responsible for planning, choosing, managing, or implementing a business alliance. Provides invaluable tips, tools, and guidance in a how-to format that will serve as a ready reference for years. Buy this book now . . . your competitors are not waiting for the paperback!"
—Michael J. Bellissimo, director, alliance operations, iPlanet—a Sun | Netscape Alliance

Mastering Alliance Strategy

Mastering Alliance Strategy

A Comprehensive Guide to Design, Management, and Organization

James D. Bamford
Benjamin Gomes-Casseres
Michael S. Robinson

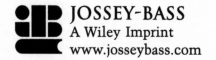
JOSSEY-BASS
A Wiley Imprint
www.josseybass.com

Published by Jossey-Bass
A Wiley Imprint
989 Market Street, San Francisco, CA 94103-1741   www.josseybass.com

Jossey-Bass books and products are available through most bookstores. To contact Jossey-Bass directly call our Customer Care Department within the U.S. at 800-956-7739, outside the U.S. at 317-572-3986 or fax 317-572-4002.

Jossey-Bass also publishes its books in a variety of electronic formats. Some content that appears in print may not be available in electronic books.

Library of Congress Cataloging-in-Publication Data

Bamford, James D., 1965–
  Mastering alliance strategy : a comprehensive guide to design, management, and organization / James D. Bamford, Benjamin Gomes-Casseres, Michael S. Robinson.
      p. cm. — (The Jossey-Bass business & management series)
  Includes bibliographical references and index.
  ISBN 0-7879-6462-X (perm. paper)
  1. Strategic alliances (Business)   2. Strategic alliances (Business)—Case studies.   I. Gomes-Casseres, Benjamin.   II. Robinson, Michael S.   III. Title.   IV. Series.
  HD69.S8 B36 2002
  658'.044—dc21
                                                    2002012105

Printed in the United States of America

FIRST EDITION
HB Printing   10 9 8 7 6 5 4 3 2 1

The Jossey-Bass
Business & Management Series

Contents

Part Two: Managing Alliances
Working Together

Leading the Relationship

Getting Out

Part Three: Competing in Constellations
Managing Networks

For Carol Lynn, Elliott, and Alex

For Susan and Rachel

For Kristine, Emma, Olivia, and Madeline

Acknowledgments

Every book is the work of a team, but this one is more so than most. Our team consisted not just of us, our contributors, and our publisher but also of a long stream of advisers, experts, and staff that helped shape our ideas, sharpen our judgment, and open our eyes to new perspectives. Their insights are the essence of this book.

We owe enormous gratitude to the staff of *The Alliance Analyst*— a publication that Jim Bamford and Mike Robinson founded and ran. The material for this book simply would not have existed but for the small team of writers, designers, and production staff, including Don Durfee, Cheryl Melchiorre, Marcia Meyerowitz, Jorge Sandrini, Kelly Schwab, and Demetra Taleghani. For eight years (1994–2001), they delivered a publication that had no equal in the field. The spirit of that team lives in this book.

At *The Alliance Analyst* we were also fortunate to have access to hundreds of managers, consultants, academics, and readers—all striving to make alliances work better and willing to share their thinking with us. We particularly want to thank Reginald Jones, Malcolm Riddell, and Steve Forbes for their early encouragement to embark on the publishing journey, and Charles Roussel for his friendship and enduring support. Special thanks are due to David Ernst for joint work through the years, his tenacity in engaging in content, and for his substantial contributions to this volume.

From the start, Ben Gomes-Casseres was a close adviser to *The Alliance Analyst*. He too was fortunate to learn from experts. Many colleagues at the Harvard Business School and at Brandeis University encouraged his research on alliance constellations; among them, Peter Petri, Lou Wells, and David Yoffie deserve special thanks. In teaching executives, Ben got a chance to test his ideas and in the process came to understand the managerial challenges of alliances better. Tom MacAvoy was a particularly helpful guide in this process. These teachers and audiences shaped the comprehensive conception of alliance strategy in this book.

Finally, we each are lucky to have our wives and children on our personal teams. Sometimes their questions about alliances, as observers, have prompted us to dig deeper and explain better. More often, it was simply their support, as family, that enabled us to do our best work. This book is dedicated to them.

October 2002   JAMES D. BAMFORD
Washington, D.C.

BENJAMIN GOMES-CASSERES
Lexington, Massachusetts

MICHAEL S. ROBINSON
Sydney, Australia

Mastering Alliance Strategy

Introduction

What Is Alliance Strategy?

Alliances have come of age. In the last ten years, they have gone from being a peripheral tool of management, used mostly to enter restricted overseas markets, to a centerpiece of corporate strategy and competitive advantage. Today, many companies have portfolios of twenty or more alliances—and some have more than a hundred. Because of this, it is now common to see alliances account for 20–50 percent of corporate value—whether measured in terms of revenues, assets, income, or market capitalization. Alliances are fueling the success of a wide range of firms, including British Petroleum, Eli Lilly, General Electric, Corning Glass, Federal Express, IBM, Starbucks, Cisco Systems, Millennium Pharmaceuticals, and Siebel Systems.

As alliances moved from periphery to center of corporate strategy, the discussion surrounding them changed subtly. Executives are no longer asking "Why do an alliance?" but rather "How do we make our alliances succeed?" Over the years, numerous studies have shown that between 30 percent and 70 percent of alliances fail—that is, do not meet the goals of the parent companies. Whatever the number, it is clear that in many companies alliance performance lags far behind what could and should be achieved.

How can managers improve the performance of their alliances? Those involved usually have a unique story for why their alliance is troubled; popular among the reasons cited are unclear strategies, poor partner choice, weak or unbalanced alliance economics, dysfunctional governance, clashing corporate cultures and goals, and lack of sufficient operating staff skills and parent commitment. Although these explanations for alliance failure may be true in one case or another, we believe that they are expressions of a larger syndrome: companies are taking too narrow a view of what it takes to make an alliance succeed.

A simple memory aid will help. Instead of focusing on "the strategic alliance," we believe that managers should develop a comprehensive "alliance strategy." The term *strategic alliance* stands for a deal, a new venture, an organization—often one that is announced with some fanfare. An *alliance strategy* represents much more than the deal—it is an intent, a dynamic process, and a logic that guides alliance decisions. A strategic alliance without an alliance strategy is doomed to fail. Now that alliances are central to strategy, we must adopt this more comprehensive view of how they work.

The Four Elements of Alliance Strategy

This book discusses issues and presents guidelines for management of the four key elements that should be part of every alliance strategy: alliance design, alliance management, using a constellation of alliances, and building an internal alliance capability. Representative questions in each the elements are shown in Exhibit I.1.

Alliance Design

The business strategy of a firm or division must shape its alliance strategy and, ultimately, the design of every alliance. Corning Glass has long used alliances to exploit its glass technology in different vertical markets; this meant allying with Samsung in television glass, with Dow in silicones, and with Siemens in fiber-optic cabling. Cisco Systems uses alliances to scout for new technologies, with the intent of bringing these technologies in-house if they prove successful. Even though these are very different uses for alliances, in each

EXHIBIT I.1   Issues in Alliance Strategy.

Design of an Alliance

- Why use an alliance, as opposed to relying on internal resources, acquiring a company, or buying services and products on the market?

- What is the scope of the alliance, that is, what is included and excluded? Which markets or products, technologies, and business systems does it include?

- What are the criteria and methods for selecting a partner?

- What are the options for structuring the alliance, and what effects will these structures have on governance and value sharing?

- How should the alliance be negotiated, that is, what are the priorities, who should be on the negotiating team, how will the relationship be affected by bargaining, and so on?

Management of an Alliance

- How should the relationship be launched, that is, what should be done in the first 30 to 180 days?

- What is the process for making decisions in the alliance when issues arise that have not been resolved in advance, as they surely will?

- How will operational decisions be made within the alliance, on both routine business and new strategic directions?

- How will the performance of the alliance and the relationship between the parents be measured and monitored, and how will these measures be linked to individual incentives?

- What is the process for adjusting the alliance design (or even terminating the alliance) as the partners accumulate experience working together?

Design and Management of an Alliance Constellation

- Where in the business value chain and in the market space of the company should the alliances be formed, how many alliances should there be, and of what type?

EXHIBIT I.1   Issues in Alliance Strategy, Cont'd.

- What should be the relationship among the various alliances and partners in the constellation?
- How will interactions among alliances of different divisions be identified and managed?
- How should the company's multiple linkages be structured; for example, should there be a loose network, a stand-alone consortium, or an equity joint venture?
- How will the company's constellation compete with rival constellations and to whom will added value ultimately flow?

Development of an Internal Alliance Capability
- Who in the corporation should be responsible for specific tasks in alliance design, alliance management, and in coordinating the alliance constellation?
- What skills, human resources, processes, tools, and systems are needed in each area?
- How centralized or decentralized and how formal or informal should the alliance capability be?
- How will the corporation capture and disseminate learning from its own experience with alliances?
- What will encourage incorporation of alliance thinking into the general management of each business?

---

case the role and design of the alliances is consistent with a clear business strategy. By *alliance design* we mean identifying the role of the alliance in the business strategy; setting the goals, rationale, and scope of the alliance; determining the criteria and method for selecting a partner; and crafting the structure and processes for sharing value and decision making in the alliance.

In Part One of the book, issues of alliance design are covered in two sections. The first section deals with the links between strategy and alliances. It contains perspectives and advice on how to set strategic goals for an individual alliance, how alliances add value to a strategy, and how strategy shapes the general design of an alliance. The second section deals with key challenges in selecting a partner and designing the structure of the alliance. Among these challenges are how to collaborate with a competitor, how to negotiate an alliance, how to combine the legal and business aspects of an alliance, and how to differentiate between vendors and partners.

One broad conclusion from these chapters is that alliance designers must think beyond the narrow concerns of their day-to-day functional tasks. Lawyers must understand business objectives, competitors must also think like collaborators, negotiating teams must do more than bargain for the last dime, everyone must define risk broadly, and so on. By the same token, the task of designing an alliance should not be relegated to deal makers or some group of partnership specialists. Instead, alliance design must be an integral part of strategy making and business leadership.

Alliance Management

Even with the benefit of a good design, an alliance will never take care of itself—the partners must make continual investments of effort and adjust their relationship in response to new circumstances. The success of an alliance thus depends as much on the unfolding relationship between the partners, including the personal relationships between managers, as on its initial design. A prime example of this is Xerox's forty-year-old joint venture with Fuji Photo Film in Japan, which yielded benefits way beyond initial expectations because the partners were flexible and forward-looking in managing their relationship. Guidelines and case studies on alliance management are in Part Two.

In a real sense, the initial deal is merely an *opportunity* to develop an alliance—it declares the ground rules for the growth of the relationship that should bring value to the partners. Unfortunately, the tendency of an alliance to change dramatically over time is often misinterpreted as a weakness. At the extreme, change can lead to exit, resulting in the high divorce rate of alliances. But this attention to termination rates or general instability misses a central point—the stability of the alliance ought not to be a goal in itself; only the success of the alliance strategy matters.

The three sections in Part Two show how excellent practitioners manage the relationships between partners. The first section covers the basic mechanisms for working together and governing an alliance relationship. These mechanisms recognize that alliance managers have less exclusive control than they have in internal decisions, and that they must find ways to make joint decisions. That, after all, is the soul of an alliance. The second section gives evidence and advice on the role of alliance leaders, from top-level champions to day-to-day managers. Finally, the third section covers exiting from alliances—why alliances end and how to prepare for a graceful separation.

These chapters show that success in alliances is as much an organizational challenge as a strategic one. In fact, studies that have attempted to find which factors are most important in the success of individual alliances invariably have yielded a split decision: organizational issues in alliance management are about as important as strategic issues in alliance design. These two sets of issues determine the fate of individual alliances. In the remaining chapters of the book, we address ways to maximize value in a whole program of alliances.

Alliance Constellation

Because most business strategies include more than one alliance, success often depends on how the whole collection of alliances fits together. This collection of alliances has been called a *constellation;* it often acts as a distinct unit of competition. In fact, in many industries, competition has been transformed from a battle of firm against firm to one of group against group. Probably the best known example of this type of competition in the early 2000s was the battle among the airline constellations Star and oneworld. Part Three gives perspectives and lessons that help in designing and managing an effective alliance constellation.

Constellations are often important for companies in systems- or network-type businesses. At a minimum, business units that use multiple components will depend on multiple supply alliances, and business units that sell in multiple vertical or country markets will use a collection of allies to reach different customer sets. Airline alliances among various national carriers are examples of this strategy. Similarly, when a critical mass of sponsors is important to future market acceptance—as it is in many high-technology sectors—firms will often try to sign up many allies quickly. Standards battles in computer software, consumer electronics, and communications are good examples of such constellations.

But being involved in multiple alliances is not sufficient in these situations; the firm must also manage the constellation as a whole. In principle, two alliances of a firm may either complement each other or they may conflict with each other. The same is true, in spades, of a network of many alliances. A poorly designed and managed constellation can entangle the firm and waste scarce managerial bandwidth—the conflicts among partners will overwhelm any potential value to be gained from multiple partnerships. Good coordination, on the other hand, can save resources and diversify options for growth.

Part Three focuses on firms with extensive networks of partners, but many of the guidelines from this part are also applicable to firms with just a few partners. It examines two different forms of constellations. One is the portfolio of alliances of a firm, such as Coca-Cola's portfolio of bottlers. Another form is a collection of firms allied with each other, such as the groups of firms in Visa International or Colliers International. With both of these forms of constellation in mind, the first section in this part of the book outlines how strategic goals shape group design, how multipartner alliances may be governed, and how constellations spread and grow. The second section describes how constellations have flourished in three very different industries.

As these chapters show, constellations take many forms and are used for various purposes, just as is the case with individual alliances. In the same way, designing and managing constellations requires decisions, capabilities, and structures that are related to those important in individual alliances. But the complexity and scope of constellations adds new challenges.

Alliance Capability

Firms that use alliances as extensively as do our constellation pioneers have also discovered another important lesson: the success of external alliances often depends on having a supportive internal infrastructure. This lesson is by no means limited to firms with many alliances. Unfortunately, proofs abound in every organization. Managers involved with external relationships can all testify to how important it is to get internal organizational support for these relationships.

A good alliance strategy therefore starts at home. The firm must not only define a business logic for its alliances, keep an eye on the future, and manage the group of partners well, it must also align its organization to this strategy and invest the right resources in it. Firms that are doing this are frequently cited for their alliance capability. In some industries, such as pharmaceuticals, the early 2000s saw a rivalry among firms to become "partner of choice" by building an internal capability that would make them attractive to technology providers. The essence of this capability is that alliances are made part of the everyday functioning of the company. They are not special deals relegated to a group of alliance experts.

A firm that truly values its alliance capability will seek ways to share best practices among its business units and to develop special expertise where it is needed. The best practitioners therefore record the lessons from their own alliance experience, assemble tools for future alliance designers and managers, and train managers involved in alliances. Finally, a good internal infrastructure identifies and mediates the internal conflicts that can pit one alliance against another.

Part Four shows how leading firms have built their alliance capabilities and draws lessons from their experience. It covers such issues as how alliance knowledge can be managed, how alliances across business units can be coordinated, how managers can be trained for alliance work, and how the health of an alliance might be measured and tracked.

The evidence suggests that there are many ways to build an alliance capability. What works depends on the organizational culture of the company—some firms use extensive data storage and sharing tools, others do just fine with personal interaction and a minimum of technical overhead. Some firms place alliance management under a centralized organization, say at the corporate level, while others prefer to distribute responsibility for alliances across all business units. Furthermore, the degree to which a company is willing to invest in a permanent alliance capability, or indeed needs to do so, also depends on its organizational and strategic circumstances.

The Arc of Alliance Strategy

Superior performance comes from managing this whole array of issues. To help keep track of these issues, we designed the Arc of Alliance Strategy shown in Figure I.1. The four elements of the alliance strategy arc rest on a foundation that is the general strategy and organization of the firm. This arc represents an integrated view of what it takes to succeed with alliances. It is also a road map for this book.

Although mastery of these individual elements of alliance strategy is essential, it is the overall workings of the arc that drive success. Within the arc, the strongest links are between alliance design and management. The success of one clearly depends on the other. The design must set the stage for management, and management must strive to bring to fruition the goals set at design. These two elements apply to every alliance of the firm, and carry roughly equal weight in the success of any given alliance.

The other alliance elements shown—alliance constellation and alliance capability—apply to the collection of alliances of the firm.

FIGURE I.1   The Arc of Alliance Strategy.

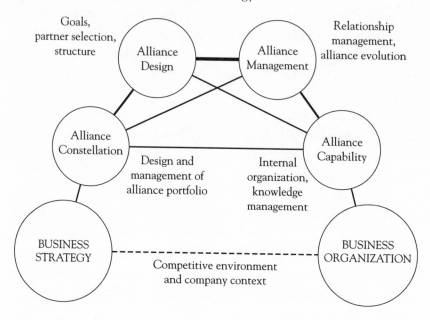

Here too, there are important interdependencies. On the left side, constellation design often sets the stage for the design of individual alliances, because it influences goals and partner selection criteria. On the right side, the firm's alliance capability often determines how it will tackle alliance management. Weaker links exist between the management of the alliance constellation and the management of individual alliances, and between capability and design.

Finally, it is clear from this diagram that the whole arc rests on two broad foundations—the strategy and organization of the firm. These elements go well beyond alliance strategy and are influenced by considerations in other fields, such as marketing, finance, production, and so on. Broad strategic decisions help determine the constellation strategy of the firm, and broad cultural and organizational norms influence the way the firm will manage its alliance capability. The business model of the firm, in other words, shapes the arc of alliance strategy.

Using the Arc

How should managers navigate this arc? That depends on where one starts. Logically, one must reason up from firmwide strategy and organization to the top elements. But, practically, that is not how most managers will learn to master alliance strategy.

Most readers will come to this book with urgent needs at the top, and only later will address the broader elements at the bottom. Certainly, for newcomers to alliance strategy, it is more effective to start at the top—first understand the key success factors in design and management, and then work your way down to the broader implications for the firm. That is why the parts of the book are ordered as they are.

We encourage readers to enter at any level and move around this space. One can just as well read the book backward. Start by asking: What capabilities do we need? How do we design the overall constellation? And, only then: What are the implications for alliance design and management? But such an approach already assumes a good understanding of alliance strategy.

What is most important is to understand the logic and to keep a view on the whole arc. Wherever one sits, that element will doubtless loom largest and most important. That is why deal makers in business development think their alliance design activities are the keys to success and why operational managers in the alliance feel that it is their implementation of the deal that really matters. Both are right. And both sets of specialists must deepen their skills and advocate their views. But the specialists must also be generalists. They must know where their piece fits in the totality.

That is why alliance strategy is an essential part of general management. No general manager of a business unit or division or company would be content to leave financial decisions to the financial managers and marketing to marketing departments. So too, alliance strategy is too important to be left to alliance managers. It must become part of natural thinking in every general manager's mind.

This holds for top management too. Senior executives are not immune to tunnel vision, notwithstanding their role as overall company leaders. They too are sometimes fooled into adopting too narrow an approach, centering perhaps on striking this or that deal with such-and-such powerful ally. That is only one move in a dynamic alliance strategy. In addition, leaders of the firm must evaluate their total portfolio, ensure that there is follow-up management, and sustain performance by building lasting capabilities. This book is for them too.

Definition of Alliance

Before launching into the book, one bit of terminology is needed: What exactly is an alliance? In our definition, alliances can be used to fulfill a broad range of corporate goals, including gaining scale, reducing costs, accessing new skills, products, or markets, and sharing risk. In fact, any goal of corporate strategy can, in concept at least, be achieved with an alliance. The real question is whether such a goal is best achieved with an alliance or another organizational approach.

Answering that question requires understanding what kind of organization an alliance is. Here too, our definition covers a wide range of forms, from classic stand-alone equity joint ventures and non-equity relationships, including enhanced supplier agreements, contractual research collaborations, marketing affiliations, licenses, and multipartner consortia. What do these arrangements have in common?

Three characteristics. First, all alliances are agreements between two or more separate firms that involve ongoing resource contributions from each to create joint value. Typical partner contributions include technology, staff, customers, brands, capital, and equipment. Second, all alliances are in some sense an "incomplete contract"— a phrase from the economics of law that refers to an agreement in which the terms cannot be completely specified and agreed at the outset. As a result of these first two conditions, all alliances share a third characteristic: joint decision making to manage the business and share the value.

Why do firms enter into such loose agreements, and willingly endure the difficulties and risks associated with all three characteristics? In simple terms: the alternatives are less attractive for the given situation. One alternative to an alliance is an arm's-length contract. In many situations, such contracts do not provide sufficient incentives for firms to collaborate deeply. Another alternative is a merger or acquisition. In many cases, such an approach is infeasible, or too expensive or risky. As an arrangement short of merger but deeper than an arm's-length contract, an alliance may strike just the right balance.

Mastering Alliance Strategy

So, how do you *master* alliance strategy? As in other activities, mastery comes from deep understanding, frequent practice, and some wisdom from others. This book is designed to help on each of these fronts.

This is not a book of best-practice formulas—we don't believe in the cookie-cutter approach to management. Instead, we have gathered here what we consider the best thinking that is also useful in practice. Best-practice formulas have limited shelf lives and narrow applicability; best thinking, on the other hand, prepares managers for sustaining good practices even when the situation changes.

Best-practice surveys used to be all the rage a few years ago. But companies that invested in these surveys have come to realize that no matter how successful a practice is in one company, it may be completely wrong for others. The effectiveness of a management practice depends critically on its organizational and strategic contexts. To know what works for you, therefore, you must first understand not only *what* another company is doing, but *why* its people are doing what they are doing. Then, you must know how to translate the foreign experience to your own company.

That is where best thinking comes in. This book gives practical approaches, frameworks, examples, models, and other tools to spark your thinking. The result, we hope, is a deeper understanding of how alliance strategy works, why some companies do what they do, and what you might consider doing in your company. But the work of applying it to your own organizational and strategic context remains yours.

Sources of Wisdom

Most of the chapters in this book are based on articles in *The Alliance Analyst*, a management strategy newsletter that from 1994 to 2001 documented every few weeks what leading companies were doing and thinking with their alliances. The three authors of this book were instrumental in driving that publication—as editor, adviser, and publisher.

Many of the original articles were written with or about experienced practitioners. Over the years, we interviewed more than a thousand executives, many on multiple occasions, and in the process came to understand their issues deeply. The original articles have been revised, updated, and edited for this book with one goal in mind: to sharpen their lessons and advice. What remains is alliance wisdom accumulated over eight years and filtered down to its essence.

Many of the case studies are presented here as histories. They are not intended to portray how individual companies operate today or to rank one company over another. Instead, they were chosen for the timeless lessons they teach. Many of the companies described have continued to develop their alliance practices or taken different directions. But their experience will serve as a guide for others.

How should readers use this book? Browse it, read what is most intriguing, and most of all, discuss and debate the implications for your firm. The varying and sometimes even contradictory views of different contributors have not been forced into a common pre-scription, intentionally. Each may see the world slightly differently, but they are here because their views will help you find the answers that work best for you.

You already recognize that your company cannot succeed if it tries to do everything by itself—you know you need alliances. But you will not be helped by a strategic alliance here or there; you need a comprehensive alliance strategy. This book will help you craft one. The rest, as they say, is practice.

PART ONE

Designing Alliances

—

Setting Strategy

1

Envisioning Collaboration

David Ernst

During the last decade, alliances have become part of the corporate lexicon. Managers routinely talk about alliances. Books on the topic keep filling the bookshelves, while financial newspapers and magazines cover the swelling number of deals. Even companies that once shunned alliances are turning to them at some level and in certain parts of their business.

Yet alliances remain underappreciated. For starters, few managers understand the extent to which alliances contribute to market value. Many of the world's largest companies now have more than 20 percent of their assets tied up in alliances. Many others depend on alliances for 30–50 percent of their research expenditures or annual revenues. At the same time, many companies have not developed an informed point of view about how alliances create value or how to design them to succeed. To help remedy this situation, I focus on two topics:

- *How alliances capture value.* Alliances offer an enormous opportunity to create value. There are six basic ways in which companies can use alliances to create value. Managers should ask how many of these the company is using to date, and whether there might be some missed opportunities.

- *How to avoid the seven alliance sins.* Despite the potential, alliances often do not work. Between 30 percent and

60 percent of alliances do not succeed. To improve the odds of success, companies need to understand the common alliance sins and take steps to avoid them.

First, a definition. An alliance is a relationship between separate companies that involves joint contributions and shared ownership and control. What makes alliances so unique is that independent companies must coordinate their actions and resources as well as share risks and rewards. Alliances usually involve some degree of exclusivity and are often, but not always, temporary vehicles. Seen on a continuum, an alliance is an organizational form between a full acquisition and a loose relationship based on an informal agreement; it may be a joint venture, a non-equity contract, a minority equity stake accompanied by an operating relationship, and so on.

The nature of alliances has changed quite a bit in the last ten years. In the past, most alliances were joint ventures to enter overseas markets or funding mechanisms for collaborative research. Today, alliances cover all kinds of joint ventures and many flavors of non-equity alliances. Some of the most common non-equity alliances include co-branding, co-marketing, strategic outsourcing, cooperative bidding, and joint purchasing. And the number of deal structures is continuing to expand, with many variations appearing in different sectors.

How Alliances Capture Value

There are six broad ways that companies use alliances to create value: building new businesses, accessing new markets, acquiring skills, gaining scale, improving the supply chain, and creating networks.

Alliances to Build New Businesses

Alliances can be a powerful tool for building a new business. Microsoft and NBC created a successful joint venture to compete in cable and Internet-based broadcasting. First Data Corporation formed a series of joint ventures with banks to perform credit card processing. Philips and Sony used an alliance that pooled their patents to develop the compact disc—and then licensed the product as an open standard. As a general rule, alliances can be useful to build a new business when the risks are high, skills are incomplete, or speed is essential.

Alliances to Access New Markets

Alliances are also a powerful means to access new markets. Traditionally, such alliances have focused on accessing new geographic markets, such as Japan or Brazil. But what we are seeing now is leading companies using alliances to access new product and customer markets. Think about Starbucks Coffee, which has leveraged a brand and a concept through a whole set of alliances (see Figure 1.1). Some of the Starbucks alliances are geographic (to enter such markets as Japan, Korea, and Singapore), some are with customers like United Airlines and Westin Hotels, some are with retail formats such as Marriott, and some are with complementary producers such as PepsiCo and Dreyer's Ice Cream. Done well, alliances can allow a company to remain focused on its core product or service while reaching a huge number of new customers.

Alliances to Access Skills and Learning

Alliances are also a powerful tool to create skills and learning—the building blocks of future competitive advantage. A number of large food companies formed alliances with a leading online grocer to learn what it would take to sell food over the Internet. In a similar spirit, major pharmaceutical companies routinely form alliances with biotech companies to access skills, ideas, and technology that can be transformed into commercial drugs. Alliances can be a wonderful way to access these critical building blocks. During the last twenty years, leading electronics firm Samsung has accessed various skills and technology platforms through multiple joint ventures and

FIGURE 1.1   Starbucks Coffee:
Creating Value Through a Set of Alliances.

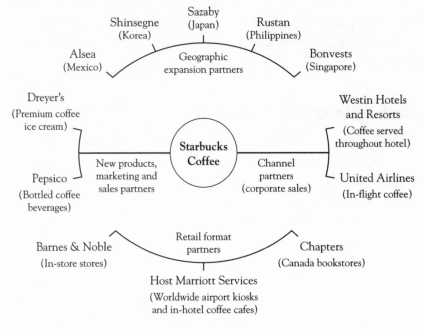

Source: Press reports; McKinsey analysis.

licensing agreements. Of a hundred or more new businesses it has started, at least twenty-five have gotten their start through joint ventures. Even when joint ventures (JVs) haven't been the vehicles, the licensing arrangements have allowed Samsung to access critical skills and technology.

Alliances to Gain Scale

Alliances can also be used to gain scale—much like traditional mergers and acquisitions. For example, First Data Corporation has formed JVs with a number of banks to gain scale in credit card processing. Arrangements like these allow partners to consolidate overlapping businesses, reduce costs, and increase scale. Several factors may lead companies to choose an alliance over an acquisition to fulfill these goals: acquisition premiums are often high, most joint ventures are tax free, alliances do not come with a cost for goodwill, and companies don't have to give up control of their business.

Alliances to Improve Supplier Effectiveness

Done well, alliances can transform the relationships between a company and its suppliers. Mercedes has done this with its successful M-class sports utility vehicle in the United States. The firm shifted much of the risk, capital investment, and effort to long-term suppliers. Mercedes reduced the number of suppliers and signed long-term contracts with the remainder. In return the firm insisted that suppliers speed up development time and invest their own money in developing some modules for the vehicle. Mercedes is not alone. Companies from a range of industries are taking part of their value chain and shifting it out to their suppliers to reduce costs and risks while increasing innovation and quality.

Alliances to Create Advantaged Networks

The best companies use their portfolio of alliances to create value beyond the individual relationships. Duke Energy was one of the world's leading utilities in the 1990s, with a price/earnings ratio consistently higher than that of many competitors. Stable short-term earnings have helped, but more important is its growth story—one that has long been supported by alliances. For example, Duke brings expertise in operating power plants into a joint venture with Fluor Daniel that builds, owns, and operates power plants worldwide.

How to Avoid the Seven Alliance Sins

Many alliances don't succeed. Various studies, including those done by McKinsey, point to success rates between 30 percent and 60 percent. The question is: How do firms get alliances into the successful group? As a place to start, companies need to understand the seven common alliance pitfalls: unclear objectives, lack of a detailed business plan, decision gridlock, aligning with a weak or competitive partner, unmanaged cultural clash, failure to learn or protect core capabilities, and failure to plan for alliance evolution.

How do companies avoid these pitfalls? Companies operating successful alliances tend to have a definite approach to how they develop alliance strategies, select partners, structure the deal, and plan for evolution.

Have a Clear Strategy

The next time you are forming an alliance write down on one piece of paper, and only one piece of paper, your definition of success for the alliance in three years' time. What are the financial goals? What are the strategic goals? How are these goals going to be measured? What are the goals and measures for the partner? Crispness of objectives is key.

Second, ask yourself, Do we really need an alliance? In many respects, alliances are terrible vehicles. You don't have decision-making control. You don't get all the rewards. You don't know how long it is going to last. You don't know whether your partner will change objectives or become your competitor. Only use alliances when you need to—when going it alone will take too long or cost too much, when you need more control and alignment than is possible with an arm's-length contract, or when seeking very specific capabilities. Sometimes you may want to use a joint venture if it is the only way to buy or sell a business.

Choose Your Partners Carefully

Our work points to a number of general observations here. First, choose financially strong partners. Alliances between two strong partners have a success rate that is twice that of alliances in which even one of the partners is weak. If executives have to spend attention on fixing a weak core business they will not have the time to focus on the alliance.

Second, for alliances that are not aimed at consolidation, find partners with strengths very different from your own. Kentucky Fried Chicken and Mitsubishi may sound like strange bedfellows, but their alliance makes a lot of sense. KFC wanted to sell fried chicken in Japan and needed to know where to buy or lease real estate. Mitsubishi happened to have that capability. Because the two companies are so different, their alliance posed limited threat of competition, conflict, or a buy-out. The joint venture recently celebrated its thirtieth birthday.

Third, screen for cultural fit. About twenty indicators can be used to give managers a strong sense of the important cultural differences with a potential partner. For example, managers may want to ask: What are the partner's values? Is their objective to maximize revenue, to maximize share price, to maximize profits, or are they really focusing on cash flow? What does the organization look like? If it is an oil company, is it organized by assets, by region, or by function? If it is a pharmaceutical company, is it organized by function or therapeutic area group? Is it a highly centralized or decentralized company? Is it hierarchical? What is the share of base-pay versus performance or bonus? What kinds of schools are employees hired from, and what is the turnover rate? Companies should not be looking for partners with corporate cultures identical to their own. But they should have an awareness of cultural differences and pick partners where the differences are not too great. This can go a long way toward avoiding cultural problems down the road.

Fourth, think about how bargaining power will evolve with a potential partner. This is just as important in non-equity deals as in joint ventures. Consider an alliance in the automotive products business. The emerging market distribution partner had a license to the product. The producer was a global company whose brand was on the product and whose technology was used. It became clear to the distribution company that it had a $300 million business that was completely dependent on the license belonging to its partner.

Its managers were thinking about a pan-regional strategy in the Americas, but the license expired in two years. They needed to re-negotiate the alliance while the partner's switching cost was still high, because in two years it was going to be lower. So thinking about bargaining power is absolutely crucial.

Choose the Right Structure and Govern Accordingly

Executives need to think about structuring alliances in a way that is very different from mergers and acquisitions. It is not about price and value. It is about scope and strategy, and governance. In alliances, legal and financial arrangements follow rather than lead. There is often a trade-off between how much value you get out of a structure and the complexity and commitment of that structure. For example, two companies were considering a joint venture. Joint ventures can be very complicated, so they looked at the alterna-tives. One of the companies found that a contractual joint pur-chasing and cross-selling alliance would allow it to capture about $150 million in value. One of the companies could have captured slightly more value with an alternate structure, but its leaders felt the added complexity outweighed the benefits.

Setting up an effective governance structure also is crucial. About half of alliance failures result from governance issues. For example, a Japanese and U.S. company had a joint venture in the United States where the R&D and manufacturing personnel re-ported to the Japanese parents, while sales and marketing was handled by the U.S. parent. A customer asked for a change in the product, and promised a very large order on completion of that change. What happened? The salespeople talked to the R&D staff, who "negotiated" the product change through a series of discus-sions with the parent and the potential customer. But by the time a decision was reached the customer had decided to go with a com-petitor who could make decisions more rapidly. Joint venture suc-cess required a decision-making structure that was more cohesive.

There is no one-size-fits-all answer to alliance governance. If you are setting up a joint venture, then you have three basic governance models from which to choose: independent, dependent, and interdependent. The independent model is often the preferred choice because it allows those running the alliance to treat the venture as an autonomous business, to set up a strong organization, and to make most of the main business decisions, including those relating to hiring, firing, pricing, annual planning, and capital expenditures. Dow Corning is a classic example of an independent joint venture, and Airbus is now migrating toward this model.

A second model is the dependent venture. Fuji Xerox is perhaps the best known case: a forty-year-old joint venture where one partner, Xerox, took the lead in contributing essential technology patents and other assets and making ongoing operational decisions. (According to press reports this model has remained unchanged, despite Xerox's recent sale of part of its equity stake in the joint venture.) Many oilfield joint ventures follow this model as well, with one of the partners acting as the operator and the others as more passive financial investors. The third model is interdependence. These ventures cannot escape having multiple levels of ongoing interaction and resource flows between the venture and the corporate parents. For example, Toshiba and Motorola had a joint venture where they relied on Toshiba for DRAM technology and on Motorola for microprocessor technology. Motorola has since purchased Toshiba's interest in the joint venture.

All three models can work. Choosing among them depends on a number of factors, including the parents' goals and the nature and relative value of their contributions. When the partners choose the interdependent governance model, it is essential to work through clear roles and responsibilities and decision-making rights.

Plan for Evolution

The lessons for joint venture evolution are pretty well known. Almost 80 percent of terminated joint ventures end up as a sale to one of the partners. The data suggest how important it is to think through the evolution up front, and at minimum lock in a pricing formula in the event of termination.

Planning for evolution is also essential for non-equity deals. If you are committing exclusive rights you should think about exit. Case in point: a U.S. consumer goods company signed an exclusive ten-year license with a leading player in a significant Latin American country. At the time it was a great deal. However, a number of problems arose: the local partner did not perform, competitors started attacking the market, and there was no exit clause. The U.S. company had committed all of its sales potential in a major geographic region for a substantial period of time with no way out. Thinking about an exit is quite important whenever you have locked up your intangible assets or customers in an alliance.

Prepare for Scope Expansion and Restructuring

The most successful alliances, from licensing deals to joint ventures, tend to evolve and grow. Executives need to be ready. How will the alliance grow? What kinds of conflicts will that create? What is the natural lifecycle of the technology or product? Will the alliance need to be escalated from a licensing deal to a joint venture? Will additional partners need to be added? A whole mind-set about alliances and their evolution is absolutely crucial to future success. Alliances are not necessarily a success if they last a long time. Yet if executives don't think about alliance evolution, the chance of success is slim.

Conclusion

Alliances are powerful creators of wealth. Their success rates are quite mixed, though. What is most important is crisply defining success for each and every alliance. Other key factors include choosing strong and complementary partners, having a balance of bargaining power, tailoring the scope, structure, and governance of the deal, and effectively managing alliance evolution.

Further Reading

Joel Bleeke and David Ernst. *Collaborating to Compete*. New York: Wiley, 1993.

Yves Doz and Gary Hamel. *Alliance Advantage*. Boston: Harvard Business School Press, 1998. Chapters 2 and 3.

David Ernst and Tammy Halevy. "When to Think Alliance," *McKinsey Quarterly*, 2000, *4*, 47–55.

Source

This chapter is based on "Mr. Ernst's Third Go Round," *The Alliance Analyst* (October 1998), which was derived from a speech given to a strategic alliance conference in London. The article was edited and updated for this book.

2

Finding Joint Value

Charles Roussel

Consider the dozen successful alliances your company has undertaken in the last few years. You know you've done some good R&D alliances. You've set up some winning co-promotion and co-marketing agreements. And you've established some manufacturing alliances that have reduced the cost of sales. Although you know in your gut that these alliances are adding value, you have applied no systematic performance measurement to individual alliances or to the alliance portfolio. You are not alone.

For most executives, alliances exist at the periphery of corporate strategy. They are not viewed as central to a company's approach to creating value in the marketplace. That is a problem because alliances are everywhere.

How Much Value Do Alliances Add?

Measuring alliance value has traditionally relied on rumor and hunch. Witness equity analysts' reaction to Walt Disney forming an alliance with Pepsi in 1998. Pepsi would supply all soft drinks for the Club Disney, Disney Quest, and ESPN SportsZone ventures. The agreement also called for Disney and Pepsi to co-market their products. In many analysts' minds the alliance called into question Disney's long-standing, much-touted agreement with Coca-Cola. The market began to speculate on problems in the Disney-Coke relationship and over time imputed a lower value to the Disney-Coke alliance.

This loose approach to alliance valuation is understandable, given that alliances only recently entered the mainstream of management interest. If you go back to the early days of the stock exchanges, market value was also based largely on rumor and hunch. But just as the market has institutionalized equity analysis, so there are now better ways to value alliance performance.

Accenture worked with professors Tarun Khanna and Bharat Anand of Harvard Business School to develop the Partnership Value Assessment model, or PVA. Based on a study of two thousand alliance events done by Khanna and Anand, the project created a model to help its clients evaluate alliance options. The model isolates the effects of an alliance announcement on the stock market valuation of the affected companies in the days and weeks following the announcement.

The study sample consisted of alliances where at least one of the partners was a U.S.-based firm, as comparable data were not always available for non-U.S. firms. The study methodology assumed that capital markets were relatively efficient, correlating stock prices with the fundamental values of the companies. Further, the study focused on selected industries: electronics, pharmaceuticals, consumer products, communications, and chemicals. The findings are summarized in the following sections.

Alliances Can Both Create and Destroy Value

The fifteen most active value creators in the study created $72 billion in shareholder value over two years. But the study also showed that alliances can destroy value. The fifteen most active value destroyers destroyed $43 billion. For example, most alliance-intensive pharmaceutical companies do a good job running their alliances. Take Abbott Labs. Over seven deals, Abbott created $3 billion in market value for shareholders. That represented a 2 percent return on stock price. On the other hand, another company's alliance destroyed nearly the same amount. Although performance varies tremendously across companies, over time alliances tend to create value.

Being Good at One Kind of Alliance Doesn't Mean Being Good at Another

Take AT&T. AT&T lost $5 billion in value through its licensing agreements. But it created $10 billion in value through its joint ventures. IBM is in the reverse situation. IBM created roughly $12 billion through its licensing agreements and lost close to $7 billion through its joint ventures.

Strong Firm Management Does Not Imply Alliance Success

Taking a high market-to-book value as a proxy for good management allows testing how well-managed firms do with alliances. It turns out that high-market-to-book-value firms lost $355 billion through their joint ventures and created a relatively negligible $1 billion through their licensing agreements. Low-market-to-book-value companies created $102 billion in value through their joint ventures and $438 billion through their licensing agreements.

There seem to be two reasons for this. First, well-managed firms are often centralized, hierarchical, and bureaucratic—characteristics that can hinder alliance success. Second, poorly managed firms benefit disproportionately from their association with better-run companies. They enjoy a learning effect.

Certain Alliance Types Create Value in One Industry but Not in Another

R&D joint ventures in the electronics industry create value, but in the chemicals industry they don't. Production joint ventures create value in the communications industry but not in the computer industry. In the pharmaceuticals industry, marketing joint ventures yield the greatest return, while R&D joint ventures and licensing agreements by large firms tend to lose value.

Each industry has its own hierarchy of alliance types (Figure 2.1). In the computer industry, for instance, licensing agreements with small firms tend to create the most value. In the chemicals industry, where overall returns are lower for all forms of alliances, joint ventures and licensing agreements tend to create the same modest amounts of value.

Company Size Affects Alliance Performance

A big company does not necessarily reap more value from an alliance than a small company does. This is true when a big company licenses its technology to a small company or vice versa. On average, those situations led to a 20 percent increase in the stock price of the small company, but no change in the stock price of the large firm. This is surprising and significant. One possible explanation is that big companies have not invested in the infrastructure needed to take advantage of alliances—skill building, knowledge management capabilities, formal job descriptions, and formal scorecards. In other words, they are not learning as much as a small company might from similar relationships.

Looking Overseas for Alliances Is a Good Idea—Sometimes

The benefits of cross-border alliances vary by industry. If you are Merck and you license one of your compounds through a European company, you will on average derive more value than if you license that compound to a U.S. company. Conversely, if you are IBM and you license your server technology to a small vertical-solutions developer in Europe, you'll derive less value than if you licensed it to a U.S. company.

Which types of overseas alliances create the most value? Although joint ventures yield more value overall than licensing agreements, a joint venture with a domestic partner will generally yield

FIGURE 2.1   Value Creation in Different Types of Alliances.

Value Hierarchy: Pharmaceutical Alliances

Marketing joint ventures: 8–9%*

Production joint ventures: 5–6%	Small firms' licensing: 8–9%

Marketing and R&D joint ventures: 1–2%

R&D joint ventures: negligible	Large firms' licensing: negligible

Value Hierarchy: Computer Alliances

Small firms' licensing: 8–9%

Marketing and R&D joint ventures: 7–8%

R&D joint ventures: 2–3%

Large firms' licensing: 1–2%

Production joint ventures: negligible	Marketing joint ventures: negligible

Value Hierarchy: Chemical Alliances

Production joint ventures: 3–4%	Small firms' licensing: 3–4%

Marketing joint ventures: 3–4%	Marketing and R&D joint ventures: 3–4%

Large firms' licensing: 1–2%	R&D joint ventures: 1–2%*

Note: Numbers are based on average across sample, and only indicate the range of stock effects experienced by participants in the days following an alliance announcement. The effect is expressed as a percentage of the company's stock value before the alliance. For joint ventures, percentage returns for large versus small firms were not explicitly calculated. Small firms, due to their smaller equity base, will typically have larger percentage returns.

*Sample size less than 10.

more value than a joint venture with a foreign partner. Given the cultural and distance barriers that often exist in overseas alliances, this should not be surprising.

Further Reading

B. N. Anand and T. Khanna. "Do Firms Learn to Create Value? The Case of Alliances," *Strategic Management Journal*, 2000, *21*, 295–315.
Erin Anderson. "Two Firms, One Frontier: On Assessing Joint Venture Performance," *Sloan Management Review*, Winter 1990, pp. 19–30.

Source

This chapter is based on "The Search for Alliance Value," *The Alliance Analyst* (September 1998), which was derived from a speech given in London in July 1998. The article was edited for this book.

3

Managing Risk

Thirty years ago, if you asked the chief executives of large companies why they used joint ventures, they would likely say: "To share risk." In fact, the modern joint venture format was all but invented by oil companies to do just that. Exploring for oil was a risky endeavor and a series of dry holes could be costly—better to share these costs with a partner, even if this also meant sharing the rewards of a successful strike.

Today, executives are likely to offer a more complex answer to the same question. Risk sharing will feature among the motivations for alliances, but it may not be as important as gaining access to complementary resources, influencing industry standards, or beating rivals in the rush to market. What they may not realize is that in these strategies too, alliances are a way of managing risk. Modern alliances not only help companies share the costs of risky projects, they also help them hedge risks, mitigate the costs of responding to unpredictable trends, and, most important, buy and shape options to exploit future opportunities.

Unfortunately, this raises an unpleasant paradox. To manage the business risks they face, companies are choosing an organizational strategy that is itself notoriously risky—many joint ventures and other alliances end in nasty divorce or mutual disappointment. In a sense, alliance strategies enable companies to buy protection from business risk only by taking on additional *relationship* risks. The tragedy for many companies is that they have no comprehensive framework with which to evaluate this trade-off. The risks of managing alliances are fairly well known, but the roles of alliances in managing business risk are not. Here we will focus on the latter and briefly summarize the former.

Uncertainty and Alliances

The strategic risks that companies face stem from uncertainty in their technological, market, and competitive environments. This means that they cannot be confident of the payoff of a given strategic move, such as investment in a new plant or development of a new product. What can they do? One approach is to minimize the damage of a negative outcome. Another approach is to avoid committing to a definite strategy until the future is clearer. Yet a third policy is to try to influence the uncertainty itself. Sometimes a combination of policies can be used.

Alliances can help in all these approaches to strategic risk. To see why, we must begin by defining *alliance*. An alliance is a unique organizational structure to enable cooperation between companies. It comes in many forms, from simple joint ventures to complex consortia and ever-changing co-development agreements. Regardless of the form, the alliance governs an ongoing, open-ended relationship between companies that themselves remain separately owned. One-off, arm's-length deals with clear terms and conditions are not alliances; neither are complete mergers or acquisitions. The beauty—as well as the challenge—of an alliance lies precisely in its flexibility and the partial commitments of its members.

Managing Strategic Risks with Alliances

As a rule, alliances enable companies to make incremental commitments to an unfolding strategy, a useful feature when environmental uncertainties preclude decisions that are more definite. In addition, the partial commitments involved in alliances leave a company with resources to invest in more than one such arrange-ment, thus spreading and diversifying the risk. At the same time, however, the open-ended nature of an alliance means that if not managed carefully, it can unravel and nullify all the potential ben-efits. If the partial commitments of members are not enough to compel them to act cooperatively, the alliance can be a recipe for strategic gridlock. The two sides of this coin are reviewed separately.

Lower Exposure to Risk

Involving many partners in a risky venture reduces the exposure that each has to the possibility of failure. This technique is as old as cap-italism—the English East India Company used it in the seventeenth century to finance risky voyages. In the twentieth century oil explo-ration companies often teamed up. In today's high-tech economy the explorers are not sailing to distant continents or drilling the earth—they are colonizing the sky or probing the depths of DNA and atomic structures.

A prime example is Iridium—the consortium of electronics, aerospace, and telecommunications companies that launched sixty-six satellites into space and initiated the first round-the-world tele-phone service in late 1998. The enterprise cost more than $5 billion and filed for voluntary bankruptcy within a year.

Why? Many answers have been offered. Prime among them is that the project was overtaken by technological and market trends that were not foreseen when the initiative was launched. Being at the leading edge of technology and aiming to serve a market that did not yet exist brought huge risks for Iridium. Motorola, the U.S. mobile telecommunications manufacturer, and its partners did well to lower their exposure to the possibility of failure. They are not alone. All the remaining satellite-communication projects under way are led by consortia of players seeking to share risk. Even Microsoft's Bill Gates has teamed up with mobile phone pioneer Craig McCaw and Motorola to share in the next-generation Teledesic project.

This case shows why alliances can be valuable in lowering a company's risk exposure. Aside from the presence of uncertainty, the project itself is large and "lumpy"—a company cannot decide to launch just one satellite in an effort to lower its exposure. Similar conditions exist in bioengineering research and in the push to create ever smaller structures on semiconductor chips, an area where alliances abound.

Hedge Your Bets

Another useful feature of alliances in bioengineering and semiconductors is that they allow companies to hedge their bets among two or more competing technologies. This is also a chief reason why alliances in the dot-com world proliferated so rapidly. In this strategy, not only is the company's exposure to failure in any one project reduced but, more important, its chances of succeeding somewhere are increased.

Microsoft used this strategy too. The company invested in a slew of companies offering competing solutions to address the coming convergence between the TV and the PC. No one knew exactly how this would occur. So Microsoft invested in AT&T to spur the roll-out of high-speed Internet access over telephone lines, in Nextel Communications to develop wireless Internet access, and in Comcast to promote access over cable systems. It is likely that one or more of these options will pan out and that others will not. Either way Microsoft is likely to have at least one winning bet. It may then use this to raise the ante on competitors.

Alliances are most useful in hedging bets when there is uncertainty among competing future outcomes. This kind of uncertainty is common in the dot-com world, in which there are likely to be one or only a few winners. In these winner-takes-all markets, it pays suppliers, customers, and providers of complementary technologies to ally with several parties to secure a place in the triumphal parade.

Reduce Your Transition Costs

In both hedging and risk-sharing strategies, the company takes a passive role after forming its alliances. As events unfold, the company is protected from excessive loss because of its portfolio of alliances. However, alliances are also used in the more active management of risk, as the next three sections reveal.

One common use of alliances is to change the capabilities and strategic position of a company. Xerox, the U.S. printer and copier manufacturer, and Corning, a leading U.S. glass and systems manufacturer, are among enterprises that are well known for having used joint ventures to enter new markets abroad and gain access to new technologies.

Other companies have used mergers and acquisitions for the same purpose—Daimler-Benz did so in acquiring Chrysler, becoming a German-U.S. automotive group. When should a company, under pressure to change business capabilities or market position, use an alliance and when an acquisition? Differences in cost apart, these alternative strategies manage risk differently.

Two risks are inherent in any effort at transforming a company's business: the risk of setting off in the wrong direction and the risk of stumbling badly, even when headed in the right direction. Using alliances rather than acquisitions can mean lower transition costs in both situations. An alliance lets a company test out the new direction and then retreat gracefully if it proves to be the wrong move. This is generally less costly than acquiring a company and then divesting it. An alliance also helps transfer knowledge and skills gradually while a partner maintains an interest in the business; an acquisition can well kill the spirit that promised to renew the acquiring company.

A case in point involves AT&T, the U.S. telecommunication carrier. For decades, computer and telecommunications companies had thought that someday their technologies would merge. However, in a scenario akin to the TV-PC convergence described earlier, no one knew when or precisely how this would happen. Even

faced by this big uncertainty, AT&T charged ahead to acquire computer company NCR for $7.5 billion in 1991. As it turned out, there
was little synergy between the two and AT&T spun off its acquisition in 1996, after the latter racked up more than $3 billion in losses.
An initial alliance to test the idea might have saved money, time,
and effort. Taking smaller steps can help managers gauge the terrain
better and assist them in avoiding premature fatigue.

Buy Options on the Future

An alliance at an early stage of industry transformation can also be
seen as a way of acquiring an option on future developments. The
company first invests in an alliance and then has the option either
to exit or get more deeply involved after it sees how the business
develops. The cost of entering a relationship is relatively small in
this case, as is the cost of exit, but the value of the option to grow
the relationship may be high—a point worth a brief detour into
financial options.

An option, in the financial world, is the right to buy or sell a
security within a given period at a prearranged price. It is not a definite commitment do anything. If the option is not exercised within
the period, it expires. The chief value of the option comes from the
flexibility it offers to act in the future as new events unfold. Conse-
quently, the higher the uncertainty in the environment about
future events, the higher the value of this flexibility.

Corning Glass used alliances as options to explore and ultimately
take leadership in optical fibers. When it started research on this
technology in the 1970s, the idea of transmitting information in the
form of light pulses through a glass fiber had not been tested outside
the laboratory. Corning used a series of early alliances with telecommunications companies and research outfits to reduce technical
uncertainties and develop a commercial solution. After it gathered
new information, Corning launched a second wave of alliances, this
time with early users and manufacturers. Its most important manufacturing ally was Siemens, which became a 50 percent partner in

Siecor, the optical cable company that soon rose to a dominant position in the industry. By 1999, Corning's interest in optical fibers had grown such that it preferred to exercise its option to fully own and manage the business, and it bought out Siemens's share. Corning did not buy Siemens's shares at a prearranged price because it did not have a formal option on those shares. Even when alliances don't include formal options as part of their structure, they can be viewed through the lens of options thinking.

Manage Business Risk Directly

In our next strategy, alliances can actually reduce business risks directly by improving a project's chances of success. This strategy is often complementary to the others; a company may do what it can to make a project succeed, while also hedging its bets in case of failure.

The pharmaceuticals industry has many examples of this type. Sometimes major pharmaceutical companies make multiple investments in biotechnology start-ups and in university laboratories primarily to share risks and hedge their bets. At other times, however, they get deeply involved in shaping the agenda of a start-up or coaching it in marketing, the regulatory process, and other matters that can make or break a new drug. Often this direct management of risk is reflected in complex sequences of decisions and milestone payments, designed to guide the start-up while also creating an option-like flexibility for the larger partner.

The deal between Abbott Laboratories, the U.S. drug and medical products maker, and Japan's Takeda Chemical Industries is a good example. In 1977 they formed TAP Pharmaceuticals, a U.S.-based joint venture that initially would have access to all of Takeda's R&D for use in the U.S. market. This was a classic use of the options approach to alliances, as it was uncertain which compounds would turn out to be commercially viable in the United States. Abbott did not just sit by and watch the uncertainties resolve themselves. Instead, it helped TAP develop a marketing strategy and sales force and manage the long and complex approval process at the Food and Drug Administration. With Takeda's compound and Abbott's contributions to management, TAP Pharmaceuticals eventually developed Prevacid, a blockbuster drug that accounted for approximately $2 billion in sales in 1999.

Here too alliances were useful in dealing with the risks inherent in the project. Another important way in which today's alliances reduce business risk directly, particularly in hotly contested Internet technologies, is by helping rivals agree on common standards. However, the risk protection offered by alliances is never free. Aside from the out-of-pocket costs of forming and managing alliances, the organizational strategy itself implies taking on additional risks.

Managing Relationship Risks in Alliances

Management lore on alliances is full of anecdotes of messy relationships and of allies that turned into rivals. We need not emphasize that a poor structure or partner choice can doom an alliance from the start, nor that insufficient attention to post-deal alliance management can ruin a promising relationship. Still, it may be useful to recap how companies can manage the relationship risk in their alliances:

- *Avoid co-opetition.* The risk of conflict is high in alliances between rivals.

- *Define the scope carefully.* Even among companies that are not direct rivals, good fences make good neighbors, to borrow a phrase from the poet Robert Frost.

- *Do not ignore governance.* Careful structuring of the alliance in advance of the deal and continual adjustment thereafter is key to building a constructive relationship.

- *Build multiple bridges.* Enable relationships among partners to grow at many levels of their organizations.

- *Do not trust trust.* Personal chemistry is good and needed, but it is no substitute for monitoring mechanisms, cooperation incentives, and organizational alignment.

- *Success begins at home*. Without a support system within your own organization, your external alliances are doomed to fail.

- *Do not stare at the downside, watch for the upside*. Failed alliances do not achieve what they set out to do, but successful alliances achieve much more than their original goals planned for.

These guidelines for alliance success have one thing in common: they treat the alliance as an evolving organization embedded in a dynamic strategy. An alliance, in this view, is much more than "the deal" that is typically announced with much fanfare in the business press. Every manager has seen how excessive focus on the deal can lead to neglect of the strategy behind the deal. Why are we participating in an alliance? How will we manage it? How does this alliance fit our overall constellation of allies? How will we support it internally? These key questions go well beyond the closing of a deal. Effective use of alliances to manage risk requires such a dynamic perspective.

Further Reading

T. K. Das and Bing-Sheng Teng. "Managing Risks in Strategic Alliances," *Academy of Management Executive*, 1999, *13*(4), 50–62.

Timothy Luehrman. "Strategy as a Portfolio of Real Options," *Harvard Business Review*, Sept.-Oct. 1998, pp. 89–99.

Source

This chapter is based on "Alliances and Risk" by Benjamin Gomes-Casseres, *Financial Times* (May 2000). The article was edited for this book.

4

Entering Emerging Markets

Ashwin Adarkar, Asif Adil,
David Ernst, Paresh Vaish

Global companies are looking to emerging markets for growth. Companies in emerging markets are looking for ways into the burgeoning global economy. Alliances can seem the obvious solution for both sides.

For global companies, limitations on foreign ownership make alliances the only route into some markets. In other markets, alliances provide an appealing way to accelerate entry and reduce the risks and costs of going it alone. U.S. company Aetna Insurance, for example, invested $300 million in a joint venture with Sul America Seguros, Brazil's largest insurance company. The aim of the Brazilian-based alliance was to accelerate growth and introduce new products in health, life, and personal insurance and pensions. Aetna agreed to contribute expertise in products, information technology, and servicing, while Sul America provided local knowledge, an extensive distribution network and sales system, and its leading market position. (This joint venture has recently been restructured following ING Baring Group's acquisition of Aetna.)

Companies in emerging markets can find the idea of an alliance equally attractive. For those in a position of strength, it can be a powerful vehicle for growth or a way to leverage low-cost manufacturing or a unique distribution network. Samsung of Korea has used several hundred technology licensing arrangements and joint ventures as vehicles to build a world-class electronics company (Figure 4.1). Of

FIGURE 4.1   Selected Samsung Alliances, 1970s–1990s
(25 of 96 new businesses started via joint ventures).

1970s Consumer electronics	1980s Semiconductors	1990s Multimedia
Joint ventures with Sanyo, NEC, Corning (>$700 million sales)	Joint ventures with Texas Instruments, DNS, Towa	Joint ventures with Hewlett-Packard, GTE
		Equity investment in AST, Array, IGT, CAI
More than fifty technology licensing agreements, including RCA, JVC, Kelvinator, Matsushita, Toshiba, Philips, Casio	More than ninety technology and cross-licensing agreements, including Micron Technology, Sharp, Intel, Texas Instruments, NEC, Toshiba, General Instrument, Oki	More than thirty technology licensing agreements, including Sega, Microsoft, Philips, Motorola, Mindscape
		R&D consortium with LG and ETRI for next generation TDX
	R&D consortium with LG, Hyundai for next generation DRAM	

Note: Given the time span involved, some of these alliances have ended.
Source: Press reports; McKinsey analysis.

almost a hundred new businesses it set up between 1953 and 1995, a quarter were initiated via joint ventures. In other cases, alliances may be the only way—short of selling the company outright—for an emerging-market player to survive once the home market has opened to new entrants bringing global brands or technology.

Some are successful. Nintendo and JVC both allied with Gradiente, a leading Brazilian electronics company, to manufacture or market products under their own brand names as well as the Gradiente brand. The alliances helped Nintendo and JVC build volume rapidly in an important market, while helping Gradiente to become a profitable company with revenues of over $1 billion and its own skills, market position, and manufacturing capability.

Yet both the popularity of alliances between emerging-market and global companies and their apparent win-win character can mask their difficulty. They are hard to pull off and often highly unstable—much more so than alliances between companies from similar economic and cultural backgrounds. Many have failed to meet expectations or have required extensive restructuring. Indeed, in recent years, numerous high-profile joint ventures in Asia and Latin America have been dissolved, restructured, or bought out by one of the partners.

Why are joint ventures in emerging markets so difficult? The answer lies in the fact that multinationals and companies in emerging markets must overcome formidable differences if they are to develop successful alliances.

First, most global companies are considerably larger than their emerging-market partners; they possess deeper pockets and, often, broader capabilities. This makes it hard to find equal, complementary pairings—a balance that is the hallmark of successful and enduring alliances. Among alliances undertaken in India during the mid-1990s, the global company typically had thirty times the revenue of its local partner.

Other difficulties result from ownership structure, objectives, culture, and management styles. State-owned enterprises can make frustrating negotiating partners for multinationals because they have no single decision maker; instead they have to seek approval from a range of political constituencies. But a multinational can be an equally frustrating partner for a family-owned business if its country manager has to seek approval for decisions from other senior managers, while the patriarch or matriarch of the family business can make decisions unilaterally. Different types of companies also have different agendas. The family-run business may be more interested in ensuring a steady stream of dividends for shareholders than in maximizing growth of short-term shareholder value.

These challenges do not mean that emerging-market alliances should be avoided. But they do raise the stakes. Before entering these deals, therefore, prospective partners should ask three questions: Is an alliance really necessary, or would an outright acquisition, direct investment, or contractual relationship suffice? How sustainable will an alliance be, given the partners' ambitions and strengths? And how should the strategy and tactics they adopt reflect the distinct challenges of alliances between global and emerging-market companies?

When Is an Alliance Necessary?

Given the differences between partners and the complexities of managing a relationship, a reasonable (but rarely asked) question is: Why are we forming an alliance in the first place? If the main benefit of an alliance would be inside knowledge of customers, government, and suppliers, for example, the global company should ask whether it might be possible instead to hire five or ten key people who would bring those relationships.

Acquisitions can be equally effective for emerging-market companies. Many companies have responded to globalization by looking to joint ventures or broad-based technology licensing arrangements with international partners, particularly when they needed to bridge a technology gap. Other emerging-market companies are experimenting with virtual alliances—piecing together the technology or abilities they seek without forming an alliance. One large Indian textile manufacturer aspired to enter the clothing business but lacked manufacturing technology and marketing expertise. Rather than form an alliance, it cobbled together what it needed by hiring experienced people, persuading the equipment manufacturers to serve as technical consultants, and licensing certain technologies. The company grew by 150 percent during the first four years of the program. Such a strategy would not suit all companies, however; the learning and coordination of relationships it involves call for highly developed skills and consume a great deal of management time. These alternative approaches are especially relevant when technology is readily available and global brands are not needed.

How Long Will the Alliance Last?

When an alliance *is* deemed necessary, both companies should assess at the outset how the partnership is likely to evolve and whether it is a marriage of equals that will endure—or something else. Achieving an equal balance in an emerging market is particularly challenging because of the differences in size, culture, skills, and objectives that we have mentioned. Such alliances are also vulnerable to rapid regulatory change.

Two factors influence the sustainability and likely direction of an alliance: each partner's aspirations—that is, the will to control the venture—and relative contributions. Aspirations can help tip the balance. Does the global partner desire full control in the long run? If it does, the alliance is likely to wind up in acquisition or dissolution. Or does it want a permanent alliance in which the local partner provides specific elements of the business system? Is the emerging-market player's focus on the home market, or does it harbor global ambitions? If it does, and it wants to compete on its own against the multinational, conflict will be inevitable.

Ultimately, though, the evolution of an alliance will be driven by each partner's strengths and weaknesses, and by the relative importance of its contribution. Examples of valuable contributions might include privileged assets (ownership of mining rights or oil field reserves, for example); advantaged relationships such as access to regulators, operating licenses, and exclusive distributor relationships; or intangible assets such as brands, marketing, manufacturing, technology, management expertise, and patents.

Usually the global company contributes intangibles such as technology, brands, and skills that grow in importance over time. The local partner's contributions, on the other hand, are more likely to be local market knowledge, relationships with regulators, distribution, and possibly manufacturing—assets that may fade in importance as its partner becomes more knowledgeable about the market, or as deregulation undermines (sometimes overnight) the value of privileged relationships or licenses.

Manufacturing cost leadership can also be fleeting in a globalizing economy. If the local partner essentially provides an escort service, it will almost certainly become less important. A survey of Chinese joint ventures indicated that Chinese partners systematically deliver less value than expected in terms of sales, distribution, and local relationships.

To assess whether an alliance will be a marriage for life and how it will evolve, partners in emerging markets should catalogue the current contributions of each partner, plot how they are likely to shift, and negotiate to ensure that the venture will be sustainable or to protect shareholders against a change in power. Figure 4.2 provides a worksheet for recording the contributions of each partner.

FIGURE 4.2 Assessing Bargaining Power.

Determining Factors	Importance of Factor		Balance of Power	
	High	Low	Firm	Partner
Product or process technology	☐	☐	☐	☐
Brand ownership	☐	☐	☐	☐
Channel control	☐	☐	☐	☐
Manufacturing capacity	☐	☐	☐	☐
Ability to invest in the business	☐	☐	☐	☐
Local relationships (such as regulators)	☐	☐	☐	☐
Global relationships (such as global suppliers; global customers)	☐	☐	☐	☐
Management control	☐	☐	☐	☐

Source: McKinsey & Co.

Four Paths of Development

Emerging-market alliances tend to evolve along one of four paths (Figure 4.3). The first is that trod by *successful long-term alliances* such as Samsung-Corning, established in 1973 as a 50-50 joint venture to make CRT (cathode-ray tube) glass for the Korean electronics market. Samsung needed a technology partner to pursue its strategy of integrating vertically into electronics components and materials; Corning wanted to expand in Asia. In 2002, the joint venture was still going strong and had expanded into neighboring countries and industry segments.

The second path involves a *power shift toward the global partner*, often followed by a buyout. Take the case of two consumer goods companies that formed an alliance to target the Indian toiletries market. At the outset, their contributions were balanced. The global company brought an international marketing group, world-class

FIGURE 4.3 Four Possible Futures for Alliances in Emerging Markets.

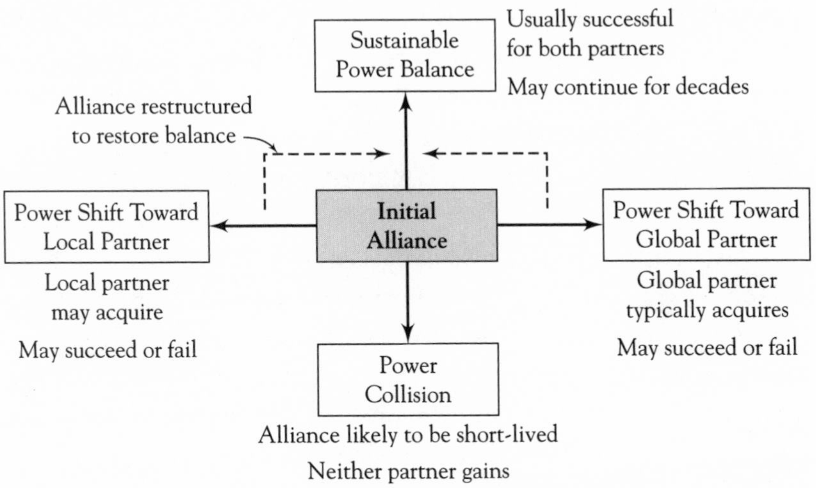

Source: McKinsey & Co.

management systems, and additional volume to fill local manufacturing capacity. The local company brought the technology to make
soap from vegetable fat (the use of animal tallow is banned in
India), low-cost manufacturing, local market knowledge, and established products and brands. The global company wanted access to
an enormous and potentially lucrative market; the Indian company
aimed to increase its capacity utilization and enhance management
and marketing skills and systems.

Gradually, however, the balance of power shifted. The global
partner succeeded in getting an organization up and running and
gained local acceptance for its product, whereas the Indian company was prevented from filling its capacity by slower than expected
sales. Moreover, the expected transfer of skills and systems to the
Indian partner never materialized, while its own brands, which had
been transferred to the joint venture, suffered. The alliance was dissolved by mutual consent.

The third path sees a *shift of power toward the emerging-market
partner*. Local partners do sometimes build their bargaining mus-
cle, increase their ownership stake, buy out their global partners,
or exit the alliance to form other partnerships. Sindo-Ricoh illustrates how a power shift toward a local partner can lead to the
restructuring and continued success of an alliance. Sindo became
Ricoh's exclusive distributor in Korea in 1962. Over time, it built
low-cost manufacturing capability, expanded the relationship to a
50-50 joint venture, then took majority ownership with a 75 percent stake.

The fourth path is *competition between partners, followed by dissolution or acquisition of the venture by one of them*. A 50-50 joint venture between GM and Daewoo to manufacture cars in Korea lost
money until Daewoo acquired it outright. The partners had incom-
patible strategies: GM wanted a low-cost source for a limited range
of small cars; Daewoo aspired to become a broad-line global auto
manufacturer. (In an interesting twist of fate, GM agreed in 2002 to
acquire a controlling interest in Daewoo, which had fallen into

bankruptcy.) Conflict and collision often result when the partners fail to agree on whether the joint venture or the parent companies will compete in related product areas or in other countries.

Recognizing what path an alliance is following and how its balance of power is shifting is critical to ensuring that both partners have the opportunity to satisfy their objectives. Our research in Asia and Latin America—and a growing body of experience—identifies some practical steps that companies can take to address the challenges of emerging markets.

Strategies and Tactics for Emerging-Market Companies

Companies in emerging markets must recognize that they may be vulnerable over the long term because of inherent power imbalances. Indeed, our research suggests that global partners are more likely to wind up with control when the balance of power shifts. On the other hand, emerging-market partners may possess sources of value that cannot easily be replicated in the short term, such as customers, channel control, local brands, control over key supply sources, and relations with officials and government regulators. They should make the most of these bargaining assets. Above all, they should invest to ensure that they last.

Before a company can develop a strategy to build power, it must set objectives for the alliance that reflect its objectives and a hard-nosed assessment of its own strengths. Is its goal to become a world-class operator able to compete in some areas with global companies on their own turf? Is it to develop a sustainable home-market alliance based on an enduring source of strength? Or is the alliance a defensive measure to protect the business against threats from global brands or technology? And is it acceptable—or even inevitable—that the alliance will evolve toward a sale? When the aim is to develop a genuine alliance or build a platform for growth, strategies to maximize power include a number of tactics.

Invest Today to Build Power for Tomorrow

The most critical issue for local companies is how to establish a sustainable source of value and thus maintain the balance of power. Among the most effective ways to do this are developing your own brands, controlling distribution, securing proprietary assets, and acquiring local competitors.

Develop Your Own Brands. Recent experience suggests that local brands can be more powerful than their owners tend to believe. In Brazil, electronics producer Gradiente laid the foundation for more balanced partnerships by building name recognition and sales volume that match those of global brands. A Venezuelan building products manufacturer entering a joint venture with a global partner retained its own brands in several segments in which the global technology was not required, and where craftsmen trusted the local product.

Control Distribution. Distribution is an area where emerging-market companies typically have initial advantages that can be extended to enhance their bargaining power. One industrial equipment manufacturer in Latin America increased its influence over distributors—and its clout with its global partner—by offering inventory management systems, financing, and extensive technical support. Investing to keep the advantage is crucial. In India, Rallis, a leading company that commanded dominant relationships with agrochemical dealers, started to experiment with direct distribution to farmers, potentially improving its bargaining power and leverage with its global partners.

Secure Proprietary Assets. Most industry value chains in emerging economies are beginning to have *chokehold* points—privileged assets in short supply. Locking these in can establish a continuing source of value. An Indian hotel company owned the best properties near the country's main tourist destinations, for example. And one metals company in Brazil entered a long-term arrangement with a key supplier for a crucial input that was in short supply.

Preemptively Acquire Local Competitors. Provided that these acquisitions make sense in their own right, they can strengthen a local company's negotiating hand by limiting the entry options for would-be players.

Become a Regional Hub for Your Partner

Many global companies have their hands full exploring the larger emerging markets such as Brazil and China. Few have the time and management capacity to concentrate on smaller economies. Local partners can improve their market position and their long-term stature in a partnership by becoming a regional hub. One Colombian industrial concern acquired its counterpart in Peru and is expanding in Venezuela, thereby not only increasing the contribution it makes to its alliance with a European company but also strengthening its own position by attaining economies of scale in regional distribution.

Think Twice Before Allying with a Global Leader

Global market leaders are often the most obvious partners because of their products, skills, capital, and prestige. But they usually have global aspirations too, and may well seek to tighten their control over any alliance they undertake in order to optimize purchasing, pricing, product development, manufacturing, and brand strategy. Autonomous ventures—or, worse still, ventures in which a local partner calls the shots—can be anathema to truly global players. In the words of one chemical industry executive, "How can we serve our global customers in the same way across twenty or more countries when our partner operates the business? We can't even assure our customers that they can buy the same products with the same specifications from one country to the next."

Emerging-market companies should ascertain whether a prospective partner is pursuing a global strategy or a global-local strategy with, for instance, local and global brands, strong country or regional managers, and regional product development.

Considering alternative partners is especially important if the leading global players in an industry are inclined to swallow up local partners' stakes. For example, one global consumer goods company followed a set pattern in Latin America and Asia. It frequently entered a market by allying with a leading local consumer goods company; then it introduced its own brands, systems, and managers. Later, it tended to became embroiled in conflict with its partner— and finally bought out the venture. Local firms considering foreign partners would do well to investigate the track record of the global firms.

Consider Less-Obvious Partners

A smaller, non-global company may present less of a long-term threat to a company from an emerging market. One Latin American metals producer decided to form an alliance with a medium-sized German firm rather than a world leader. The alliance has prospered for twenty years, with neither partner aspiring to take full control.

An alliance with a global leader from a different industry is another possibility. Telecom companies from emerging markets could consider allying with information technology providers to build their capabilities, instead of entering more predictable arrangements with global telecom service companies.

Emerging-market companies seldom consider taking a financial partner, yet this may make sense if they can build the internal capabilities to compete over the long term. Companies with attractive business propositions can win funding from sources as diverse as private equity funds, offshore Chinese holdings, and industrial investors.

Secure Access to Key Intangibles

Emerging-market companies should consider locking in key assets such as brands, technology, or distribution rights for ten to twenty years if possible, rather than risk losing them within a short period or being forced to renegotiate the venture. They should also think how they would survive termination of the alliance. This risk is highest when the local partner contributes physical assets and capital that rely on the intangible assets controlled by its global partner. One Andean Pact manufacturer would have lost a $200 million business had its partner rescinded the license agreement on which their joint venture was based. It therefore insisted on a clause stipulating three years' notice of termination. A less canny Latin American industrial company had to consider a shotgun wedding with a new partner when its original partner quit before it had internalized the skills to operate the business alone.

Create World-Class Alliance Capabilities

For multibusiness companies that may form as many as twenty alliances across unrelated industries, it is better to employ a few experts with well-honed negotiating skills than twenty gifted amateurs. Mahindra & Mahindra, a leading Indian business house, designated a single senior executive to work with the leaders of each business unit as they developed and managed their alliances to ensure that the lessons each one learned were transferred to the rest of the company.

We have assumed so far that emerging-market partners do not wish to sell their share of the business. In reality, they frequently do. The problem is that potential buyers can be unwilling to acquire joint ventures outright because of the importance of local operating know-how and relationships, or because of capital constraints. In this situation, a joint venture can be an effective stop toward a sale, but the negotiations should look more like an auction than a typical alliance discussion. The local company should pursue simultaneous discussions with several potential partners or buyers, each of which should be asked to develop a proposal that includes an initial valuation for a controlling shareholding, proposed dividend flow, and terms for ultimate sale.

Strategies and Tactics for Global Companies

Global companies, like emerging-market companies, need to adapt their alliance approaches to succeed in emerging markets. It's helpful to take a position early and try to shape the market. Also, think broadly about bargaining, venture structure, and partner interests.

Position Early

Several global companies became leading operators in China partly because they were early entrants into the telecommunications, automotive, and insurance industries, respectively. Procter & Gamble acquired an early leading position in the Chinese detergents market because it secured access to production assets through majority ventures, then moved quickly to establish local sales and distribution. Early entrants frequently have more opportunities to lock up the most promising distribution channels, gain access to attractive production assets, and invest to build the business before competition intensifies.

In many product categories in emerging markets, the desirable assets, brands, and distribution systems are controlled by a handful of attractive partners. Once they are spoken for, competitors may be locked out, especially if the cost of setting up alternative distribution is prohibitive (as it is for many consumer goods) and where added capacity would create overcapacity (as in chemicals).

Shape the Market

The "toe in the water" approach of seeding dozens of growth options at low cost in many markets may seem appealing. In reality, however, joint ventures established in this way often perish for lack of time or commitment. The global companies that do best in emerging-market joint ventures invest heavily and act to shape the market by introducing new business approaches or products.

Think Broadly About Your Partner's Capabilities

The flow of opportunities that local partners, especially conglomerates, can contribute may exceed the value of the initial deal. When a multinational wants access to local relationships, it may be wise to consider companies outside its industry that could play an advisory or ambassadorial—rather than operating—role. It is in this light that Camargo Correa, one of Brazil's largest family-owned conglomerates, viewed its role in an alliance with Alcoa. Camargo, a leading national construction company, had widespread relationships with industry and government. It was also involved in related industries such as the development of power projects and infrastructure. Alcoa took the clear leading role in their aluminum smelting joint venture, while Camargo assisted in negotiations with government authorities, built manufacturing facilities, and provided capital.

As most emerging economies are still at the nascent stage, industry experience may not be of lasting value in an alliance. Consider the case of a multinational seeking to join forces with a local company to enter India's nondurable consumer goods market. The key asset to acquire is distribution, but India's distribution system will probably change dramatically over the next decade. The multinational could select a market leader (and thereby educate a future competitor), but a more interesting choice might be a tobacco company, which is likely to have extensive retail distribution systems in India.

Bring All Your Global Capabilities to the Table

Global companies have a strong suite of technical skills, geographic presence, business units, and systems, but rarely bring them to the negotiating table. The losers in several joint venture negotiations in the Chinese automotive and machine tool industries offered a solid but narrow manufacturing partnership; the winners offered technology, local parts sourcing, and substantial capability building. One Latin American state enterprise selected its partner because it could provide technical expertise on the ground to improve the business. Another Latin American company places as much weight on how potential partners might help it secure growth opportunities as on the immediate business they could do together.

Avoid the "51 Percent or Nothing" Mind-Set

Having 51 percent ownership does not guarantee control. Effective control has more to do with management structure and ownership of key intangibles such as technology, relationships, and knowledge. In fact, a 49 or 50 percent stake can provide an opportunity to gain full control later, with less risk and more flexibility.

In one emerging-market joint venture, the global partner owned the brand, controlled the patented process technology, and was rapidly building its knowledge of the local market—yet it had only a 50 percent stake because its partner, while recognizing that it needed an alliance in order to introduce new products, was unwilling to sell the family silver by giving up 51 percent. The 50-50 venture nonetheless proved attractive for the global partner, given that its other options were to sink $200 million into a greenfield operation, form a partnership with a second-tier player, or forget about entering the market. Further alleviating concerns, the global partner had effective control over the most important business levers and was positioned as the logical buyer of business should the partners fall out or the family owners decide to sell.

It is often worth asking, What do we really need to make sure we can protect our interests in a 50-50 deal? The notion of control can be broken down into rights to determine specific issues—capital expenditures, dividend policies, production volumes, and human resources, for instance. Some multinationals have found creative ways to address particular issues. One leading international oil company signed a 50-50 joint venture in the Indian market after concluding that a casting vote on capital expenditures was enough to protect its interests. Another global company agreed to a 50-50 joint venture with the proviso that it would have the right to build additional capacity if its partner vetoed expansion by the joint venture.

Beware of Long-Term Licensing Arrangements Without Performance Contracts

Many global companies have granted licenses because they had no other way to enter the market, or because at the time the market was negligible. In doing so, some have tied up the value of their intangible assets without any exit mechanism or promise of fair value in return. One U.S. manufacturer granted a twenty-year exclusive license covering several large emerging markets to a single company in the region, with royalty fees set as a percentage of revenues. When its partner underperformed and competitors proliferated, it had little leverage to renegotiate the arrangement.

Recognize That Aims of Family Owners May Differ from Aims of Public Companies

For one family owner of a profitable business, assuring an annual dividend of $20 million was one of the key terms of its alliance agreement—far more important than maximizing the value of each partner's contribution. Other family owners may be concerned that their name will stay with the business and that the deal should not be seen as a sale, even when they want to transfer control. And there is usually some sensitivity about preserving operating roles for qualified family members. Acknowledging these wishes may cost little and be worth millions. It can make the difference between being the chosen partner or one of the runners-up.

Emerging-market alliances can create sustainable growth platforms for both local and global companies. But they pose different challenges from those faced by alliances in mature markets, and are often less stable. Before getting caught up in the heat of negotiations, companies should ensure they have a clear strategy and endgame in mind. They should also determine not only how many chips prospective partners bring to the deal, but how the value of those chips will evolve.

Further Reading

Benjamin Gomes-Casseres. "Joint Ventures in the Face of Global Competition," *Sloan Management Review*, Spring 1989, pp. 17–26.

Kenichi Ohmae. "The Global Logic of Strategic Alliances," *Harvard Business Review*, Mar.-Apr. 1989, pp. 143–154.

Michael Y. Yoshino and U. Srinivasa Rangan. *Strategic Alliances: An Entrepreneurial Approach to Globalization*. Boston: Harvard Business School Press, 1995. Chapter 3.

Source

This chapter is based on "Entering Emerging Markets: Must They Be Win Lose?" *McKinsey Quarterly* (1997), Number 4. The article was edited for this book. Used with permission.

5

Putting Strategy
Before Structure

Despite all the talk about "strategic alliances," the strategy behind many alliances gets lost in the fever to secure a partner and get the deal done. That ignores one of the key lessons from successful alliance practitioners: think carefully about strategy before you worry about the details of the deal.

To be sure, alliance performance hinges on a large and diverse set of key success factors, some of which are captured in Exhibit 5.1. Yet it is a clear alliance strategy that, more than any other factor, shapes success (see Introduction, too). Indeed, the importance of a clear alliance strategy is in part a function of the lack of institutionalized mechanisms to enforce the needed discipline—something that is not the case in other business development options. With internal growth, for example, most executives insist on keeping a tight connection to strategy, in part because the Board of Directors demands it. Likewise, they are usually good at explaining the links between their strategy and acquisitions; the investor community demands that and punishes merger proposals that lack clear strategic logic. But nobody demands that an alliance be firmly rooted in strategy; alliances occur below the radar screen, so to speak. This shallow strategic foundation has resulted in some rickety alliances. And these alliances can be dangerous, both to executive careers and to company value.

EXHIBIT 5.1 Alliance Success: Top Ten Factors.

1. *Have a clear strategic purpose.* Alliances are never an end in themselves, they are tools in service of a business strategy.

2. *Find a fitting partner.* You need a partner with compatible goals and complementary capabilities.

3. *Specialize.* Allocate tasks and responsibilities in the alliances in a way that enables each party to do what it does best.

4. *Create incentives for cooperation.* Working together never happens automatically, particularly when partners were formerly rivals.

5. *Minimize conflicts between partners.* The scope of the alliance and of partners' roles should avoid pitting one against the other in the market.

6. *Share information.* Continual communication develops trust and keeps joint projects on target.

7. *Exchange personnel.* Regardless of the form of the alliance, personal contact and site visits are essential for maintaining communication and trust.

8. *Operate with long time-horizons.* Mutual forbearance in solving short-run conflicts is enhanced by the expectation of long-term gains.

9. *Develop multiple joint projects.* Successful cooperation on one project can help partners weather the storm in less successful joint projects.

10. *Be flexible.* Alliances are open-ended and dynamic relationships that need to evolve in pace with their environment and in pursuit of new opportunities.

Alliance formation has three main elements: strategy, partner selection, and deal structure. Although all three are interrelated, they are not equals but rather subsidiaries to each other: strategy determines partner selection, and strategy and partner selection shape the deal structure. Another way to think about this is that the fundamental strategy behind an alliance changes rarely or only slowly and that partners stay for the life of the alliance (at least in bilateral alliances). In contrast, structure is often fluid; typically, it will be adjusted over time to pursue new goals or account for new partner capabilities.

Business Strategy Must Set Goals

How should companies go about developing and implementing an alliance strategy? The process must start with an assessment of the firm's external competitive environment, its internal capabilities, and its business goals. Only once these are meshed should executives develop tactics and policies toward partner selection and alliance structure. Asking questions such as these is often useful:

1. What capabilities are required for any player to succeed in the competitive environment? Think broadly about the key success factors in the business.

2. Do we have these capabilities internally? If not, is it feasible for us to develop these capabilities in a timely manner and at reasonable cost?

3. If not, are these capabilities available in other firms? If so, how can we gain access to these external capabilities?

4. Is an alliance the only option? It usually isn't. So ask: Can we buy the skills? Should we acquire a firm? Is there some transaction that will give us access to the capabilities?

Going outside the firm to gain access to capabilities should thus be an integral part of the initial strategy. Unfortunately, many alliances are launched with less than a back-of-the-envelope analysis. Inexperienced alliance practitioners are too often opportunistic or reactive at this early stage. Alliance ideas may filter down from golf outings and executive retreats. Alliance opportunities are pitched by myriad companies to multiple parts of the firm. Often, prospective partners are well into negotiations before someone cobbles together a strategy to justify the alliance. Such an approach is bound to fail; strategy must come first.

Once the strategy is in place, and a clear need for an alliance has been identified, then a partner needs to be chosen and a structure crafted. Of course, likely partners may have come to the fore during the strategic analysis, but it is important to evaluate explicitly what each possible partner might bring to the alliance. This is the second most important step, and here again, companies tend to lack discipline. Partner choice is often essentially ad hoc.

Partners Must Help Reach Goals

Partner selection typically happens in one of three ways: A company responds to an unsolicited proposal, executives call close industry contacts, or the choice is made based on some evaluation of who is the market leader in a business. In many cases, these are insufficient ways to select a partner; more analytical rigor is required.

For example, partnering with a market leader does not make sense in all situations. Imagine you work for a small software company that has developed a new program relevant to certain industries. Indeed, the program has the potential to revamp the way business is conducted in those industries. In this case, partnering with a market leader may not make sense. Market leaders have much to lose and little to gain by introducing the product. A better approach would be to partner with an aggressive, up-and-coming player.

Another factor often ignored in partner choice is the second-order or third-order connections, that is, connections between the partner and third-party firms. A partner may look good on its own, but may be tied to your competitors. Or it may be competing so vigorously with your friends and allies that tying up with it is likely to turn erstwhile friendly firms into enemies. Remember, every choice of partner implies some potential partners that were not chosen; how will they feel about the new alignment in their industry? Executives need to take a broader view of who is connected to whom in their industry.

Criteria for Selecting Partners

Managers should not forget the more usual partner selection concerns: Can we get along with a particular company? What is its
management like? Do our cultures fit? Have we had a successful
relationship in the past? These issues are still important, though it
is surprising how little time most companies devote to them.
Exhibit 5.2 shows one set of criteria that can be used in partner
selection. As with any management tool, the criteria need to be
adjusted to fit the situation, but the general categories shown are
likely to be important in most situations.

EXHIBIT 5.2 Partner Selection: Balance Capabilities and Goals.

	Company A	Company B
Complementary Capabilities • Product and market • Technology and capital • Global network and local customers		
Conflicts of Interest • Overlapping geographic markets • Competing sources of production • Transfer pricing across companies		
Compatible Goals • Market access . . . product access • Local knowledge . . . technology • Time savings . . . cash generation		
Targets and Missions • Common rivals • New market, new technology • Time horizons • Value		

Identifying and signing on the right partner goes a long way toward ensuring effective alignment of interests in an alliance. If the partner match is fraught with conflicts of interest, no structure in the world is going to make a workable alliance. The built-in friction, strategic and otherwise, is too great. Having said that, structure does play an important role as it aligns incentive structures, establishes governance mechanisms, and allows for evolution over time.

Structure Must Maximize Cooperation

Most managers equate alliance structure with financial and legal arrangements—for example, valuation of partner contributions, value-sharing mechanisms, transfer pricing, exclusivity, product and market scope, length of contract, and exit provisions. Although these are essential elements of an alliance structure, we've found that three other elements—incentive alignment, decision processes, and evolution—are critical in creating a structure that produces success.

Incentives for Cooperation

The value that a partner derives from an alliance—and thus its incentives to cooperate—can vary from cash to product supply to competitive positioning in the market to learning, as shown in Figure 5.1. For each type of goal, different measures might be applied.

Financial people are usually interested in and good at measuring returns in the form of short-term cash flows—the bottom left corner of the diagram. They also understand the value of products that the alliance is supplying to the company. But it is rare that companies have developed ways of measuring long-term value associated with market positioning or learning.

That is a problem because alliances are often based on desires to improve capabilities (learning) or market positioning. Without appropriate measures the alliance's progress can't be tracked, managerial adjustments can't be made, and stakeholders—whether they be shareholders, customers, or employees—can't be motivated.

FIGURE 5.1 Measuring the Return on Cooperation.

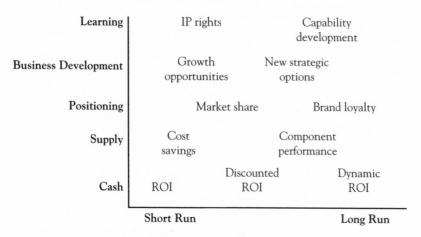

	Short Run		Long Run
Learning	IP rights		Capability development
Business Development	Growth opportunities	New strategic options	
Positioning		Market share	Brand loyalty
Supply	Cost savings		Component performance
Cash	ROI	Discounted ROI	Dynamic ROI

The news is not all bleak. A handful of companies evaluate and monitor their alliances against regular business planning goals. Nonconventional performance metrics, such as Eli Lilly's surveys of partner satisfaction, are gaining increasing use. While these practices are still the exception, they are likely to become the norm over time. Even if some goals cannot be measured by a financial rate of return on investment, it is important to establish qualitative and quantitative targets and metrics.

The question of how to measure performance is intimately tied to the strategy behind the alliance, as is everything else in alliance design. It is important to go back to the fundamental strategic question: What is the alliance trying to achieve? In the case of a learning alliance, performance metrics may focus on access to new technologies, rights of discovery, improvement in R&D cycle times, effectiveness of knowledge capture, minimization of knowledge leakage, and so on. The performance metrics must be tied to the alliance's strategic intent, be measurable, and be well communicated. A marketing alliance could have performance metrics ranging from market share to customer access, insight into customer needs, and product design. It all depends on the goals.

Governance: The Soul of an Alliance

In addition to incentives for cooperation, successful alliances have a governance process that enables joint decision making. To see why this is critical, it's necessary to go back again to fundamentals—in this instance, defining clearly what the term *alliance* means.

In common parlance, observers often define alliances by their structural type: A joint venture, a consortium, a joint R&D program, a co-marketing arrangement, and so on. This focus on structure rather than strategy again misses the point. Fundamentally, an alliance is a way of managing an open-ended agreement between two companies. This is the definition that has gained ground among leading researchers in the field. It is a bit abstract, but it pays to understand what it means.

An open-ended agreement is one in which not all terms, conditions, and contingencies are defined at the outset; instead, it is accepted that the agreement will change and evolve over time and fill in some of its apparent gaps. An alliance is thus a way of sharing the task of making decisions in the future and provides a way to govern future negotiations between the firms—it is a recognition that the initial agreement is in some sense incomplete.

Partners in an alliance do not leave terms open-ended by choice or because of sloppy legal work. In fact, if all the terms of an exchange between two firms can be completely specified and agreed upon at the outset, the firms need not form an alliance; a simple purchase order or legal contract will do. But for many reasons, such completeness is often not possible. Typical conditions that lead to this kind of incompleteness in alliance contracts are rapid changes in technology and markets, uncertainty in what the joint project will require, difficulty in measuring inputs and outputs, and so on. These conditions make it impossible to foresee all decisions that will have to be made in the future and to write clauses to cover every contingency. If two firms want to work together under such conditions, then they need to engage in an open-ended agreement with a process for managing joint decisions as the need arises.

The key to making alliances work, therefore, is effective governance of the "open end." It is the role of alliance governance to help determine information flows, establish decision-making rules and processes, delineate executive responsibilities, integrate partner operations, and so on. If executives get this correct at the outset, they will have to spend less time in the alliance management swamp later on.

There is no end to the practical mechanisms that can be used to shape alliance governance under such conditions. Many of the chapters in this book address these mechanisms. One example of a complex governance task facing a large information technology company illustrates some of the possibilities. This company had developed a large number of alliances to handle logistics and after-sales service. The company realized after signing on all these partners that its network was in fact too large, too loose, and too uncommitted. Effective governance of the group was well-nigh impossible. So it shrank the group and tightened the governance structures. It created subcommittees around key issues and promoted an all-inclusive alliance council forum.

The company then used incentives carefully to shape the decision-making process. It instituted a simple, effective incentive program that encouraged the partners to work together to minimize costs of delivery. For example, if suppliers were able to deliver a service below current cost, the company shared the gain with them. Once the financial incentives were in place and had been shown to work, it was fairly easy to build a set of common processes and practices to promote other goals.

The Alliance Must Evolve

It is clear from this example, and from all the other evidence in this book, that the structure of an alliance cannot stand still—it must evolve to adapt to changing conditions and needs. This, again, is usually well accepted by practitioners. What is often overlooked is that change is seldom unbiased—it tends to favor one partner over another. In other words, as the alliance evolves, it is not uncommon to see one partner gain influence at the expense of the other. The balance of power in governance can shift over time.

What can companies do to avoid losing influence in an alliance? Three things are key: keep an eye on your own strategy, monitor the value gained from the alliance, and continue to invest in yourself. For example, if the goal of the alliance is to learn, then executives should realize the key to increased influence is the ability to absorb and implement knowledge. Notice that these key factors are not related to the original structure of the alliance; instead, they arise out of the strategy behind and around the alliance. Put starkly, majority ownership in the structure of an alliance usually cannot ensure dominance in influence; only sustained leadership in technology, market position, and financial power can do that.

The NUMMI joint venture between GM and Toyota is a great example. Equity was split 50-50. Toyota brought a manufacturing process and a design, and GM brought market knowledge, labor knowledge, and a plant. It sounded like an even match. But when you look at the companies' commitment and intent you find a different story. Toyota managed the plant itself and was exposed to daily learning by doing. GM, on the other hand, sent a rotating group of visitors to look at the plant one or two days per week. Toyota was seeking to break into the American market and was desperate to understand what it would take to compete. GM wanted to understand Japanese production techniques but had little ability to overhaul its Detroit plants.

Not surprisingly, Toyota learned more than GM. Over the life of the alliance, the balance of power continued to shift toward Toyota. No amount of governance restructuring by GM would be able to right the imbalance.

The NUMMI joint venture remained in force because GM did continue to get something out of it, though it did not fulfill the high hopes managers had for it at the start. But often, an alliance evolves to the point where it no longer yields value to a partner that is commensurate with the contributions the firm must make to the venture. This situation can sometimes be turned around by restructuring the alliance to yield new benefits, or the alliance can simply be dissolved.

From the point of view of strategy, such a dissolution, or exit, is a perfectly reasonable outcome. But here again, an excessive focus on alliances as ends in themselves has led to much concern with alliance divorce rates. Not a few academics and consultants have conducted statistical studies using alliance stability as a measure of success. This focus on termination rates misses the central point: *alliances are a means to an end, never an end in themselves.* Alliance longevity by itself is of little relevance—strategic success is what counts.

Sometimes the strategy will call for using alliances as transitory mechanisms on the way to a full acquisition or full divestiture. At other times, particularly in the case of technological uncertainty, alliances may be used as positioning markers or R&D bets. Such a strategy is no different from an internal investment program where companies hedge their bets or pursue parallel projects. The flexibility—and thus instability—of alliances is often a strength, not a weakness.

Strategy must lie at the heart of every alliance. The business rationale for an alliance, the fit between partners, the incentives for cooperation, and the governance mechanisms—like everything else about the alliance—depend critically on the alliance strategy behind the deal. Executives often know this but lose sight of it in the heat of the battle to hammer out a deal and run an alliance. More explicit and continual strategic reflection and analysis will help.

Further Reading

Yves Doz and Gary Hamel. *Alliance Advantage*. Boston: Harvard Business School Press, 1998. Chapters 4 and 5.

Benjamin Gomes-Casseres. *The Alliance Revolution: The New Shape of Business Rivalry*. Cambridge, Mass.: Harvard University Press, 1996. Paperback reprint, 1998. Chapters 1 and 2.

Source

This chapter is based on "Strategy Before Structure," *The Alliance Analyst* (August 1998), which was derived from an interview with Benjamin Gomes-Casseres. The article was edited and updated for this book.

Building the Foundation

6

Collaborating with Competitors

Corporate managers and analysts have long understood that alliances among competitors introduce considerable risks. For instance, one study estimated that U.S. companies lost $50 billion a year by collaborating with foreign competitors in 1995. And yet alliances among competitors are more popular than ever, accounting for an estimated 10–30 percent of alliances in 2000, depending on how broadly one defines competitor. Ray Noorda, CEO of Novell, even coined a new term to describe the process of collaborating with a competitor: "co-opetition."

Alliances involving co-opetition come in many forms and touch virtually all industries. Arch-rivals Eastman Kodak and Fuji Photo Film together with other companies poured $1 billion into a ten-year research program to reinvent the modern camera. Dow Jones and Reuters folded together their online service and database businesses to gain greater scale. Pillsbury, Kellogg, and Nabisco all worked with online grocery pioneer Webvan to learn how to sell their food products online. And DaimlerChrysler, Ford, and General Motors invested millions of dollars in Covisint, the automotive business-to-business exchange.

There are many reasons why co-opetition is important. One is the rise of the Internet and the concomitant need for competitors to come together to define and expand a new market. Another reason is the blurring of industry boundaries. As a result, many companies move from one sector to the next looking for innovative ways to exploit their core competencies. Microsoft is not a telecom company or a bank, for example, but it has formed alliances with players in these sectors and clearly sees both as areas for future expansion.

Unfortunately, few companies have mastered the art of managing the balance between cooperation and conflict. In part, this failure stems from insufficient awareness of the causes and challenges of co-opetition; in part, it is because managers have lacked effective responses to these challenges. To address these twin problems we investigated why leading companies were collaborating with competitors and how they were managing the distinct risks involved.

Drivers of Co-opetition

Understanding co-opetition requires a more appropriate definition of *competitor*. Today, with the speed and uncertainty of change, firms need to think not in terms of competitor versus noncompetitor but of the degree of competitive threat. To help do this, they may use a broad radar screen that identifies the future strategic direction of both traditional and nontraditional competitors (Figure 6.1).

FIGURE 6.1 The Competitor Radar Screen: Example of an Electric Utility.

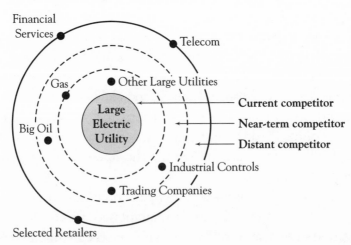

Source: Adapted from Adrian J. Slywotzky. *Value Migration*. Boston: Harvard Business School, 1996.

Having identified potential competitors from a broad scan, managers must seek to understand the potential value of collaborating with a rival. Among the many reasons for alliances, three are well known as motivations for collaboration among rivals: setting standards, sharing risks, and entering emerging markets. These old drivers of co-opetition have not faded away. Alliances to create standards have risen in importance as industrialized economies shift from heavy industry to high technology. Alliances to enter emerging markets—to access new consumers or to secure low-cost production centers—have spread to China, India, Southeast Asia, and Latin America. So too with risk-sharing alliances aiming at developing new semiconductor processes or biotechnologies. In addition to these traditional reasons for co-opetition, however, four new reasons emerged in the late 1990s that accelerated the prevalence of co-opetition: expanding product lines, reducing costs, gaining market share, and creating new skills.

Expanding Product Lines

Companies often form alliances to extend their product lines. When First Union wanted to offer its traditional banking customers a broader product suite, it entered an alliance with Charles Schwab. This alliance allowed First Union to provide its customers with OneSource, the Schwab-branded basket of mutual funds, and helped position First Union as a one-stop financial service provider and differentiate it from other banks.

But the new alliance also introduced a potential competitor. While Schwab was not a traditional bank, its broad financial service product portfolio offered customers an alternative to First Union. Again, the partners in this type of alliance would do well to recognize the relationship as a form of co-opetition, and manage it accordingly.

Reducing Costs

Alliances to combine similar assets and reduce costs are common. Since direct competitors tend to have similar types of assets, they often make the most efficient partners for this purpose. In the middle to late 1990s, the popularity of cost-reducing alliances appeared to be on the rise. Many of these ventures were in traditional, capital-intensive industries such as machinery, oil and gas, and chemicals. After the market shakeout of 2000 and 2001, New Economy companies too started to turn to this type of alliance. Sony and Ericsson, for example, combined their mobile handset businesses in a bid to reduce costs and become more competitive against market leaders Nokia and Motorola.

Gaining Market Share

In the New Economy sectors and elsewhere, companies have often formed alliances to increase market share and, in the process, generate powerful network effects. An example is the multipartner joint ventures in the auto and retail industries to create online business-to-business exchanges. The reason that direct competitors like DaimlerChrysler, Ford, and General Motors or Carrefour and Sears Roebuck have been willing to work with one another is that such alliances are the only way to attract a large number of suppliers and customers from the outset, and hence create the scale and network effects needed for success. Once again, firms need to manage these relationships as co-opetition.

Creating New Businesses

Many alliances among rivals are formed to combine complementary capabilities and create wholly new sets of skills. A prominent example is MSNBC, the joint venture between NBC and Microsoft in the online and cable news business. When the alliance was formed, NBC contributed traditional broadcasting skills and assets to the alliance, while Microsoft added substantial online and technical expertise. Together, they aimed to create skills in a new medium that merged TV and computing.

At first glance, this alliance appears to be between noncompetitors. But a broader view of the firms' strategies might lead to a different conclusion. Microsoft had been expanding into the communications business, with alliances with Comcast and AT&T, and

NBC had been moving outside traditional broadcasting. Were the two partners in MSNBC thus in direct competition? Perhaps not. But as traditional industry boundaries continue to blur, the potential for competition between them becomes more likely. The partners therefore need to manage this alliance as a form of co-opetition.

Managing the Risks of Co-opetition

As a general rule, co-opetition does not so much create new risks as it intensifies risks found in other alliances. For example, all alliances face the risk of noncooperation: that is, that the partners will be unable or unwilling to agree on decisions, or will be extremely slow in doing so. In alliances between competitors, however, the chances of this outcome increase, since the partners are inherently more suspicious of one another. Likewise, most alliances introduce the risk of technology leakage—that is, proprietary skills or processes being inadvertently revealed in the course of cooperation, creating essentially free competitive benefits for the partner. In alliances with competitors, this risk increases as well. The reason: a competitive partner is more likely to be on the lookout for these skills and processes and, because of its familiarity with the business, will be better positioned to understand and transfer them.

How do companies manage these and other risks? At one level, companies can affect the outcome through deal structure and partner selection. Northwestern University professor Ranjay Gulati has found that the more risk an alliance introduces, the more likely the firms are to use an equity-based structure. So, when forming alliances with competitors, firms often prefer a joint venture or some sort of equity swap to promote commitment and tie the partners together. Gulati also found that when partners had a prior relationship the risk level was lower, because the partners both had more trust and more to lose from cheating.

Consider also the payoff structure of the alliance. What are the returns to each partner from cooperating and cheating, and what is each likely to get if the other party cooperates or cheats? The outcomes of these possibilities define the rules of the game, and that in turn influences whether each partner will cooperate and compete. Consider the alliance between IBM and Dell Computer. IBM agreed to supply components to Dell, a bitter rival in the personal computer business, in a deal that was potentially worth $16 billion over several years. One reason that the firms went public with the potential value of the deal was to show IBM employees that there were considerable benefits from cooperation and reduce the chances of noncompliance.

Another helpful practice is to expand the relationship gradually. Consider a pair of U.S. and Japanese firms that were both allies and rivals in the semiconductor business. The firms started their relationship slowly, initially forming a two-year research alliance that was divided into a series of phases and contained graceful exit points along the way. As this cooperation proved a success and the competitors grew accustomed to working with one another, the firms expanded the duration and scope of the relationship. Other alliances have followed a similar path of cautious evolution.

Although these and other general approaches are worth considering, companies also need to manage the risks specific to the individual alliance. After all, not all alliances with competitors introduce the same risks. Some alliances, such as the consolidation joint venture between Dow Jones and Reuters, must guard against the risk of a fire sale—that is, one partner buying out the other at a below-market price. This is not a serious threat in standard-setting alliances like Advanced Photo Systems, where Eastman Kodak and Fuji Photo Film should have been more concerned about noncooperative decision making or telegraphing future market moves. The following are five common risks in co-opetition, each of which demands a different managerial response.

Risk 1: Technology Leakage

A common risk in co-opetition is that a company's core technology or process will fall into a competitor's hands. Professor Kathryn Harrigan of Columbia Business School argues that for alliances between competitors to work "a certain amount of information has to be forth-coming from you, and there's the danger that the knowledge you have released into the hands of your competitor will come back to haunt you." One leading bicycle manufacturer knew this all too well. In the late 1980s, the firm formed alliances with Chinese and Japanese firms to manufacture its product at a lower cost. The company taught its partners everything it knew about building bicycles. Over time, the alliances disappeared and the partners emerged as direct and formidable global competitors.

Reducing such risk means controlling information. One approach is to limit the scope of the alliance. One U.S. firm did just this in a semiconductor manufacturing joint venture with a domestic com-petitor. The firms simply split the output of the shared production line, and did not share any intellectual property. Another method is to draft contracts that clearly define who owns which technologies, and how these technologies can be used. The joint venture contract between Xerox and Fuji Photo Film forbids the Japanese partner from us-ing Xerox technology for anything outside the venture. Contracts have their limits, though. Such documents can be hard to enforce, especially in countries with loosely enforced intellectual property laws. And they may have little effect on changing the behavior of engineers and others working with the partner from day to day.

There are other ways to regulate information flows. One is to create rules for employees that describe what they can and cannot discuss with the partner. Another technique is to appoint a gate-keeper—an employee who acts as an information funnel to and from the partner. One large electronics firm did just this, creating the posi-tion of technical program manager as the contact point for any and all discussions with a partner with respect to technical issues.

Some firms prefer to use a black box. Under this approach, the firm provides a finished component to the partner, who agrees to not open the box. A related approach is to contribute competencies, or bundles of skills, rather than disaggregated skills or assets. For exam-ple, McDonald's is well known for its competence in retail site selec-tion. In forming a co-location alliance with another retailer, such as a convenience store operator or oil company, McDonald's might be well served to maintain full control of this contribution, and not allow its partner to see how it makes its decisions. As a general rule, bundled competencies are extremely hard for partners to replicate.

Risk 2: Telegraphing Strategic Intention

Alliances with competitors can also tip a partner off as to the firm's future strategic plans. Sometimes, this happens through the direct transfer of information to the partner. Witness the banks that formed an alliance in the 1990s to define a new platform for Internet banking. Our interviews with those close to the venture suggested that the alliance allowed some firms to gain a broad and deep understanding of competitor strengths, weaknesses, and future business direction.

Other times the transfer is less explicit—but perhaps more troubling. Protracted interfirm relationships of any type create an ability to predict future behavior. How much do you know about your partner's wider plans in the business arena of your alliance? The partner may have revealed nothing to you outside of the scope of your alliance. But surely, by virtue of working closely together, each firm gains an intimate understanding of how its partner thinks and is now better able to predict its behavior. Only the nimblest companies step clear of these dangers. So much information can be inferred. To capture it, partners need only be vigilant observers.

Companies can reduce—but not eliminate—such risks by better managing information flows. For instance, senior management should convey to managers what information is strategic and develop guidelines for sharing this information. Management may also want to consider limiting the number of staff with direct contact to partners or establishing a separate site for the alliance that is away from the parent company.

Risk 3: Customer Defection

Companies are understandably touchy about putting current or potential competitors into contact with their customers. In so doing, they expose themselves to the very real risk that the partner will use its increased brand awareness, customer understanding, and direct personal relationships to steal customers away at some future date.

How do firms manage this risk? There are a number of potential approaches. One is to insist on jointly interacting with customers, never ceding full contact to the partner. Another is to demand reciprocal access to partner customers, a "mutually assured destruction" approach to collaboration. A third approach is to limit the threat of customer defection by allowing partners access to customers only when selling a jointly owned product.

A more common approach is to allow customer contact only when the alternatives are few, and the partners share a deep commitment. For example, two European firms created a joint venture to market high-speed trains in Asia, a new market for both firms. To some extent this was a risky strategy, but when weighed against the alternatives of less revenue and higher costs, the risks appeared worth taking.

Risk 4: Slow Decision Making

Alliances with competitors are more likely than other alliances to result in slow decision making, shallow cooperation, or even abandonment. The last was the outcome in a joint venture between General Electric and Rolls Royce to produce jet engines. The companies were direct competitors, selling similar products into similar markets. Ultimately, the partners were unable to cooperate; they canceled their venture when Rolls Royce announced its intention to introduce a jet engine that competed with the joint venture's engine. Alliances with competitors often become "a zero-sum game," according to one prominent Silicon Valley attorney. "Every inch of the way they're trying to get the same thing you are. Instead of having a complementary, synergistic relationship, there will be conflict over every issue, from who manufactures the product to who has the customer relationship."

At other times, alliances with competitors do get off the ground, but then suffer from slow decision making once in the air. One way to avoid this, suggests Columbia's Harrigan, is for the companies to focus their efforts at different points along the value chain. "If you can actually agree on who does what well, you can divide up the job description—you make it, I sell it." Pharmaceutical firms frequently structure their alliances this way—a small biotech firm develops and produces a drug, and a large pharmaceutical company sells it. Direct competitors can also cooperate on precompetitive research—that is, work that does not provide immediate commercial advantages for any of the partners. SEMATECH, Advanced Photo Systems, and U.S. Car are all examples of such alliances.

In addition to these approaches, it is essential to concentrate on the basics of sound decision making. This means identifying from ten to fifty of the most important decisions that the alliance will face, and defining which decision makers will participate in those decisions. (See Chapter Eleven, "Making Joint Decisions.")

Risk 5: Business or Asset Fire Sale

Alliances between competitors also create the risk of a fire sale—that the firm will be forced to sell its interest in the alliance at a below-market price. According to a McKinsey study, nearly 80 percent of all joint ventures are acquired by one of the partners within seven years. This figure may even be higher when the partners are competitors, and therefore simultaneously possess more interest in the other's business and less appetite for long-term cooperation. All too often, firms do not carefully think through the implications of this endgame, however, and fail to lock in a price or pricing formula for their assets during the initial negotiations and structuring. The result: because third-party buyers have much less interest in the assets once they are tied up in a joint venture, the firm is left with one real buyer (the partner) who then is in an extremely strong position to acquire the assets at a favorable price.

In addition to agreeing up front on a sale price, firms should consider other actions to avoid falling into a fire sale. One approach is to favor an independent joint venture structure, which will reduce the costs and complexity of a sale, as well as increase the interest of other buyers. Another approach is to avoid joint ventures altogether.

One prominent lawyer argues that small companies should avoid traditional joint ventures with larger competitors, because whereas the small company puts its core business into the venture, the alliance may be only a short-term distraction for the larger partner: "Sometimes I tell my clients," he says, "Let's not do the joint venture. If what they really want is to buy our business, let's give them distribution rights for an agreed period. At the end of that period, they can either buy the company or we get the rights back. That may cap our upside, but it probably also makes the buy-out more likely. And it avoids the risk of getting bogged down in a joint venture that you can't get out of."

Co-opetition is here to stay. To succeed, companies, at a minimum, must manage the risks of such alliances, developing a toolkit of best practices suited to different situations. In alliances with competitors, blind trust is not enough.

Further Reading

Adam M. Brandenburger and Barry J. Nalebuff. *Co-opetition.* New York: Currency/Doubleday, 1996.

Gary Hamel, Yves L. Doz, and C. K. Prahalad. "Collaborate with Your Competitors—and Win," *Harvard Business Review*, Jan.-Feb. 1989, pp. 133–139.

Robert Reich and E. Mankin. "Joint Ventures with Japan Give Away Our Future," *Harvard Business Review*, Mar.-Apr. 1986, pp. 78–86.

Source

This chapter is based on several articles in *The Alliance Analyst*, especially "Into Coopetition" (March 1997), "Lucent Views on Coopetition" (May 1997), and "Growing Up in Coopetition" (May 1997). The articles were combined, edited, and updated for this chapter.

7

Crafting the Agreement

Lawyers and Managers

David Ernst, Stephen I. Glover, James D. Bamford

Crafting an alliance can throw lawyers and executives into a bitter struggle. Lawyers often want to limit risks and create future options for the corporate parent. They tend to favor alliances that are narrow in scope and long on contractual detail. Executives, on the other hand, tend to be more concerned with building successful businesses. They are more focused on growth and often argue for broad-based alliances with running room for scope expansion. In addition, ownership structure and decision rights, for example, are a familiar battleground: while lawyers often shun 50-50 joint ventures because of the risk of deadlocks in decision making, executives often see them as ideal for encouraging trust and independence.

Tension between lawyers and executives may not be unique to alliances, but it is more extreme here than in other business development strategies. In acquisitions, for example, legal and business views tend to be more closely aligned on the objectives of minimizing liabilities, seeking the lowest acquisition price, and easing the integration process. The same is true in divestitures: lawyers and business leaders want to maximize the price to the firm and minimize disputes after closing.

But when forming an alliance, managers and lawyers often part ways. Indeed, many executives believe it best to keep the legal team away from the alliance negotiation for as long as possible. This is a mistake. The best firms combine legal and business best practice when structuring alliances. To show how this works, we've focused on five essential deal terms: ownership, scope, structure, valuation, and exit. Each area demonstrates how the traditionally divergent views of lawyers and executives can be combined into a powerful model for forming alliances.

Ownership: Allocating Decision Rights

Companies entering an alliance are often concerned about their share of economic ownership in a venture. In part this comes from a desire to maximize financial rewards, but it also stems from a belief that ownership determines the extent to which the firm will control (or have influence over) critical venture decisions. A McKinsey study of more than five hundred alliances involving large U.S., European, Asian, and Latin American companies found that many ventures fail because of unclear decision-making rights. Creating smooth decision-making processes can be particularly difficult in a 50-50 alliance, where both partners often have equal influence, and where the managing board is composed of an equal number of directors from each corporate parent.

Yet 50-50 alliances have a substantially higher success rate than those with uneven ownership—50-50 deals succeed 60 percent of the time, whereas majority-minority deals meet the financial and strategic expectations of the parents in 31 percent of the cases examined. Moreover, 50-50 joint ventures have a somewhat longer life span than those with uneven ownership (Figure 7.1). The McKinsey study concluded that in 50-50 ventures where both partners are equally committed, the partners are more likely to work harder to make the venture succeed. Also, 50-50 ventures are typically more independent of the parents than are majority-minority deals.

The Lawyer's Perspective

Lawyers typically advise against 50-50 joint ventures, recommending that the client take a majority position and management control. This ensures clear decision power (translation: we decide)

FIGURE 7.1 Lifetimes of Joint Ventures.

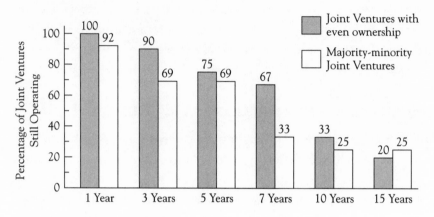

Source: McKinsey & Co.

while also protecting the parent's interests (translation: since we decide, we can easily protect our interests). And sometimes, these solutions are acceptable to both partners, especially when there is a large disparity in their strengths or contributions, or when one of the partners sees the venture as a potential step toward divestiture and is therefore willing to cede control of a non-core business.

But companies do not always heed the lawyer's counsel against 50-50 joint ventures. Frequently, neither partner is willing to turn over control to the other side. When ownership is split 50-50, lawyers will attempt to protect parent interests by drafting a detailed joint venture contract specifying that both partners will have equal seats on a governance board. Although the joint venture CEO will be given day-to-day operating responsibility, the board will have veto power over a list of key decisions, which typically include acquisitions or divestitures, the annual budget, capital expenditures in excess of a specified amount, strategic plans, changes in product or market scope, transfer pricing to and from the parents, appointment of the top two to five officers of the venture, and designation of auditors.

If either partner vetoes a key decision, the contract will often specify a cooling-off period, an obligation to use best efforts to work out the differences, referral of the issue to a higher level within the parent organizations, or possibly outside mediation or arbitration. If all of these conflict resolution devices fail, the venture may be terminated under prearranged conditions.

The Executive's Perspective

Some executives approach the issue just as lawyers do: try for majority ownership and a controlling vote on the board and, at a minimum, reserve the right to veto key decisions. Others look beyond the matter of economic ownership and focus on decision-making control, for instance, by identifying a few key issues and agreeing how each will be resolved before the agreement is signed.

Consider a U.S. firm and a Latin American firm that were negotiating a joint venture to manufacture and sell the U.S. firm's product in Latin America. The U.S. firm was concerned that its local partner would be unwilling to fund the construction of a second regional plant. Under the terms of the typical agreement, the local firm would be able to block the investment by virtue of its veto power on the board.

To address this situation, the U.S. firm made several alterations to the standard alliance agreement. First, the partners agreed in advance to a plan for capital expenditures, including plant expansions, for the first several years (again, subject to performance conditions). Second, the partners agreed that in the event one partner wished to fund expansion while the other did not, then either partner could fund the incremental investment and in return would receive a larger share of ownership and dividends in the joint venture. If one partner wished to invest and the other partner was not willing to have its ownership stake diluted, then the investing partner could build the plant as a wholly owned entity and sell the product in a specified set of markets outside the core focus of the joint venture.

This solution was carefully tailored to fit the immediate circumstances. However, it illustrates the typical conflict situations that are likely to arise and the possibility of crafting creative solutions that fit with the business strategy and protect parent interests while also increasing the odds that the joint venture does not fail as a result of conflicts and decision gridlock.

The Best of Both Worlds

Since clear decision making lies at the heart of successful alliances, both partners can derive substantial benefits from combining the best of legal and business best practice. The ideal approach contemplates using five mechanisms.

Separate Economic Control from Decision-Making Control. It is natural to assume that economic control (what percentage of the venture the firm owns) will be same as decision-making control (how much say the firm has in decisions). But there is no reason that this needs to be so. In the energy industry, one consolidation joint venture had a 65-35 split in terms of economic ownership but operated as a 50-50 partnership on all decisions. Conversely, a joint venture in the office equipment business was 50-50 in economic control, but one partner operated the alliance and controlled all major decisions.

Seek the Casting Vote or Veto Power on Certain Decisions. It is often possible to protect parent interests simply by having real influence over one or two decisions. One leading international oil company signed a 50-50 joint venture in the Indian market after concluding that a casting vote on capital expenditures was enough to protect its interests. In other cases, firms have focused on decisions that involve changes in the basic venture goals, quality control, and regulatory and fiduciary responsibilities. In focusing on the control of a few decisions—rather than control of the entire venture—firms will be more flexible in deal making and more successful in their alliances.

Agree in Advance on Ten to Fifteen Key Decisions. With some decisions, it is both possible and advisable to reach agreement before ever forming the venture. One candidate for such treatment is capital expenditures. As mentioned earlier, partners can develop a capital expenditures plan, including investments in product development, manufacturing, and new markets, for the first several years of the alliance. Other times, firms may want to agree in advance on transfer pricing, venture staffing, and dividend policies. In scripting certain decisions, partners will uncover potential areas of conflict and speed decision making once the alliance is operational.

Develop a Decision-Making Map. Smooth decision making depends on a clear understanding of roles in different decisions. To promote this understanding, the partners should consider developing a decision-making protocol—a road map of the twenty to fifty most important decisions that the alliance will face. This protocol will spell out which decision makers (JV CEO, JV board, EVP of operations, and so on) will be involved in which alliance decisions (annual budget, spot discounts to customers, and so on) and the nature of the involvement (propose, consult, decide, and so on) in those decisions. In most cases, it is possible to develop such a decision-making road map during a workshop at the outset of the alliance.

Create Conflict Resolution Mechanisms. Partners should include opt-out or wild-card provisions in the alliance agreement to avoid or resolve conflict after it arises. For example, the JV agreement might allow one partner to fund investments while diluting the other's ownership stake. Alternatively, it might allow one of the partners to take on activities within the initial scope of the alliance if the other parent does not empower the alliance to do so. As a third example, the alliance might be allowed to buy crucial inputs or sell its output on the open market if the parents fail to reach agreement on transfer prices. All of these creative decision-making strategies may prevent termination.

Structure: The Form of the Alliance Tie

Potential partners must determine what sort of legal structure will hold them together. At the most basic level, this is a choice between a "newco" joint venture and a non-equity (contractual) alliance where no new entity is created. As a general rule, joint ventures are favored when the partners seek to make deep combinations of tangible assets (technology, equipment, factories, and so on). And since joint ventures often take substantial time to form, start up, restructure, and undo, they are preferred when the alliance is stable in direction and expected to last for at least several years. In contrast, non-equity alliances are generally favored when planned integration is less deep, or centers around intangible assets (brands, ideas, and so on), which can be hard to value. Non-equity alliances are also favored in short-term or fluid situations.

The decision on venture structure is more complex than the choice between joint venture and non-equity alliance, however. Below these basic options lie more choices. For instance, in the United States, firms must select one of four joint venture structures: corporation, general partnership, limited partnership, or limited liability company.

The Lawyer's Perspective

In choosing an alliance structure, lawyers tend to focus on four dimensions: liability, governance, tax, and regulation. Traditionally, the main concern has been liability—how much exposure the company has to lawsuits and other large downside risks. This focus led to a preference for joint ventures—and in particular the corporate, limited liability, or limited partnership forms, which limit the firm's liability to the amount of its venture investment. By contrast, a non-equity alliance or general partnership joint venture may expose all the assets of the corporate parent to the liabilities of the alliance.

In recent years, lawyers have revised this view somewhat, adding sophistication to their arguments. Experienced lawyers now tend to follow new guidelines. (Tax and corporate laws are unique to each country. This discussion focuses on the United States. In addition, specific tax and accounting rules tend to change frequently, so the practitioner should seek the advice of counsel.)

Liability Concerns Are Not Primary. Through appropriate structuring, partners can achieve limited liability even if they opt for the general partnership or contractual joint venture forms. For example, if the partners choose a general partnership, they can establish new wholly owned corporate subsidiaries that will be the partners in the venture. If the partners choose the contractual form, they can form new corporate subsidiaries that will enter into and perform the contract. As long as the new subsidiaries are adequately capitalized and the venture participants adhere to corporate formalities, the partners should enjoy the protection of the corporate shield.

Neither Is Governance. Different entities certainly use varying management structures (a JV corporation is managed by elected officers and overseen by a board of directors, a partnership is run by general partners), but the partners can typically achieve their governance goals under a range of structures. If the partners of a 50-50 joint venture want a group of four individuals to govern the venture, they can establish a corporation with a four-member board of directors, a limited liability company with a four-person board of managers, or a general partnership with, again, a four-person managing board. In a contractual alliance, the partners can create an alliance steering committee with two representatives from each partner.

But Taxation and Accounting Treatment May Be. In most cases, the key tax question will be whether the entity is taxed as a corporation or a partnership. Owners of corporations will be subject to double taxation—income will be taxed not only when it is earned by the joint venture corporation but again when it is distributed to the venture shareholders. By comparison, the income of entities that are treated as partnerships will not be subject to double taxation. Instead, they will be taxed only at the partner level. (Tax and corporate laws are unique to each country. This discussion focuses on the United States. In addition, specific tax and accounting rules tend to change frequently, so the practitioner should seek the advice of counsel.)

Entities that are taxed as partnerships also offer greater flexibility than the corporation with regard to the allocation of gains or losses. Thus, for example, under certain conditions the partnership documents might provide that one party will receive 50 percent of the gains generated by the partnership but 99 percent of the losses, or they might provide that one partner will receive 80 percent of the profits while holding 50 percent ownership.

A venture partner may be interested in consolidating the joint venture for tax or accounting purposes. The tax and accounting consolidation and income reporting rules generally will apply in the same way whether the venture is a corporation, limited liability company, or a partnership. If the partner owns an 80 percent or greater equity interest in the venture it should be able to consolidate for tax purposes, and if it owns a greater than 50 percent equity interest or otherwise exercises control it should be able to consolidate for accounting purposes.

Payments from a venture to a venture parent may be treated differently for tax purposes depending on whether the joint venture is a corporation on one hand, or a limited liability company or partnership on the other—thus, if the partners expect the venture to make substantial dividend payments to the parent, they should consider this issue in making their structure decision.

Regulation Often Is. Under the rules applied by the U.S. Department of Justice and the Federal Trade Commission under the Hart-Scott-Rodino Act, the formation of a non-equity alliance or a joint venture that is a general partnership, limited partnership, or limited liability company ordinarily is not a reportable transaction. The formation of a corporate joint venture, by contrast, is reportable if the partners or the contributed assets meet certain size tests. Where the partners are concerned about potential delays due to antitrust review, the partnership or limited liability company form of joint venture may thus offer significant advantages. (Obviously, avoiding a Hart-Scott-Rodino filing does not insulate the alliance from antitrust challenges.)

The Executive's Perspective

Executives faced with a broad range of alternative structures can become overwhelmed and spend a great deal of energy making a choice. In other cases, they arrive with preconceived notions about the ideal structure and are unwilling to consider alternative forms. Both approaches present obvious drawbacks. Partners should be flexible about the choice of structure and willing to consider alternatives that will help them achieve their underlying business goals.

Executives should focus on business issues that will affect the choice of structure. Do they want an alliance that is an autonomous business like Dow Corning, or does the success of the alliance depend on integrating parent assets? Do the partners plan to make additional capital investments? If successful, will the alliance last for three or more years? Is one partner likely to sell its interest to the other partner or a third party, or will the venture be spun off to public investors?

The answers help partners decide whether to establish a joint venture or a contractual alliance. If they answer yes to any of these questions, then establishing a joint venture may be useful.

The Best of Both Worlds

These perspectives can be combined by taking three steps. First, encourage the executives to articulate what concerns the structure should address—for example, autonomous management or the possibility of a spin-off. Listing these concerns will help determine whether the partners should form a separate entity and how that entity should be governed. The executives should also be the ones leading the discussion about governance procedures and board composition.

Second, lawyers should be asked to identify the governance, tax, regulatory, and liability concerns that favor one form over another. This is clearly within the scope of their professional expertise. Third, work together to generate the answer. Choosing the optimal alliance structure is a collaborative act—between the partners, and between the executives and lawyers. The answer must address the strategic and managerial concerns that so consume executives, while at the same time satisfying the tax, liability, and regulatory issues that matter so much to lawyers.

Scope: Where the Alliance Begins and Ends

Another essential task is defining the scope of the alliance—what the venture and the partners can and cannot do. Defining scope requires the partners to establish boundaries of geography, product categories, customer segments, brands, technologies, and fixed assets between the alliance and the parents. They must identify the activities in which the alliance may engage and those reserved for the parents. They must decide how the alliance can use the parents' technology and other assets and who can use those assets that the alliance develops.

The Lawyer's Perspective

Lawyers often want to define the scope of an alliance narrowly and reserve the right for the parent to expand into related areas in the future with or without the partner. This cautious approach can be enormously helpful in reducing risk. For example, one U.S. manufacturer granted a twenty-year exclusive license covering several large emerging markets to a single company in the region, with royalty fees set as a percentage of revenues. When its partner underperformed and competitors proliferated, it had little leverage to renegotiate the arrangement. A more cautious approach—limiting the scope to specific countries, signing a nonexclusive agreement, setting a shorter term, or building in minimum performance requirements—would have been a much better strategy.

Lawyers understand that defining scope narrowly has drawbacks. First, it can interfere with ongoing venture development, especially if technology licenses from the parents are too restrictive. Second, to the extent that a narrow scope means that the alliance will depend on the parents for resources (for example, marketing and sales support and sourcing of key components), transfer pricing issues will loom as a continuing source of conflict. And third, a narrow scope limits the alliance's ability to respond to change—to adapt to new market conditions.

The Executive's Perspective

Executives often want to create a broad and autonomous venture with running room for growth. As one joint venture CEO said: "The parents should put all of the relevant activities and markets into the pot, pay me based on the profitability of the JV, and leave me alone to run the business. Otherwise, conflicts are guaranteed."

Executives understand that defining alliance scope narrowly may reduce risks and prevent a big giveaway to the alliance or other partner. But executives also recognize that a narrow scope may reduce the likelihood that the alliance—and hence the parents—will succeed in the long run. A McKinsey study involving the 150 largest multinational corporations showed that 65 percent experienced major conflicts in the first years of an alliance. Many of the successful joint ventures in the study were substantially expanded in scope. Looking at the 49 percent of cross-border joint ventures that failed to meet the strategic and financial objectives of the parents, one of the most common causes of failure was that the parents did not scope the alliance broadly enough. An obvious solution is to scope an alliance narrowly at first and then expand it at the appropriate time. But this is much easier said than done. Restructuring an alliance to expand its scope can be even more time-consuming than the initial negotiations.

The Best of Both Worlds

Five approaches can help to bring the "best of both" from legal advisers and business managers when structuring an alliance. Alliances should build in room for growth, and companies should select partners that are not competitors. They should establish exclusive agreements only when necessary, and they should anticipate the probability of changes in scope and negotiate them in advance. In addition, they should define how each of the parents will use the technology developed by the alliance.

Create Room for Growth. The partners should minimize the potential of conflicts between their current businesses on one hand and the business of the alliance on the other, by giving the alliance sufficient scope to grow for some period of time. For large joint ventures, this period should be at least three to five years. The corporate parents should also restrict their right to engage in activities within that scope during that time. For a more fluid non-equity alliance, this period may be much shorter.

Select Partners That Are Not Competitors. This step will reduce disputes over the activities of the alliance and ensure commitment. Collaborating to compete need not mean collaborating with direct competitors. McKinsey has found that alliances between direct competitors are more likely to fail and more likely to terminate within the first three years than alliances involving parents that are not direct competitors.

Establish Exclusive Arrangements Only When Necessary. When compelled to establish an exclusive arrangement, partners should link the term and scope of the exclusive arrangements to performance requirements and exit triggers.

Anticipate and Negotiate Changes in Scope in Advance. When possible, partners should agree on the conditions under which the product, market, technology, and value chain scope will be changed. For example, a European manufacturer of vehicles negotiated an alliance with a Korean company aimed at distribution throughout Asia. However, the initial geographic scope of the venture was confined to a single country, with plans to expand to other countries after Korean sales were established.

Define How Parents Will Use Technology Created by the Alliance. There are a number of ways to do this: by geographic area, product category, or end-user customer segment. Two chemical manufacturers, for example, might decide to collaborate to develop a new type of plastic, with one of the firms having the right to sell to the automotive segment, and the other retaining rights for all other customers.

Valuation: Sorting Out Economic Interests

Structuring an alliance introduces a series of valuation issues—how much each partner's contributions are worth, what economic interest in the venture the partners will receive in return for these contributions, and how the partners will value the output of the alliance. These valuation questions are complex and important.

The Lawyer's Perspective

When it comes time to make proposals regarding value, a lawyer's reflexive response is to negotiate aggressively to minimize client resources devoted to the alliance and maximize its share of future profits or other outputs. Of course, lawyers recognize that larger parent contributions may benefit the alliance and thus ultimately help the client. But fundamentally, lawyers approach valuation from the perspective of the client. Lawyers do not act as an advocate of the alliance—indeed they are ethically barred from doing so, except in the rare case in which specifically retained for this purpose. The result is that lawyers, by taking aggressive positions on behalf of their client that result in a win-lose outcome, may interfere with the creation of a strong business.

The Executive's Perspective

Some executives are more likely to advocate valuation solutions that create a strong alliance. For example, they might provide a generous valuation to certain partner assets in order to create such benefits as partner trust. Executives may also be quite willing to value assets (or set transfer prices) on favorable terms for the alliance, and thus improve its chances of sustainable business success. But executives also understand that creating a strong alliance makes sense only if the result is consistent with the goals of the company—that is, maximizing shareholder value for the parent company. And thus executives understand the value of careful analysis and aggressive negotiation on behalf of the parent.

The Best of Both Worlds

When it comes to valuation, the executive's desire to develop a strong alliance and the lawyer's advocacy on behalf of the parent both have their place. But a real concern in resolving valuation issues is that it is very difficult for a single team of dealmakers to advocate for the alliance and at the same time negotiate on behalf of the parent. To combine these views, consider *establishing three deal teams*. Each company would have a separate negotiating team—a group of executives and lawyers assigned to protect parent interests and analyze the alliance from the parent's perspective. Their focus is on valuing and negotiating required capital contributions, expected return on the parent's investment, and zero-sum issues such as equity split and initial contributions.

A third team would consist of executives from both sides. Its role is to protect the interests of the alliance—to develop a business plan and determine how the alliance can maximize synergies, including resource requirements such as cash, assets, technology, and management. This team should be permitted initially to develop its own plan without significant input from the negotiating teams.

Discussions about value and capital contributions are likely to be adversarial and disruptive, especially if these negotiations take place before the benefits of the alliance are established and trust is built between the partners. They will interfere with the development of the spirit of cooperation that is essential to the creation of a strong alliance. Once the benefits have been validated, the negotiating teams should test whether the partners can agree on valuation and other deal terms.

Exit: Preparing for the End

An alliance is rarely a permanent arrangement. McKinsey's analysis shows that the average life span of a joint venture is about seven years, with more than 75 percent of terminated joint ventures acquired by one of the partners. Given these statistics, even partners with a high degree of confidence in the longevity of their alliance should consider exit provisions to protect their interests.

The Lawyer's Perspective

Lawyers recognize the need to negotiate exit clauses and will almost always insist that these clauses be included in the alliance agreement. They will ask their clients to identify the events that will trigger a right to exit. These triggers might include a change in control of one of the parents, the inability to agree on a key issue, the failure to achieve an important business milestone, breach of contract, or a sunset date after which either partner can terminate the alliance upon notice to the other.

Lawyers will also ask their clients to discuss how the exit should be made once an exit right is triggered. In joint ventures, it is common to propose "put" provisions, under which one partner has the right to require the other to purchase its interest. Lawyers may further suggest that partners be given the right to sell their interests to third parties once exit rights are triggered. And they may recommend that this transfer right be subject to a right of first refusal, under which the non-selling partner would have an option to acquire the interests of the selling partner before the selling partner may transfer its interests to a third party. Alternatively, the lawyers may suggest that the exit be effected by selling the alliance in its entirety or conducting an initial public offering.

Finally, good lawyers will ask their clients to focus on termination-related valuation issues. If the partner is going to sell its interest to the alliance or other partners, what price should be paid? Frequently, firms adopt "buy-sell" provisions under which one of the partners sets a price and the other partner then chooses whether to buy or sell at this price. Alternatively, lawyers may suggest the use of an outside appraisal (by one or more investment banks or advisers) to set a "fair price."

The Executive's Perspective

Executives tend to approach exit provisions differently. Many want to defer detailed discussion on the grounds that such discussions can reduce trust. The very act of suggesting exit provisions, let alone debating their content, can seem like a proof of bad faith. Executives may want to avoid discussion of exit provision for a second reason: it forces an uncomfortably blunt assessment of whether the parent is the natural buyer or seller of the assets. If the parent is the natural seller—say, because the business really does not fit the company portfolio but cannot be sold for an attractive price today—this can be embarrassing for the managers running the business.

The Best of Both Worlds

As with most other elements of alliance negotiations, both lawyers and executives have perspectives that should be combined in the integrated negotiation plan.

Address Exit Up Front. Given the importance of exit provisions in determining the terminal value of the alliance, the partners should consider them in detail in the negotiations. Recognizing the sensitivity of the issue, however, it makes sense to discuss exit provisions after the business team has confirmed the value of the alliance and the overall terms of the deal. Moreover, it is best if a separate team consisting of financial and legal staff negotiate the exit provisions, using guidance from the business team. This way, the managers who have to work together after the ink is dry can avoid being in the middle of a tense prenuptial negotiation.

Be Careful with "Buy-Sell" Provisions. Using this device to set alliance value upon termination has become quite common in recent years. But it is appropriate only when each partner is just as likely to be the buyer or the seller.

It is dangerous for a company that is likely to be the seller to agree to a "buy-sell" provision. Once the alliance is under way, it will be very difficult to conduct an open auction to sell the business. The partner that is likely to be a buyer will be in a very strong bargaining position, because it will have had the opportunity to meet customers, absorb know-how, evaluate the true economic value of the business, capture much of its synergies, and learn how to operate the venture as a stand-alone business. In theory, a third company could buy the joint venture, but this rarely happens. The bargaining power of the likely seller is at its strongest on the day before the alliance contract is signed.

Assess Who Is Likely to Be Buyer or Seller. It is often possible to anticipate which of the partners is more likely to be the acquirer by looking at how closely the alliance's business is connected to each partner's core activity and at the ability of each partner to invest. It also helps to consider which of the parents controls patents and technology and which of the partners controls the customer channels. If the company is likely to be the seller, it should try to negotiate a valuation approach that either locks in the current value of the business as a floor price or sets a future valuation based on a formula.

Conclusion

Both lawyers and executives have much to offer in crafting alliance agreements. Best business practices suggest that some of the typical lawyers' concerns—the desire to define scope precisely and the reaction against 50-50 joint ventures—are overblown. Similarly, the lawyers' views on such issues as exit mechanisms and structure can provide significant help to the executives. A good working relationship between the two parts of the negotiating team should increase the likelihood that the resulting alliance will be well designed and successful.

Further Reading

George T. Geis and George S. Geis. *Digital Deals: Strategies for Structuring Partnerships*. New York: McGraw-Hill, 2001. Chapters 6–10.

Source

This chapter is based on "Tug of War: Combining Legal and Business Best Practice" by David Ernst and Stephen Glover, *The Alliance Analyst* (July 1997). The article was edited for this book.

8

Negotiating the Deal

Companies often make critical mistakes in negotiating alliances. Sometimes a firm will simply cut a bad deal; other times a firm may take too long in negotiations. One U.S. pharmaceutical company concluded that it could create $1 billion per year in additional value if it reduced by 50 percent the time it took to negotiate alliances with biotech partners. Still other firms fail to link the negotiation strategy to the nature of the intended relationship, and in so doing assume an overly adversarial or cooperative stance in negotiations.

How do companies avoid these and other problems? In search of answers, we drew on the experiences of John Kalb, at IBM at the time, and Marilyn Hartig of Bristol-Myers Squibb, two leading alliance practitioners. The best alliance negotiators, we have concluded, address key issues in three areas: preparing for negotiation, building the negotiating team, and conducting the negotiations.

Preparing for Negotiation

Before entering into discussions with a potential partner, managers should develop a clear understanding of the firm's aims, constraints, and position in the alliance—and develop a strategy for the negotiation.

To do this, managers should start by creating an "alliance aims and constraints sheet"—a one-page document that summarizes what the firm really wants out of the alliance. The purpose of the document is to focus managers on what really matters and to avoid negotiation battles over issues and provisions that are peripheral to the firm's true aims. It can also be helpful to develop a "gives and gets analysis"—a basic scorecard of what contributions the firm will make to the alliance and what it expects from a partner (Exhibit 8.1). These documents create the basic rationale for the alliance and provide a strong anchor to the negotiation process.

Prior to negotiations, it is also important to determine an overall negotiation strategy—that is, agree on the tone and tenor of the pending discussions. At this stage, negotiators are well advised to consider not only the hard economic issues to be tackled but also the softer human questions. After all, in most cases, the result of the negotiations will be an alliance in which managers from the two sides will have to work together. A strictly adversarial approach therefore does not work except for deals designed to end up essentially as arm's-length vendor relationships.

The overall negotiating strategy need not be a choice between "hard" and "soft" bargaining. In fact, skilled alliance negotiators often prefer a mix of the two. In Chapter Nine Jeff Weiss and Laura Visioni describe a "two-track" negotiating approach that is at the same time "hard on the issues" and "soft on the people." The idea is to tackle the tough economic issues while laying the foundation for a constructive and amicable relationship between the partners.

The best alliance negotiators will also develop a negotiation road map—a chronology of the different phases of negotiations. While at IBM, John Kalb often approached alliances in three phases. Phase One was courtship: "That typically is a very warm and friendly exercise," he notes. "In some ways, it is defining the pie." Phase Two turned to alliance economics—that is, how to measure and divide the value in the proposed relationship. This introduces tension into the discussions. Kalb recommends making a clear indication when this phase arrives: "I frequently tell potential

EXHIBIT 8.1 Partner Contributions.

Our Firm

Formal contributions
(as contracted)

What?   When?

☐ _____   ☐ _____
☐ _____   ☐ _____
☐ _____   ☐ _____

Informal contributions
(not in contract but needed for alliance success)

What?   When?

☐ _____   ☐ _____
☐ _____   ☐ _____
☐ _____   ☐ _____

Partner Firm

Formal contributions
(as contracted)

What?   When?

☐ _____   ☐ _____
☐ _____   ☐ _____
☐ _____   ☐ _____

Informal contributions
(not in contract but needed for alliance success)

What?   When?

☐ _____   ☐ _____
☐ _____   ☐ _____
☐ _____   ☐ _____

partners at the beginning, 'Look, I'm not negotiating with you. I'll ring a bell when we go into negotiation, so that you know when we are defining the pie.'"

Phase Three was documentation. Once the broad concepts have been worked out, the companies need to get the details down on paper. This often introduces a level of emotion and pressure that wasn't there in the first two stages, according to Kalb. It doesn't last very long, but is characteristic of almost all deals. "I would say in Europe, there is a fourth phase," Kalb notes, "to renegotiate again, just to make sure that you were serious the first time." When managers have a negotiation road map, they are much more likely to negotiate with the appropriate tone and tenor, and focus on the relevant issues.

Building the Negotiation Team

Successful negotiations also depend on assembling a team with the skills to execute the deal. In general, the negotiating team should be small, with a nucleus of no more than three to five people, and contain individuals with experience negotiating and structuring similar alliances. The team clearly has to include people focusing on both the legal and the business side of the alliance; as explained in Chapter Seven, these two perspectives can differ substantially. Beyond these broad guidelines the roles of the executive sponsor, outside facilitators, and the alliance manager deserve special consideration.

Executive Sponsor

Top-performing companies will ensure that the alliance has a champion—a senior executive responsible for overseeing the negotiation and supporting the alliance once formed. According to Kalb, "If there isn't somebody at the general management level who wants to be in the deal, it is a waste of my time." But experienced negotiators say that this sponsor probably should not be the CEO. "Depending on the scope of the deal, there are many situations where the CEO is an inappropriate champion," notes Marilyn Hartig, vice president of external science and technology at Bristol-Myers Squibb, and one of the company's main alliance dealmakers. When CEOs are champions, there is no system of checks and balances, no natural mechanism to stop a bad deal. "They end up being the most expensive, the biggest, and the worst" alliances, according to Kalb. The CEO need not be the formal champion to create problems. Bristol-Myers Squibb found that deals can even suffer from the "shadow of the leader"— the CEO gets interested and voices some support, and then no one is willing to stand up in opposition.

Outside Facilitators

Companies often bring external advisers into negotiations, especially when the alliance involves complex valuation, tax, or regulatory issues. But should firms use an external facilitator to structure and lead the discussions? That may not be a good idea. At Bristol-Myers Squibb, Marilyn Hartig worked on one deal where the other party used an external facilitator: "I don't think it worked. To really facilitate a deal well, you need to know and understand the organization you are trying to facilitate for, and it is somewhat hard to do that from outside. So, if you can have someone from the inside doing that for you, it may be more effective." John Kalb often took on the facilitator role himself, particularly in the early stages of the negotiation. One of his favorite exercises was to tell the two teams to write the press releases that they would like to see coming out of the alliance for the next four years. As he explains: "It gets them out of the feel-good spirit and forces them to put something down on paper in a headline form."

Alliance Managers

Expert opinions differ on whether those who will run the alliance should be included on the negotiation team. The former head of a billion-dollar global telecom joint venture expressed one view: "You just can't afford to have the future alliance manager involved in negotiations. For every alliance you do, there are ten that you took to the brink and didn't do. Thus, to take key operating people who are capable of running a venture out of their line operating jobs long enough to go through ten negotiations for the one that finally hits means that you have taken a key operating resource and tied it up for a long period of time. Most line managers wouldn't stand for that."

Others argue that leaving the operating managers out of the negotiations risks excluding important information and reducing the buy-in of people who will later need to implement the alliance. This view argues that operating people need to be brought in early, though perhaps not sit at the negotiating table to slog it out with their future partner.

As is often the case, both sides are right. Firms would be wise to choose a potential alliance manager to include on the deal team, after the initial partner screening and discussions of interest have taken place. Likewise, in most alliances, the company will not be pulling a senior operating manager off the line to run the alliance. A large joint venture such as Pepsi-Lipton or British Petroleum–Safeway may well demand an experienced operating executive at the helm, but most alliances do not merit that level of talent. One leading U.S. software company, for example, recruits fresh MBAs from top business schools to be its alliance managers. The firm views alliances as ideal small businesses for these future leaders to sharpen their teeth on. Including them on the negotiating team can only improve the odds of success.

Conducting the Negotiation

Beyond assembling a solid negotiating team, companies need to take certain actions during the negotiations to ensure success. To be sure, alliance negotiations—like all negotiations—can be highly idiosyncratic and complicated. Here we focus on critical success factors: those actions that differentiate winners from losers.

Act Swiftly but Set Realistic Expectations

Some companies pride themselves on the speed with which they close alliance deals. Yahoo!, for example, once claimed that it only took five to ten hours to negotiate and close its average alliance. Although this is an extreme (and almost certainly reflects the standardized nature of Yahoo! alliance contracts), companies clearly need to be concerned about the speed of negotiations.

While at IBM, John Kalb discovered a strong correlation between time to general consensus and the ultimate chance of closing the deal. "Get it done in three or four months, and the hit rate is going to be 80 percent," Kalb says; "If it takes six months or more, the hit rate goes down to 25 percent. If it takes a year, it has been a nice experience, but it is not going to close." Of those alliances that do close after a year or more of negotiation, many are simply what Kalb calls "external submissions"—flawed deals that are signed because everyone is too tired to fix the problems but too tired to walk away.

While Kalb's guidelines are useful for larger alliances, a more general rule of thumb is that alliance negotiations should take no longer than 10 percent of the realistic life span of the relationship. In other words, a one-year marketing alliance should take a month or less to close, whereas a three-year research alliance could take up to a few months but not more. Alliance negotiations need a sense of urgency, but the speed of closing a deal must be commensurate with the complexity of the task.

Shape the Negotiating Environment

Certain legal documents can be important to shape the context for the negotiations. The first is a confidentiality agreement. This sets out the companies' rights and privileges with respect to the information received during the discussions. Another is a negotiation letter, which says that there is no deal until there is a written deal signed by both parties. "A lot of people pretend they have never heard of it before," according to John Kalb. "But we do get sued." Taken together, these documents can dramatically increase the openness and understanding between the potential partners, and allow them to have much more expansive and free-flowing discussions.

Another important legal document is a formation agreement. This document outlines the critical elements of the alliance—and goes much further than the letter of intent, which is usually broad and lacking in detail. Especially useful when negotiating complicated alliances, the formation agreement may cover a number of provisions, including a definition of the business and geographic scope of the alliance, the basic ownership structure, the main contractual relationships (such as licenses, loaned personnel, and supply agreements), details of any joint market or technical studies, and an overall timetable and milestones for the negotiations.

Develop a Joint Business Plan

It often makes sense for the negotiating teams to join in developing a business plan for the alliance. Consider how two large chemical companies approached the negotiations of a billion-dollar consolidation JV. After basic discussions, the executive sponsors created an exploratory team composed of six managers from each company. These managers, who would ultimately become the leadership team of the JV, were asked to spend two to four weeks developing a detailed business case for the JV, including synergy and income targets, an operating budget, initial capital expenditure program, and a launch plan for the first hundred days.

The exercise created a number of benefits. It produced a document that contained a compelling vision for the venture and mapped out critical operating practices for the JV to develop a culture distinct from the corporate parents, including a more entrepreneurial culture enabling faster decision making. It also allowed the companies to test how well they worked together—and the prospective managers to start to build a collaborative spirit.

Manage Internal Conflicts

It is common among large companies to have multiple operating units talking to the same candidate partner. Successful negotiations depend on uncovering and resolving these potential internal conflicts early. "People don't like to do it," notes John Kalb. "It threatens the life of this new idea. But it is going to come up during the final approval."

IBM had a "vendor information system" to help uncover these conflicts. When IBM started a discussion with a particular company, managers put that partner's name and IBM contact point into the worldwide database. (More detailed information was held back due to security and secrecy concerns.) At the same time, the managers searched the database to determine whether anyone else at IBM was engaged in discussions with the partner. As Kalb notes, "It is not unusual for us to meet each other for the first time in the lobby of a perspective partner's office and find that there are two or three divisions that have identified the company as a likely prospect and are in the process of trying to eventually get them."

Move Beyond the Contract

Successful negotiations do not end with the contract. After signing the agreement, it is important to ensure that the agreement leads to an operational alliance and that the company learns from the negotiation experience. One way to ensure that the alliance happens is to anchor the relationship in some form of public commitment other than a simple press release, such as partner introductions to customers or inclusion in each firm's annual report. KeyCorp, a U.S. regional bank, took this to an interesting extreme when it put its partner, Charles Schwab, on the cover of its annual report.

Learning is also essential. Experienced alliance practitioners often conduct a postmortem of the alliance negotiation process. "You'd be surprised at how useful an institutional memory is—and how impossible wisdom is to retain if you don't try to do it right then," notes John Kalb. At the time IBM tried to get feedback from the people who were involved in the deal, assessing the main issues in constructing the deal and whether they had the right support.

With sound preparation, a negotiation team that contains certain newly defined and recast roles, and a few actions to sharpen the process along the way, it is possible to avoid many of the classic pitfalls—and increase the odds of ultimate venture success.

Further Reading

Danny Ertel. "Turning Negotiation into a Corporate Capability," *Harvard Business Review*, May-June, 1999, pp. 3–12.

Roger Fisher, William Ury, and Bruce Patton. *Getting to Yes: Negotiating Agreement Without Giving In*. (2nd ed.) New York: Penguin Books, 1991.

Source

This chapter is based on several articles in *The Alliance Analyst*, especially "Negotiating Alliances: The Best (and Some of the Worst) Practices" (November 1995), "IBM on Negotiating Alliances" (April 1995), and "The Gap Between Alliance Negotiators and Alliance Managers" (November 1994). The articles were combined, edited, and updated for this book.

PART TWO

Managing Alliances

Working Together

9

Relationship Management

Jeff Weiss, Laura J. Visioni

The strength of the relationship between partners is critical to the success of every alliance. How well the partners work together affects their ability to execute strategy, adapt to change, and innovate over time. Nevertheless, many firms fail to pay sufficient attention to actually making the partner relationship work. All too often, relationship management is ad hoc and starved of resources.

In a three-year study of 130 companies that included interviews with more than 150 alliance managers, our team at Vantage Partners found clear evidence of both the importance and relative neglect of relationship management in alliances. Over half of our interviewees reported that "poor or damaged relationships" between partners was the foremost cause of alliance failure. This share is even higher (about two-thirds of the total) for companies with more than twenty alliances (see Figure 9.1). In other words, even as companies become more experienced in alliances, their relationship management capabilities tend to lag advances in other disciplines. Study participants, regardless of their company's alliance experience, reported that relationship problems manifested themselves as breakdowns in trust, accumulation of partisan perceptions, suspicions about each other's motives, festering conflicts, and strong feelings of disrespect and coercion.

FIGURE 9.1   Foremost Causes of Alliance Failure
(companies with more than twenty alliances).

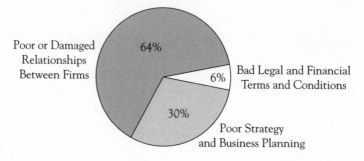

Poor or Damaged
Relationships
Between Firms   64%

6%   Bad Legal and Financial
Terms and Conditions

30%

Poor Strategy
and Business Planning

Source: Danny Ertel, Jeff Weiss, and Laura J. Visioni. *Managing Alliance Relationships: Ten Key Corporate Capabilities.* Boston: Vantage Partners, 2001.

Key Disciplines for Relationship Management

Our research also sheds light on what it takes to make an alliance relationship work. Here we will summarize six disciplines in relationship management, which are detailed further in subsequent sections.

- *Assess relationship fit.* Pay attention to the relationship from Day One. Too often, initial exploration in alliance formation focuses on what each partner has to offer, and excludes a close look at how each partner prefers to work. From the outset, partners should explore and discuss what it will be like to work together over time.

- *Negotiate on two tracks.* Frequently, the relationship is put aside as something that can be built (or fixed) after the negotiation. Instead, firms should develop a value-optimizing solution and a strong working relationship at the same time.

- *Transfer relationship knowledge to implementers.* Valuable information about the new partner is all too often held by the negotiators and rarely captured or transmitted to others. After the negotiation and before implementation, negotiators should brief implementers not only on the alliance structure and terms but also on what the negotiating team learned about how best to work with the partner.

- *Launch the relationship*. The start of an alliance is often ad hoc. Partners should launch their relationship with the same kind of discipline they would use in launching a new key initiative. They should define jointly what the relationship means and how it will be managed, instead of leaving the relationship to evolve on its own.

- *Manage the relationship*. The relationship will not remain healthy and contribute to business goals without ongoing attention. Partners should define and employ a set of common relationship management methods (for example, for decision making, conflict management, and communication). This will help maintain and improve the quality of the working relationship on an ongoing basis.

- *Audit the relationship*. Many alliance relationships are left to drift without clear monitoring. Partners should measure and monitor not only alliance performance but also the quality of the relationship on a regular basis. Doing so will detect both problems and new opportunities, while helping improve the way the relationship is managed.

These six strategies, employed systematically on a given alliance, provide the discipline required to maintain focus on the relationship and thereby to increase returns on the alliance investment.

Assess Relationship Fit

Far too often, those selecting an alliance partner look only at traditional elements of due diligence. Of course, it is critical to examine business, technical, product, and other such aspects of fit. Yet assessing how well the alliance partners will be able to work together is critical too. This involves examining at least two different things.

First, it is important to look at how the potential partner operates. How do they make decisions, communicate, resolve conflict,
manage commitments, and deal with change? Gaining an understanding of these and other operating norms—and comparing them
to one's own organization—begins to provide insight into just how
easy or hard it will be to work together. Further, jointly exploring
and discussing these differences helps the partners begin to see (and
plan for) where working together will be most challenging.

Second, it is useful to examine how well the potential partner
manages other relationships. Does its staff have a track record of
working effectively with other partners? What types of companies
does it have as partners? Are they similar to the firm itself? Different from it? If they are different, in what ways and to what degree?
How effective has the company been at bridging the gap between
how it operates and how its partners operate?

These are important questions to ask. The answers often can
help one choose the best partner. Yet even when there is only one
partner available, the answers can help the partners begin to plan
for the challenges that will need to be managed in the future.
Approaching these differences as something that needs to be managed jointly from the outset increases the chances of success in the
relationship.

Negotiate on Two Tracks

Relationship building is often left until *after* the negotiation. "It can
wait." "The negotiation is no time to build the relationship." "Let's
leave the relationship for those who are going to implement the
alliance." These are phrases that, in one form or another, we hear all
the time. Yet leaving the relationship for later just does not work.

The common practice can be attributed to a false dichotomy.
Negotiators assume (often implicitly) that they must choose between
negotiating a good deal and developing a strong relationship—that
they cannot do both at once. Thus often the negotiation of the alli-

ance becomes a battle of demands, where structure and terms are hammered out using a process that undermines, if not outright damages, the relationship between the partners. On the other hand, though much less frequently, the negotiation may involve sloppy trade-offs and concessions, made in an attempt to develop (that is, to buy) a good relationship. Either way, the partnership is in trouble from the start.

A far better approach involves negotiating on two tracks, as diagrammed in Figure 9.2. First, negotiate hard on the substance—the terms, structure, investments, and other essential elements of the business deal. Push beneath positions (stated demands) for interests (needs, aims, objectives, and fears); invent joint gain options that meet packages of these interests; and use external standards to make on-the-merits choices among the options. Second, build the relationship. In other words, create trust, respect, understanding, and a mode of joint problem solving by being "soft on the people," while still negotiating "hard on the substance." Demonstrate your trustworthiness, respect for your prospective partners, and desire to understand them. This costs nothing and it is worth doing even before you know whether they will treat you with the same respect. Chances are high that they will follow your lead. (For more on this strategy, see Getting to Yes, cited in Further Reading at the end of the chapter.)

Negotiating the substance and building the relationship simultaneously can be challenging. One way of effecting this, however, is to place this challenge front and center and make it the responsibility of both partners' negotiators.

Taking a day prior to negotiations to get the parties together to discuss the process by which they will negotiate can be helpful. Over the course of such a day, it is useful to follow a set of guidelines like the ones in Figure 9.2. That is, discuss the value of the relationship in the negotiation, explore obstacles to the relationship, craft strategies and ground rules for dealing with obstacles, think through how each side should prepare for a two-track negotiation, and investigate

FIGURE 9.2 Negotiating on Two Tracks.

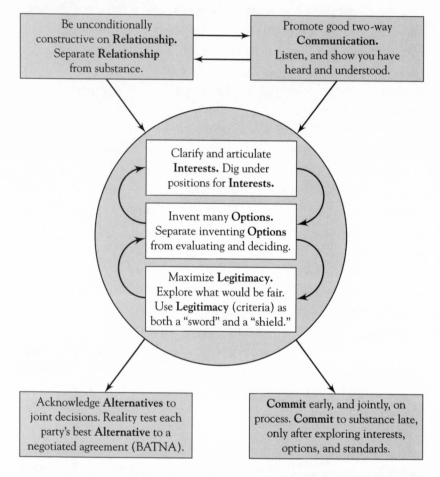

Source: Jonathan Hughes and Jeff Weiss. *Making Partnerships Work: A Relationship Management Handbook*. Boston: Vantage Partners, 2001. Copyrighted by Conflict Management Inc., 1997, and Vantage Partners, 2001.

potential sticking points. Doing these things not only helps set the foundation for an effective negotiation, it also turns the negotiation from an adversarial battle into a process of creative problem solving. As a result, the relationship will be strengthened and a negotiation can take place on both tracks.

Transfer Relationship Knowledge to Implementers

A wasteful event often occurs at the time of transition from the negotiation of the alliance to its implementation. Negotiators cut the deal and now move on, leaving implementers to begin building a new relationship from scratch. Whereas the negotiation team may brief implementers and others on the alliance terms and structure, it will rarely take the time to provide the implementers with an overview of their new partner.

The reality is, however, that over the course of negotiations, the negotiators learn an enormous amount about the partner. They gain insight into how the partner thinks and operates. They also gain insight into how this will help or hinder the success of the alliance. Further, the negotiators likely have good advice to offer the implementers. Unfortunately, this information and perspective is often left untapped. In fact, it usually departs with the negotiators.

Systematically debriefing the negotiating team can be helpful to the managers who are to implement the alliance. What have the negotiators learned about the partner and how the firms might work together? What was easy about working with the partner's representatives? What was hard? Why? What seemed to work well in working with them? What may be useful to watch out for? In what ways might our own modes of operating need to be adapted to work well with the partner? Furthermore, what elements of the negotiated deal may make it more or less difficult to work together over time? Capturing information and advice such as this and getting it into the hands of relationship managers will help make the transition easier.

Launch the Relationship

Once the alliance has been negotiated, people's tendency is to want to get on with the business of the alliance. As the partners get down to work, however, they often find themselves surprised, even frustrated. This happens even if there is a good hand-off between negotiators and implementers. The problem stems from not properly launching the alliance relationship.

As a result, partners may not understand why their counterparts behave as they do. They wonder: "Why do all decisions need to run up the management chain?" "Why don't they readily share information?" Or, they make assumptions: "They show up late for meetings because they do not respect us." "They do not provide enough people because they have more important partnerships." "They do not involve us in decisions because they do not trust or respect us." Finally, each party will begin behaving in accordance with its assumptions: "If they are not going to share with us, then we will not share with them." In turn, the counterpart reacts to this behavior, often in kind, serving only to reinforce assumptions and related behaviors.

It is far too easy and far too common for partners to quickly become stuck in a vicious cycle of action and reaction, rooted in growing misunderstanding. Even if this does not happen early on, it is quite likely to happen over time as the alliance strategy needs to change, parties come and go, or the work of the alliance gets more difficult to do. It is not hard for the relationship to get damaged, and it is not hard for such damage to spiral out of control. Many experienced alliance managers attest to the fact that trust is built one step at a time, in small increments, and yet, when the relationship is not strong and well managed, it can far too easily be lost as the result of just one incident.

To ensure the strength of the relationship, it is wise for the partners to take time right after negotiations to formally launch the relationship. Applying the same kind of discipline to the relationship that one might to the launch of a project or key initiative can make a big difference. In launching the relationship, it is useful to bring those who will manage the relationship together for a day or two to do the following:

- Review the purpose and structure of the alliance.
- Define what is meant by a "good relationship."
- Plan ways to work together.
- Define a set of relationship management roles and structures.
- Establish some common ways of thinking about collaboration and collect some tools and approaches that may help in the process.

First, it is critical for the key parties who will be managing the alliance to understand fully what the alliance is about. Together, they need to explore the arrangement, understand how the alliance is supposed to work, review its objectives and strategy, and consider what it is going to take to make it operational. Within this context, they can then begin looking at the kind of relationship they need and how they will make it work.

Second, the parties need to step back and define what they mean by a good working relationship. What are its key characteristics? What do people mean by each one? How would they know trust, open communication, engaging in joint problem solving, giving the benefit of the doubt, or any other characteristic, if they saw it? Most often the definition of a good relationship is left unstated, leaving people to walk around with surprisingly different pictures.

Even when people do take the time to define the relationship, they merely agree to nice-sounding words like *trust* and *respect*. If different people have different pictures of what these words look like in action—and they will—they risk acting in ways that they think will build the relationship, when, in fact, they do just the opposite. It is critical to explore what people really mean by their definitions, to develop understanding, and to try to develop a common picture of the kind of relationship all are striving to build.

Third, the partners need to develop approaches to enable joint decision making. In particular, it is helpful to identify differences in the ways the partners work and think, discuss the differences and how they might play out, and begin to create protocols and strategies for bridging and, in places, taking advantage of, these differences.

Exploring up front how each partner tends to approach decision making, communication, change, commitments, conflict, and difficult conversations will help the partners know what to expect. Reducing surprise is helpful in and of itself. Further, if these differences can be identified and understood by both sides, the parties can work together to establish expectations for how to manage them when they arise. They can also develop new protocols for how they will operate together. For example, to manage commitments, the partners might align around a few common guidelines: "We will push back when we believe we cannot live up to what is being requested." "We will notify affected parties immediately if we find that we cannot live up to a commitment on time." "We will not consider a commitment has been accepted or completed until there has been an explicit acknowledgment of such."

Fourth, beyond defining protocols, it is important to define relationship management structures and roles. Frequently, the partners will have created some form of governance in their contract. Often, the governance structure is focused exclusively on strategy, performance, and investment. Yet a focus on the relationship is critical as well. A steering committee should get a report on the health of the alliance at least twice a year, and should be responsible for providing advice on how to improve it as appropriate. A management committee should regularly spend time assessing the health of the relationship, continually looking for ways to build the relationship and manage change that might strain it. Operating committees should look for conflicts, resolve them, and actively manage communications.

At least one person from each company should be designated as relationship manager (or "alliance manager," as discussed in Chapters Thirteen, Fourteen, and Fifteen). This does not need to be a full-time role, but it does need to be a distinct role (separate from the role of tracking and managing the business of the alliance). The two (or more) relationship managers should work as a team, continually taking the temperature of the alliance relationship, looking for problems on the horizon, tackling partisan perceptions or other communication breakdowns, managing conflict that remains unresolved, helping each other's teams to navigate their company, and looking for ways to strengthen the way people work together. The relationship managers should be senior, seasoned people who have the skill and experience to manage the relationship as a true team (as a "we") and take a "what is best for the alliance" perspective.

Fifth, it is useful to provide some joint training for all those who are charged with making the relationship work. This develops a common mental model and behavioral picture of what working collaboratively will look like. Providing even the most seasoned people with some common tools, models, and vocabulary for solving problems together, managing conflict, and engaging in difficult conversations helps establish a way for the partners to work together. Thus equipped, the partners' leaders not only improve their interactions but also begin modeling behavior to others about how they are expected to work together in the alliance.

Manage the Relationship

To enable making the relationship work from day to day, it is useful to develop a set of common methods for working together. Challenges such as how decisions are made, conflicts are resolved, information is shared, or change is spotted and managed can be made much easier if the partners build common methodology for tackling each.

All alliances will experience conflict. Far too often, however, the way conflict will be managed is left undefined. Conflict lingers, relationships are damaged, and work slows down or even stops. To avoid this, alliance executives should develop a step-by-step conflict resolution process, a component of which should address escalation of conflict.

Many alliances have escalation paths laid out, but few of these processes are efficient in solving the problems quickly and even fewer contribute to building the relationship. They amount to simply tossing the problem to senior managers and come bundled with feelings that can damage the relationship between partners.

A good escalation process defines the steps the parties need to go through *before* they escalate, delineates the manner in which they escalate, and defines the form of what is escalated. It is best if the two parties *jointly* escalate their assessment of the conflict and suggest possible solutions. This increases the chances not only of finding a good solution but also of keeping the relationship intact.

Routine decision making may also be a challenge, not just conflict resolution. It is useful to clarify who will be involved in what kinds of decisions and in what manner. Managers should define the individuals who should be informed or consulted, and who is involved in actually negotiating key decisions. When structured well, explicit processes for making joint decisions can minimize surprises, maximize consultation, and avoid cumbersome efforts at building consensus.

In addition to the difficulties of conflict and decision making, anticipating and managing change can also be a challenge. Some changes may be tactical, for example, involving turnover among key personnel. Others will be more strategic, for example, involving a need to adapt to new market conditions that surround the alliance or one of the partners. In either case, it can be helpful to develop a method for spotting change on the horizon, planning for it, managing communication about it, and ensuring that people and processes adapt to it.

Depending on the nature of the alliance, several other organizational methods are useful to consider defining up front. In co-development alliances, for example, it is often helpful to define a process for how knowledge and intellectual property is transferred between the partners, and how that information is then managed. In short, partners need to step back, evaluate their circumstances, and determine which relationship management methods are worth creating for their particular alliance.

Audit the Relationship

No matter how well the alliance relationship is managed over time, there will always be room for improvement. Periodic alliance audits will help show where the fine-tuning is needed. When auditing the alliance, it is critical to go beyond business performance and also take a careful look at the health of the alliance relationship.

It is usually helpful to audit the relationship every four to six months, and perhaps more often for certain elements of the alliance or at times when the relationship is under strain. A relationship audit involves answering the following questions:

- How well are the partners working together?
- Does the relationship have the qualities the partners set out for themselves?
- What relationship problems are lingering?
- What might threaten the relationship in the near future?
- Do any of the relationship management methods, roles, or protocols need adjusting?
- What relationship management strategies should be changed, dropped, or extended?
- Are there reasons to change other aspects of the relationship?

To help guide the periodic audit, the partners may define a set of metrics for achieving a good working relationship. Some of these metrics may be subjective—for example, the degree to which the partners feel there is trust, open communication, or a sense of team identity. Others may be objective—for example, how quickly conflicts are resolved, or how many commitments are fulfilled in the time and manner promised. It is also useful to survey the partners to assess the effectiveness of the protocols they agreed to follow. A useful audit will go beyond tallying responses. It should help identify *why* certain protocols are being used or not used and *why* they are working or not working.

As a general rule, alliance relationships should be audited jointly by the partners and a cross-section of staff from both partners should be surveyed. Interviewees should be asked to look both at their counterpart's behaviors and at their own. They should be pushed to not simply complain or applaud but diagnose. Last, interviewees should be forced to go beyond finger-pointing and laying blame with their counterparts (or colleagues) and look at their own contribution. Joint auditing of an alliance may have the important side effect of strengthening the relationship by generating shared ownership of problems and shared responsibility for solutions.

Conclusion

Admittedly, following the six strategies in this chapter requires a lot of work. It is easier to try to leave the relationship to take care of itself, or to leave it in the hands of a few good "people people." Both strategies are common—but neither works. The relationship needs to be prioritized and everyone must take responsibility for making it work. Leaders must use discipline in building, managing, and adjusting it over time.

Further Reading

Danny Ertel, Jeff Weiss, and Laura J. Visioni. *Managing Alliance Relationships: Ten Key Corporate Capabilities*. Boston: Vantage Partners, 2001.

Roger Fisher, William Ury, and Bruce Patton. *Getting to Yes: Negotiating Agreement Without Giving In*. (2nd ed.) New York: Penguin Books, 1991.

Jonathan Hughes and Jeff Weiss. *Making Partnerships Work: A Relationship Management Handbook*. Boston: Vantage Partners, 2001.

Source

This chapter is a summary and update of the results of a larger study by Vantage Partners, published in its entirety as *Managing Alliance Relationships: Ten Key Corporate Capabilities* by Danny Ertel, Jeff Weiss, and Laura J. Visioni (Boston: Vantage Partners, 2001).

10

Governing Collaboration

Firms entering into an alliance often try to foresee and resolve in advance important management decisions that may arise in the future. For example, it is common among top-performing companies to agree on certain venture decisions, such as future capital expenditures or market expansions, in advance. But the complexity and uncertainty inherent in alliances makes this impossible to do for all but a few issues. As a result, alliances leave open many decisions that will only be addressed and settled in the future, if and when they arise. The burden of collaboration thus shifts to the governance of the alliance—the process by which managerial decisions are made once the alliance is under way.

Nowhere is this focus on governance more important than in non-equity alliances, in which the partners have no ownership link to each other. In equity-based alliances, such as joint ventures or alliances involving partial equity investments, governance is usually in place in the form of a board of directors and corporate management structure. Although managing such ventures is not trivial, the formal structures and fiduciary responsibilities that accompany equity alliances tend to ensure that governance issues are not ignored.

In contrast, non-equity alliances lack the basic ground rules for creating a governance structure. Further complicating the governance challenge, the line between governance and management is often quite blurry in non-equity alliances, given their lack of a formal "alliance organization" and dependence on cross-partner teams and committees to get work done.

Non-equity alliances are the most common form of alliance, representing an estimated 80 percent of alliances created in the 1990s. In certain industries, including pharmaceuticals, retail, airlines, and software, they are the overwhelmingly dominant alliance form. These alliances range from research alliances and licensing agreements to enhanced supplier relationships and co-marketing deals. Research on these and other alliances has shown that poor governance has been a common cause of alliance failure. A McKinsey study found that roughly 50 percent of alliance failures are related to governance. Another study, by Accenture, calculated that between $5 billion and $18 billion value was lost due to poor alliance governance in the pharmaceuticals industry alone.

What drives good governance in non-equity alliances? To answer this question, we examined three such alliances operating in the 1990s: Astra Merck–Hoechst Marion Roussel in pharmaceuticals, American Red Cross–Baxter Healthcare in health care, and one between two large U.S. companies in industrial electronics. Creating a strong governance model depends on three broad actions: determining how formal the governance structure should be, building a governance structure that works, and, recognizing that successful alliances are dynamic, managing the evolution of the governance system over time.

When Formal Governance Is Needed

How formal should the governance structure be in a non-equity alliance? In some alliances, the partners will be best served with a highly informal model—for instance, depending on an executive sponsor and a part-time alliance manager from each partner. But in other cases, a more formal approach is needed. Three criteria point to more formal structures: the alliance is highly valuable to the parent firms, the relationship between the partners is complex, and it offers a potential for expansion in the future.

Highly Valuable Alliances

When a non-equity alliance represents substantial value, there is an incentive to invest in governance structures to protect the investment. This was the case with the alliance between Astra Merck and Hoechst Marion Roussel (HMR). Formed in 1995, the alliance called for HMR to use its U.S. pharmaceutical sales force to promote Astra Merck's leading product, the ulcer drug Prilosec. As Doug Everson, former director of strategic alliances at Astra Merck, explained soon after forming the venture: "The alliance . . . focuses on a product that accounts for a vast majority of our sales. We were just not going to allow it to wander along without a high degree of oversight and dedicated supervision." To oversee the venture, the companies established a ten-person governance committee that would meet four to six times a year (Figure 10.1). Everson was directly responsible for this alliance relationship as well as other promotional alliances the company undertook.

Complex Alliances

A formal governance structure may also be needed when the relationship is complex, such as when the venture involves multiple functions or operating units. Consider the alliance between the American Red Cross and Baxter Healthcare. At its core, the alliance revolved around sharing the capacity and cost of a plasma processing plant in California. The two companies formed the alliance in the mid-1980s and committed to work together until 2005. Yet the alliance entailed more than simple time-sharing in a manufacturing plant. As Chris Lamb, vice president for plasma operations at the Red Cross, notes: "We are not just running our raw plasma down an assembly line in the morning and then turning the facility over to Baxter in the afternoon. The intent of the agreement was to develop new products as well." In addition to the alliance in plasma product development and processing, the Red Cross depended on Baxter as a supplier of blood bags.

This complexity prompted the need for a more formal governance structure. The initial agreement in 1985 set up the Contract

FIGURE 10.1 Governance Structure of Alliance
Between Astra Merck and HMR, ca. 1995.

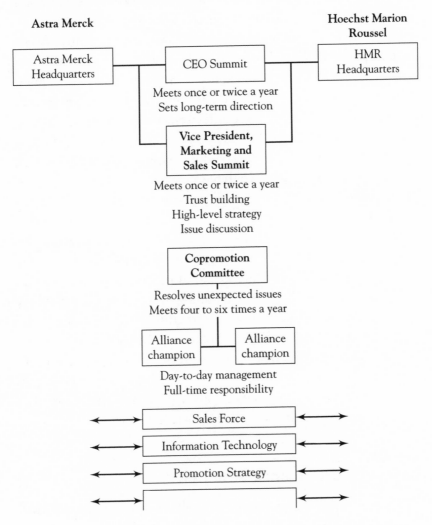

Coordinating Group (CCG), made up of four senior executives. It
also created the full-time position of contract manager—someone
to coordinate the relationship from day to day. "We did this out of
a recognition that there would be things that we couldn't anticipate," Lamb says. "We also knew that the level of existing complexity required an ongoing and formal dialogue."

Alliances with Potential for Expansion

While high value and management complexity are the two main criteria for building formal governance structures, the desire to expand the scope of the alliance can also be a motivator. Some alliance practitioners believe that when an alliance has formal governance bodies, it has a better chance to grow beyond its initial mandate. Witness the early alliance between the two U.S. industrial electronics firms. The two companies formed an alliance to cross-sell a range of products in the United States. Rather than have separate sales forces sell complementary product lines to the same customers, the companies agreed to have their sales reps carry both companies' products. This would reduce selling costs and increase the time spent with each customer.

The alliance offered substantial potential for growth. The alliance started out confined to selling in the United States, but the partners also hoped to push it into joint product development and overseas sales. In addition to expanding in scope, it was also likely that the alliance would evolve in structure. From the outset, the partners talked about someday transforming the alliance into a joint venture with its own full-time employees and independent profit and loss statement. To ensure that the alliance was maximizing its growth potential, the partners created a governance structure that included an alliance board of senior managers (Figure 10.2).

Building a Governance Structure

Having determined that a non-equity alliance merits a more formal governance structure, the partners need to design a structure that promotes fast and efficient decision making and supports the overall goals of the alliance. No one governance structure is appropriate for all alliances, but certain design principles exist—and firms would be wise to follow them:

- Differentiate three structural levels.
- Create a charter for the steering committee.

FIGURE 10.2 Governance Structure of Alliance Between Two Large U.S. Industrial Electronics Firms.

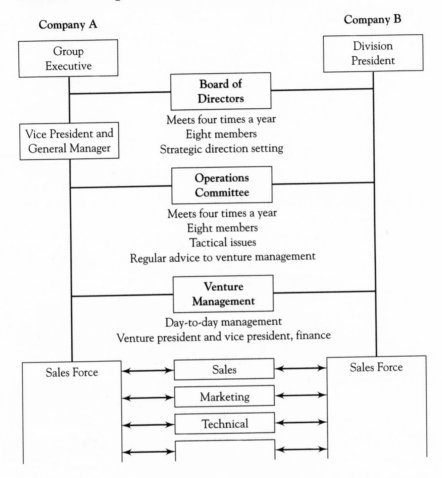

- Define individual roles on the steering committee.
- Promote continuity.
- Let responsibility determine membership.
- Don't expect the steering committee to vote.
- Ask the unasked questions.
- Create a decision protocol.

Differentiate Three Structural Levels

A unique feature of non-equity alliances is that such ventures are truly "virtual organizations"—that is, ones where essentially all decision making and work are undertaken within the loose confines of committees and joint teams. For instance, one major copromotion alliance in the pharmaceuticals industry had more than thirty committees and teams containing almost three hundred members. Designing a governance structure for such an organization requires a clear view of the overall organization, and in particular of the lines that separate governance (strategic decision making and overall performance monitoring) from management (tactical decision making and resource management) and functional operations (executing work within the various components of the alliance).

The design demands at each level are quite different. For instance, at the working level it is often a real indication of venture health and partner interdependence when the alliance contains a large number of working teams, and when these teams grow in number and change in nature over time. At the governance level, however, the exact opposite is the case. Indeed, we've found that the best-run non-equity alliances will have one governance committee, whereas less successful alliances have competing or partially overlapping committees at the strategic level—for instance, a steering and operating committee without clear differentiation in roles, or U.S. and European steering committees without a global steering committee.

Create a Charter for the Steering Committee

Having agreed to make a steering committee the main governing body of the alliance, the partners should create a charter for the group—that is, a clear articulation of its roles and responsibilities, status (for example, permanent versus ad hoc), reporting relationships to and from other elements of the alliance organization, working logistics (meeting frequency, location, and so on), key milestones, metrics, and composition. Ideally, this charter will be developed during (or before) the first twenty days of the alliance's life, and it will be captured on two to five pages.

In developing the charter, it can be quite useful to think about whether the steering committee should be a *celebrity board* or a *managers board*. To simplify, a celebrity board will contain chief executives, division presidents, and other members of top management—and it will focus on true strategic issues. In contrast, a managers board will typically contain vice presidents and be more operationally oriented. The benefit of a celebrity board is in providing the alliance with prestige and strategic advice, and in helping the alliance expand into new business areas. But it also runs the risks of being out of touch with the operational details of the alliance and growing dormant over time as senior executives lose interest. In contrast, a managers board tends to excel at overseeing current operations, and its members can often be enlisted to perform important ongoing functions of the alliance between committee meetings.

Define Individual Roles on the Steering Committee

Another characteristic of effective steering committees is the definition of individual-member roles. Our work points to a number of different roles that individual steering committee members can assume: chair (or co-chair), strategic coordinator, alliance advocate, lead director, functional lead, and facilitator. Each of these roles comes with specific responsibilities. For instance, a steering committee member designated as the "alliance advocate" would be responsible for promoting the interests of the alliance—not the parents. A "strategic coordinator" would be specifically charged with ensuring that the alliance operates effectively across key organizational and geographic gaps and promoting the long-term expansion of the alliance into new domains.

Assigning specific responsibilities to some (or all) committee members creates a number of benefits, including greater accountability and focus. Without such role definition, alliances run the real risk that steering committee members will do little more than show up for meetings.

Not all roles need to be performed by a formal member of the steering committee. For instance, in the Astra Merck-HMR alliance, the partners relied on a consultant to act as steering committee facilitator. "She was in charge of building the right chemistry between the members from the different companies, and it has been an extraordinary help," Astra Merck's Everson recalls.

Promote Continuity

Steering committee members should not face term limits. As long as the individuals are eager to participate, and provided their jobs remain relevant to the relationship, their seats should be reserved. Putting new people around the governing table every eighteen months rarely makes sense. Unlike a corporate board, the alliance board faces virtually no risk of becoming an entrenched bureaucracy or a group of CEO cronies: a governance committee may meet four to twelve times per year and, if typical, oversee an alliance with a total life of just three to five years. Mix that with all the natural turnover of an organization, and dynamism is a given. Stability is not.

Let Responsibility Determine Membership

The membership size and composition of the alliance steering committee needs to reflect the nature of the alliance. Astra Merck's alliance with HMR covered five discrete functions (marketing, promotion, field sales, national accounts, and operations management), which became the checklist for the committee search. "We looked for executives within each company who were uniquely qualified in each of those five areas," notes Everson.

Don't Expect the Steering Committee to Vote

"It is really a communication channel—a way to identify problems and to achieve consensus," explains the Red Cross's Chris Lamb of the CCG, the group that coordinated the contract alliance with Baxter. Lamb can not recall a time when the committee formally voted on anything: "What's the sense in voting when the CCG has two members from each company? A vote would never resolve a problem; it would just show that we needed to go into arbitration."

Ask the Unasked Questions

Although firms often give their non-equity alliance boards the same types of responsibilities as corporate boards (that is, the setting of long-term strategy and the monitoring of performance), they rarely think to raise the questions so common in the debate surrounding corporate boards. For instance:

- Do smaller boards work more effectively than larger ones?
- How important is diversity of board members?
- How much consideration should be given to the personality fit of board members?
- Should there be outsiders on the board?

Consider the last question. Our review of more than fifty non-equity alliances revealed only one non-equity alliance with outside board representation. This is curious. Scholarly studies of corporate boards suggest that companies with a high number of outside directors tend to perform better than others. Yet few companies have considered whether outside governors might also benefit their alliances. The reasons to have an all-insider board are indeed often strong: for instance, it may be difficult to justify the cost of outsiders, or an alliance board's primary goal may be to generate internal support for the venture, thus making outsiders particularly ineffective. However, the independent perspective of an outside board member—especially for a company's most strategic alliances—could well justify the expense or the trade-off.

Create a Decision Protocol

Good governance depends on more than a well-structured steering committee—that is, the "lines and boxes" view of governance. It also hinges on clear decision-making processes. To promote good governance, the partners should create a protocol—or road map—for how the ten to thirty most important alliance decisions will be made. To do this, the companies should first identify these decisions (for example, approving capital expenditures above $5 million, altering the alliance's product or geographic scope, approving the annual alliance plan and budget) and then create a mechanism for assigning decision-making rights to various decision makers (see Chapter Eleven).

Evolution of the Governance Structure

Unlike the corporate board, which often stabilizes in structure after the company goes public, alliance governance structures are generally fluid, needing to change as the alliance grows in scope, for example, or comes to depend on a corporate parent in new ways. How should companies think about governance evolution? Our discussions point to two recommendations: have more governance over time rather than less, and keep senior management involved.

More Governance Over Time, Not Less

One common perception is that alliances need more intensive governance in the beginning—that newness equates with importance and therefore with the need for more committees and management involvement. "Actually, it is just the opposite," notes an executive at a leading pharmaceutical company. "Our alliances usually start small and are very focused. In the past—though this will be less likely in the future—the alliances have often picked up additional areas of collaboration. And that calls for more intricate communication channels."

Many successful alliances build additional governance structures over time—though not at the senior management level. Witness the sales alliance between the two U.S. industrial electronics firms. It started with an eight-member board of directors, plus a venture president and vice president of finance. After a year, the corporate parents decided to add an operations committee. The motivation was to alleviate some of the growing pressure on the board, whose members were too busy with other company matters to fully attend to the alliance's growing volume of operational issues. The operations committee was created to handle such matters as assessing venture performance, advising the board of directors, providing day-to-day communications with the venture managers, and resolving conflicts and making important operational decisions such as aligning the corporate compensation systems of the two partners' sales staff.

Over time, the partners added further—and more tactical—governance elements. Less than two years after forming the alliance, they created an annual national meeting and quarterly regional gatherings for the sales forces. And once a week, there were conference calls where twenty to thirty sales agents and engineers shared troubles and success stories.

Keep Senior Management Involved

While senior management's role may decline over time as other individuals and groups assume added governance responsibilities, companies should not let senior management wander too far. Consider the troubles of the American Red Cross. When its alliance with Baxter was launched in 1985, the companies created a two-person committee called the Value Managed Relationship Committee to oversee the totality of the alliance. These two governors not only monitored and managed the joint plasma initiatives, they also looked after non-plasma elements of the relationship—including the sale of Baxter blood bags to the Red Cross, a supplier alliance worth upwards of tens of millions of dollars per year. Underneath the two co-chairs were a series of subcommittees overseeing specific aspects of the alliance (Figure 10.3).

It all worked well—until both co-chairs left their organizations. When this happened, Baxter and the Red Cross decided that the alliance was operating so well that there was no need to maintain the overarching governance structure. No new chairs were appointed. Some of the subcommittees continued on, but ultimately stopped meeting as well. The manufacturing piece of the alliance—arguably its most critical component—relied on its own governing body, the Contract Coordinating Group. The blood bag supplier alliance operated without a formal governance mechanism.

FIGURE 10.3 Governance Structure of Alliance Between Red Cross and Baxter, ca. 1995.

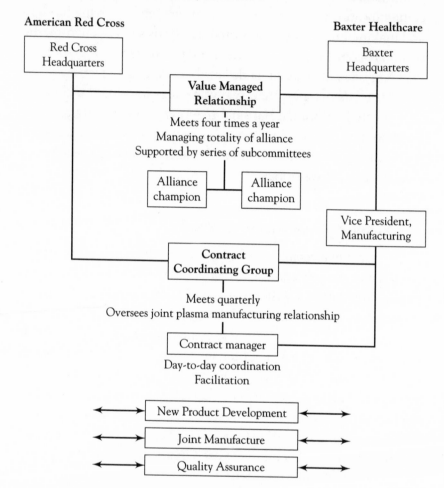

This approach seemed to work until Red Cross found itself in a budget crisis. To reduce expenses, Red Cross management called for widespread program cuts, staff layoffs, and further discounts from suppliers. As part of this process, Red Cross asked Baxter to reduce the price of blood bags. "The discussions were hostile because there was no person watching over the length of the Baxter alliance," according to one Red Cross manager. "There was no one who said, 'Hey wait a minute here, guys, this relationship means a whole lot to both organizations. Don't spoil it over these blood bags.'" Without that overarching governance structure and top management sponsorship, the discussions lacked perspective. Baxter did not understand why it should underwrite the financial ills of the Red Cross. The Red Cross representatives did not understand why Baxter couldn't cut them a little slack in a time of need.

By late 1995, one Red Cross executive feared that the blood bag alliance would end. He openly predicted that a collapse in the supplier relationship would contaminate other parts of the alliance: "While you don't unravel a twenty-year manufacturing alliance overnight, you do start going through the models, the analysis, and planning to figure out the best way for Baxter and the Red Cross to go our separate ways. And with that type of future, I think there would be some diminishing productivity, or at least creativity, knowing that the alliance had a sunset." Fortunately, that did not happen. The two sides successfully renegotiated the terms of the blood bag agreement. And the manufacturing side of the alliance barely noticed a ripple.

Did the companies consider rebuilding the broader governance structure? The near-death experience with blood bags pushed some to thinking about doing just that. "Executives from Baxter and the Red Cross are going to sit down and talk about how to work better together and prevent this from happening again," said the Red Cross manager at the time. "And I'll bet the concept of the value-managed relationship is back on the table."

Good alliance governance is an essential element of alliance success. When companies understand what drives the need for formal governance structures, what elements make for solid structures, and how these structures may evolve over time, the chances of success rise markedly.

Further Reading

Rosabeth Moss Kanter. "Collaborative Advantage: The Art of Alliances," *Harvard Business Review*, July-Aug. 1994, pp. 96–108.
Mitchell Marks and Phillip Mirvis. *Joining Forces: Making One Plus One Equal Three*. San Francisco: Jossey-Bass, 1998. Chapters 5 and 6.

Source

This chapter is based on several articles in *The Alliance Analyst*, especially "When Governance Is Good, Parts I and II" (January and February 1996). The articles were combined, edited, and updated for this book.

11

Making Joint Decisions

Francine G. Pillemer, Stephen G. Racioppo

Alliances often run into problems because partners have failed to develop an effective process for making joint decisions. The lack of a systematic structure for decision making reduces the speed of decision making, opens the door to outside influences from "shadow" decision makers, and generally creates an atmosphere of distrust.

A clear structure for joint decision making is particularly important for complex alliances with deep interdependence among the partners. To illustrate this, examine the resource flows between corporate parents and their alliance in Figure 11.1. In a simple alliance, the resource flows are intermittent and composed of hard commodities (cash, materials). In complex alliances, the flows include soft resources and services (technology, human resources, shared business systems) and occur on an ongoing basis. The result is an increased burden of governance: resources have to be valued without recourse to market prices, and the continual process of resource allocation into and out of the alliance has to be managed.

Good governance is thus increasingly the linchpin of alliance success. In the most general sense, governance can be defined as the interaction between the shareholders (the corporate parents) and venture management. In alliances, the prime task of governance is twofold—to protect the interests of the corporate parents and to promote the goals of the venture. Good governance exhibits several traits: it promotes sound decisions, it holds individuals accountable

FIGURE 11.1   Interdependence in an Alliance.

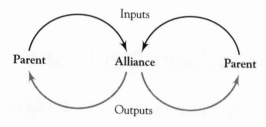

Inputs from Parents	Outputs from Alliance
Hard inputs:	Hard outputs:
• Capital	• Dividends
• Assets	• Finished products
• Raw materials	
Soft inputs:	Soft outputs:
• Staff	• Technology
• Know-how	• Know-how
• Business systems	• Market intelligence
• Technology	• Staff
• Market intelligence	
• Brand	
• Contacts	
• Customers	

for actions, it enjoys the endorsement of those who must implement the strategy, and it is systematic and sustainable.

Most managers appreciate the value of good governance, but they don't always know how to create it. One problem is that managers tend to equate governance with committees—they take a "lines and boxes" view of governance. Although this may be appropriate for corporate governance, which is conducted through the board of directors, it is downright dangerous for alliance governance. In alliances, those performing the roles of governance may or may not be formal members of committees. This inherent fluidity makes alliance decision making extremely messy without some form of understanding and structure.

Rather than focus on a board, companies need to think about a decision-making protocol—a road map for how the twenty to fifty most important alliance decisions will be made. This decision-making protocol is the foundation of good governance in alliances. Here we will review what such a protocol should cover.

Seven Steps in Joint Decision Making

Based on research in the financial services, telecommunications, energy, and health care industries we developed a seven-step process of joint decision making (shown in Exhibit 11.1). We attempted to outline a process that can be used in many different types of alliances. Even so, the unique nature of each alliance will require adjustments under each step. So, for instance, whereas a consolidation joint venture and a co-branding alliance both need a governance task force, the former may require a larger and more senior group than the latter. Thus the seven-step process has universal applicability while providing the flexibility to account for the uniqueness of each alliance.

Step 1. Create a Task Force

Partners need to think about the structure of collaboration before the deal is signed. Our work shows that partners should create a task force even before the deal is consummated and allow this small group of executives to drive the creation of the governance structure, performing the ensuing six steps.

Composition. Who should sit on the task force? The composition should represent the key constituents in the future decision-making structure. This will vary for each alliance (that is, depending on the dollar value, strategic importance, or complexity of the venture). In general, however, membership should be kept to two to four executives from each corporate parent. This ensures decision-making speed and frank discussion. Members should be selected based on a mix of characteristics and skills. This provides for diversity of views (for example, finance, marketing, operations), creative tension, and broad decision-making power. Membership should

EXHIBIT 11.1 Seven Steps in Joint Decision Making.

---

1. Create Task Force
Characteristics:
- Four to eight members
- Direct reports to CEO (for major alliances)
- Ongoing interaction
- Form immediately
- Consensus—no voting
- Drives next six steps

2. Establish Guiding Principles
Examples:
- Make decisions at lowest possible level
- Draw on best resources of parents
- Each decision maker will have a clear form of intervention

3. List Decisions
Examples:
- Annual budget
- Annual plan
- Capex
- Joint venture staffing
- Dividends
- Transfer prices
- Environmental policy
- Change in scope

4. Identify Stakeholders
Examples:
- Parent boards
- Parent CEOs
- Parent CFOs
- Joint venture board of directors
- Joint venture CEO

5. Create Decision Spectrum
Characteristics:
- Three to five modes of intervention
- No overlap of modes
- Widely understood by all stakeholders

EXHIBIT 11.1 Seven Steps in Joint Decision Making, Cont'd.

6. Appoint Decision Drivers
Characteristics:
- One stakeholder per issue
- Responsible to carry to final decision

7. Create Decision Map
Characteristics:
- Match decision to stakeholders and mode of intervention
- Perform for all decisions

---

include the lead dealmaker (for example, the vice president of business development). This provides for continuity from the negotiation stage of the alliance.

And on some occasions, membership should be extended to an outsider. A radical idea, this has proved effective when corporate parents want to protect a minority shareholder or maintain a spirit of independence for the alliance. In the oil industry, we have also seen it work to increase the perception that a joint venture is a local company, rather than the arm of large multinationals.

Meeting Structure. The task force should meet regularly and informally. This is not some board of occasional overseers, reacting to ongoing events and monitoring performance. Rather, it is a group much like the Constitutional Congress, assembled to jump-start the venture and set down a coherent and efficient trajectory for future interaction. The members of the task force should be prepared for an intense but short period of work, best performed at a location removed from their regular jobs. This period will then be followed by several less intense months of securing the support of other constituencies within the corporate parents.

Leadership and Voting. The task force should be democratic. It should strive for consensus, but be willing to move ahead with a few dissenting voices, so long as they have been heard. There is no formal voting and no chair. For complex alliances, however, it is often effective to assign areas of subresponsibility. A major co-marketing alliance in the pharmaceuticals industry, for instance, divided its ten-member task force into five areas, including pricing, advertising, and sales support, thus ensuring each area was fully incorporated into the governance structure.

Step 2. Establish Guiding Principles

The first job of the task force is to define the guiding principles of the alliance. What are the norms of expected behavior? What is the vision for the alliance? What are its operating assumptions, ideals, and constitutional tenets? Our work points to a number of places to find answers. The strategies and mission statements of the parents will help guide the task force, as will the customer value proposition of the alliance.

One alliance we examined answered these questions with a series of simple declarations. The partners agreed "to make decisions at the lowest level possible." They agreed that the alliance must "draw on the best resources of the partners, no matter which company that meant." And they were determined that "each decision maker would have a clear role and widely understood forms of intervention." Every alliance must choose its own guiding principles—though, as with the alliance cited earlier, they will be broad statements of vision, limited in number and widely communicated.

Common Problems. Common vision does not always come easily. Consider SEMATECH, the research consortium widely credited with restoring the U.S. semiconductor industry. In 1986, when the alliance was merely an idea within National Semiconductor, Intel, and other companies, a task force was created. Its mission was to define venture objectives and create an organizational framework for the alliance. The SEMATECH task force had to overcome reluctance and disagreement of some potential members who debated the product and geographic scope of the venture, as well as the spirit and procedures under which ten or more competitors would work together.

Most alliances face some major debate. In one telecom alliance, the corporate parents entered discussions with very different beliefs about control: one favored a hierarchical structure while the other believed in a flat, team-based approach. The parents needed to resolve which would guide the alliance. In contrast, a service industry alliance was torn between one parent's belief in venture independence and the other's belief in dependence, where the alliance would draw on the corporate parents for resources such as research, staff, and market intelligence.

The Process.   How do firms establish guiding principles? It is not uncommon for the task force to devote a day to drafting the guiding principles. An open-discussion format usually works best, often facilitated by an outsider. This creates a sense of inclusion and perspective. Partners should be encouraged to bring their own corporate principles for collaboration. Introducing these into the discussion can help expand the possibilities and underline the importance of universal principles. When the task force cannot agree on certain principles, it should identify two options and present them to the CEOs or corporate boards for final decision.

Step 3. List Decisions

Next, the task force should generate a list of the twenty to fifty most important decisions that the alliance will face. These decisions will range from drafting by-laws and press announcements to setting information technology strategy and environmental policies. When prompted, a task force will generate a dust-storm of dozens, perhaps hundreds, of potential decisions. It is an electrifying event, and rarely will the facilitator be able to keep pace!

Once the initial list is generated, the task force should sort decisions into categories and start to whittle the list down. Common decision "clusters" include ownership and scope, financial issues, third-party transactions, interactions with corporate parents, and human resources (see Exhibit 11.2 for samples). Once this is done, the task force can rank decisions by importance, generating a list of key decisions for the alliance.

Step 4. Identify Stakeholders

One common problem is that many alliances suffer from "shadow governance"—the influence of power brokers outside the formal governance system who, due to personal stature or resources, are the true decision makers for the corporate parent. Shadow governance has a number of causes, including incompetent leadership and an overburdened formal governance system that is unable to cope with a large volume of decisions.

Shadow governance raises several concerns. It undermines the authority of the formal governance structure, effectively converting the task force, board of directors, and other governance groups into toothless discussion forums. This lowers morale and attendance. The lack of transparency strains the alliance: partners struggle to identify and communicate with the true decision makers. At best, shadow governance slows alliance decision making. At worst, it leaves partners totally unclear on how decisions get made and, ultimately, unable to make course corrections.

The task force must entice decision makers to step out from the shadows. A key decision maker might be anyone who does one or more of the following things:

- Initiates a decision-making process
- Devises and analyzes a proposed decision
- Provides input, comment, or consultation concerning a proposed decision
- Approves a decision informally or formally, though a sign-off or vote
- Implements a decision

EXHIBIT 11.2 Key Business Decisions in Alliances.

Ownership and Scope

- Product and business line scope
- Geographic scope
- Capital structure
- Initial corporate documents
- Partner additions
- Transfers in equity
- Alliance termination and dissolution

Financial

- Annual budget
- Annual plan (beyond the annual plan)
- Capital investments
- Assumption of debt (financial guarantees of parents)
- Transfer prices
- Dividends and distributions
- Audit (oversee and approve)
- Performance measures (establish and monitor)
- Capital expenditures (above $ ___ million)
- Acquisitions (above $ ___ million)
- Sale of assets (above $ ___ million)

Transactions with Parents

- Transfer pricing
- Noncompete agreements (geographic or product)
- Agreements with one parent

Third-Party Arrangements

- Long-term contracts
- Capital leases and purchases
- Conflicts of interest (identification and resolution)
- Litigation (initiation)
- Brand name license

Human Resources

- Board of directors (appoint or remove members)
- Board of directors (authority and composition)
- Joint venture CEO (hire and fire)
- Joint venture CEO (performance review)
- CEO succession planning
- Joint venture staff (salary, hire and fire)
- Employee benefits

Environment

- Community involvement
- Litigation (initiate or settle)

We have developed several guidelines to help identify the right set of decision makers. First, don't be too restrictive: the list should include all decision makers, no matter how many there are. Concentrate on internal decision makers; external parties such as suppliers, governments, and local communities may be crucial to alliance success, but should rarely hold great sway over the internal decision-making infrastructure. Second, look for both individuals and groups. Many decision makers tend to be groups, such as executive committees or labor unions. Third, allow decision maker seniority to reflect the nature of the corporate parents and the goals of the alliance. Empowered organizations, for instance, need to include more midlevel decision makers than do hierarchical organizations. So start at the top: identify the most senior decision makers first, as they will help set the parameters of the alliance. And finally, do not assign responsibilities just yet—a rush to assign roles is likely to prevent a full accounting of decision makers.

Step 5. Create a Decision Spectrum

Most companies assume that alliance decisions will get made in one of two ways. The first is via dictate: one corporate parent has the right to make the decision and impose it on the others. The second is via consensus: the decision does not happen without full agreement. The dictator model is seen as decisive and fast but unable to incorporate many important ideas from the nondictators. The consensus model is emotionally appealing but slow and unworkable for certain issues.

Work in labor-management relations provides a third model; it transforms the two extremes into a spectrum. This spectrum shows that decision makers can have a number of different roles in the decision-making process. There is no one best way to divide this spectrum, but we've found that five roles are worth considering (see Exhibit 11.3). The middle three roles—negotiate, consult, and notify—are the heart of collaborative decision making. Each carries some sense of shared action and interdependence. They are

EXHIBIT 11.3 The Alliance Decision Spectrum.

Commit: The power to make the decision unilaterally

Negotiate: The power to make the decision in agreement (negotiation) with at least one other party

Consult: The right to be consulted in advance on the decision, but without the power to alter or to make the decision

Notify: the right to be informed of the decision once made

Delegate: No power to make the decision and no right to be consulted or informed

also the hardest to implement, with their definitions prone to differing interpretations by various stakeholders.

Negotiate. For negotiations to be productive in joint decision making, they should consist of a formal process with explicitly defined roles for parties or their representatives. It is also useful to have explicit types and timing of communications, and clear rules for how disparate views will be heard, and when. Finally, the process should define who must agree with the decision before it can be announced and who must approve the decision before it can take effect.

Consult. In addition to formal negotiation, there is a role for a formal or informal process whereby the decision maker consults with others. This means informing others about the need for a decision and stating the intention to make it, asking for views and suggestions, and then making and announcing a decision. Key points to determine are who is consulted about what kinds of decisions, and what kind of advice is needed with how much advance notice. Finally, there should be an understanding on all sides that the advice may or may not be reflected in the decision.

Notify. After a decision is made, who should be notified? This is the last element to be clarified. In addition, what they should be told, in what sequence, and what they are expected to do as a result of the decision may be specified.

Step 6. Appoint Decision Drivers

Each decision will need a decision driver. This person is not a decision maker per se, it is someone responsible for ensuring the decision is made. The decision drivers are the ones who initiate the decision, manage solicitation of input, disseminate information to others involved, communicate the result, and oversee implementation. Prior to appointing decision drivers for each decision, the task force should agree on a voting formula or tie-breaking rule for each step.

Step 7. Create a Decision Map

The task force is now ready to assemble the three main building blocks of joint decision making: decisions, decision makers, and decision roles.

We found that it is best if the task force sits down together and works through the list of decisions one at a time, determining which decision makers should be involved, and define their role precisely. Consider one decision: hiring the joint venture CEO. In one energy industry alliance, the task force selected the JV board as the decision maker with an obligation to consult with the corporate parents before any action was taken. The task force also designated the chairman of the JV to be the decision driver. This created a "decision path"—a unique trajectory and environment of influences that led to a final decision. Each decision, whether approving an annual budget, altering venture scope, or setting transfer prices, follows a unique path.

In this way, the task force can create a "decision inventory" for each stakeholder (Figure 11.2). This allows each stakeholder to see

FIGURE 11.2 Sample Alliance Decision Inventories.

Joint Venture Board of Directors

	Delegate	Keep Informed	Consult First	Decide Jointly	Decide
Approve assumption of Joint Venture debt			■		
Sign long-term contracts			■		
Set distributions and dividends				■	
Set transfer prices				■	
Approve annual plan and budget			■		
Hire and evaluate Joint Venture top management		■			
Hire and evaluate Joint Venture CEO					■
Set board agenda					■
Replace board members	■				
Appoint board of directors	■				
Sell assets				■	
Dissolve venture					■
Approve transfer of ownership					■
Determine tax strategy				■	
Determine legal strategy					■
Draft and change Joint Venture by laws					■
Determine and change geographic scope				■	
Determine and change product scope					

Joint Venture CEO

	Delegate	Keep Informed	Consult First	Decide Jointly	Decide
Approve assumption of Joint Venture debt					■
Sign long-term contracts					■
Set distributions and dividends				■	
Set transfer prices				■	
Approve annual plan and budget					■
Hire and evaluate Joint Venture top management					■
Hire and evaluate Joint Venture CEO	■				
Set board agenda			■		
Replace board members	■				
Appoint board of directors	■				
Sell assets				■	
Dissolve venture	■				
Approve transfer of ownership	■				
Determine tax strategy				■	
Determine legal strategy				■	
Draft and change Joint Venture by laws	■				
Determine and change geographic scope			■		
Determine and change product scope			■		

the range (and limits) of its authority over the alliance, including the list of decisions where it will serve as the decision driver. To carry this model to its full potential, the task force should link the incentives of each stakeholder to the successful exercise of its defined authority—and to the discipline to stay within the confines of it.

Conclusion

Governance has become a word like *trust* or *culture*—clearly important to alliances, but considered too soft to measure and too fluid for disciplined process. Alliance governance, certainly, is not as linear as running an assembly line, but it does deserve more rigor and formality than it usually gets. Our seven-step process provides a basis for collaborative decision making. And given the rising importance of alliances, such a methodology will prove a source of enormous competitive advantage for firms who heed its simple logic.

Further Reading

Robert E. Spekman, Lynn A. Isabella, and Thomas C. MacAvoy. *Alliance Competence: Maximizing the Value of Your Partnerships*. New York: Wiley, 2000. Chapter 7.

Source

This chapter is based on "A Structure for Collaboration," *The Alliance Analyst* (December 1999). The article was edited for this book.

12

Managing Without Control

Gene Slowinski

An alliance begins after the contract is signed. From that point forward, more than half of all alliances fail. Of those that do survive, many linger in a pool of unmet expectations and acrid disappointment. The critical question for a corporate strategist then is this: Once the contract is signed, how do we build an alliance with the power to endure?

That is a difficult process. It is more challenging than conceiving the initial strategy or negotiating the deal. To manage an alliance effectively, a company faces two management imperatives. First is internal preparation: in other words, asking, How do I prepare my company to work with yours? Second is managing no-man's land: How do we cross the organizational boundaries? Answer these two questions right, and you're a hero.

Recognizing the Key Links

Traditionally, alliance strategists have focused their attention on how to manage the relationship between Company A and Company B (Figure 12.1). But many soon came to realize that it was not the whole of these organizations that were forming, advocating, or managing alliances; rather, alliances were led by small groups within each company. Here we focus on this key link between the groups of people in an alliance. It is clear from this perspective that successful

FIGURE 12.1 Managing the Organizational Interface.

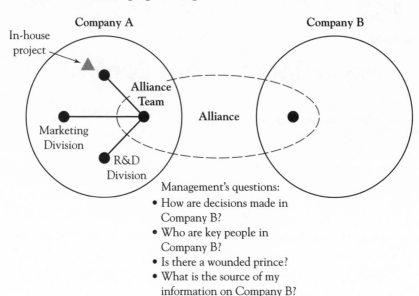

Management's questions:
- How are decisions made in Company B?
- Who are key people in Company B?
- Is there a wounded prince?
- What is the source of my information on Company B?

alliance managers not only manage the relationship with the partner, they also build strong relationships with internal groups—groups that can provide essential resources at critical times.

These managers not only look outward to their partners but also inward to their own companies. For example, say the manufacturing division of Company A is crucial to a given alliance. In most companies, the alliance manager walks up to Harry, the head of manufacturing, and at the last minute demands: "Harry! I need your best people for this alliance with an outside firm." And Harry grumbles, "Yeah, right."

Harry's reaction does not have to be hostile. The best alliance managers go up to Harry in advance and say, "Hey, Harry, I am about to form an alliance, where do you see yourself fitting in? How can we work with you on this relationship?" Now, Harry behaves very differently, and may actually become a champion for the alliance.

Warding Off Internal Competition

An alliance always competes with in-house projects for scarce resources. The triangle in Figure 12.1 flags another undertaking—an in-house project run by a woman named Sheila. For the last five years, Sheila and Harry have bowled together every Thursday night. So here the alliance manager is saying to Harry, "Harry I need your best resources for this outside relationship with this outside firm." Meanwhile, Sheila is saying, "Harry, I need your best resources."

Who wins? The in-house project wins every time. Alliances get below-quality resources for marketing, below-quality resources for manufacturing, and below-quality resources for research and development. In such a position, it shouldn't be surprising that alliances seem to be bleeding to death. Alliances die the death of a thousand nicks, getting bumped at every turn.

New Power Needed

Faced with such obstacles, an alliance manager must command significant power. There are really two types of power relevant to alliances: formal power and informal power. Let me turn to an example from my own background at Bell Laboratories. Every division manager at Bell Labs had the same amount of formal power: they could hire and fire, they had a $50,000 sign-off on purchase orders, and so forth. In this respect, they were all equal.

Informal power, however, was an entirely different story. Informal power can be defined by asking the question: When someone speaks, do people listen? When I worked at Bell Labs one division manager had so little informal power that when he spoke no one listened, not even the people who worked for him. Two doors down another division manager had so much informal power that when he spoke everyone jumped, even people outside his division.

Operating managers need huge amounts of this type of informal power to make their alliances function. They must be able to work inside their own company and marshal the resources that will allow the alliance to be successful. And what if an alliance manager doesn't command such informal power? Well, you haven't nicked the relationship, you've cut an artery. It is all over. Shut down.

Sound tough? It gets tougher still. All the organizational steps just mentioned for Company A must be occurring at Company B, and at the same time. It is the only way an alliance will work.

Dialogue of Actions

Alliances are not about communication—at least not about senior management talking to one another. If you ask me, just about all the senior manager at Company A needs to do is to pick up the phone every few months, call the senior manager at Company B, and say, "You know, I am as committed to this relationship today as I was the day we started it." That's it. Click, hang up the phone.

Actually, alliances expire or expand depending on the way lower-level employees interact with each other. Alliances are about people, not institutions. Witness the best alliance I have seen. Two West Coast electronics companies—one large and one small—formed an alliance spanning research, manufacturing, and distribution. Soon thereafter, an earthquake seriously damaged the large company's facilities. The large company's research manager called his opposite number at the small company and said, "Hey, do you mind if I send my scientists and engineers to work in your facility for the next six months while my operation is under repair?" The answer was, "No problem, send them down." Three outcomes resulted from that decision to transfer people. Number one, the goals of the alliance were achieved ahead of time. Number two, new ways for cooperation were identified. And number three, the large company's scientists and engineers didn't want to go back.

There's a message here. The reason why this alliance is so successful is that the people working in it had an opportunity to see each other day after day and interact at an interpersonal level. They got to know each other, to trust each other, to like each other, and to see what it was like to work together.

When you are in the early stages of an alliance, go to your human resource department and ask them to arrange a way to meet your partner on an interpersonal or social level. You can give an alliance an eighteen-month head start by spending time teaching people inside the alliance about the best practices of managing these relationships—and the pitfalls—and then spending some time listening to people. It is an opportunity for you to get your alliance off to a really quick move out of the blocks.

Building Bridges

An alliance manager must provide a bridge over no-man's-land, that space between Company A and Company B. Begin building this connection by asking a handful of questions:

• *How are decisions made in your partner's firm?* It is critical to link up the two decision-making structures and ensure that the communication is getting through. Decisions may be made one way in Company A and an entirely different way in Company B. In one case, a small firm president described his company's operating style as a flat, team-oriented approach. His partner's organizational approach, in contrast, was full of little kingdoms. The result was that the small firm was forced to negotiate with various parts of the large company, from legal and purchasing to research and development. The misunderstanding stymied cooperation. Decision-making linkages are hard to find, but look for them, because when they are found, they are a windfall.

• *Who are the key people?* Many alliances have mystery people floating around in the background. Usually, they are supporters of the venture. When you look inside a partner's organization, you may well find someone (or several someones) pulling strings you don't know about—somebody who is probably out of the regular alliance loop. Who are they? Find out who they are and try to make contact. They don't exist in every alliance, just often enough to look for them.

• *Is there a wounded prince?* The wounded prince is the person in your partner's firm who says, "The alliance is doing my job!" And, more privately, "and it is doing it better than I am." The wounded prince type is threatened by your existence, and such people are wonderful saboteurs. You can take a great deal of power away from a wounded prince by simply identifying who he is.

• *Am I getting my information just from my partner?* Talk to other partners. Talk to suppliers. Talk to vendors. Talk to anybody your potential partner has a relationship with. The answers may not be perfect guides as to how your partner will act in your alliance, but they will give you a good indication.

• *What is it about me that is driving you bananas?* Alliances are dynamic, vibrant, living creatures. They change all the time and, most important, they can be made better. I suggest that alliance managers ask their partners about ongoing irritations every three months: literally, ask, "What is it about me that is driving you bananas?" The first time that question is asked, the partner will come back with a laundry list. Twenty percent of the items are unchangeable because they are determined by the structure of your organization. But the other 80 percent are not difficult to adjust, and making these changes in the relationship will make working together a lot easier. And once you make these adjustments, you get to submit your own list. If done right, these lists will get shorter and the relationship will get stronger.

Transferring Know-How

In many cases, an alliance's primary goal is to transfer technology or know-how from one company to another. Sounds simple enough, but it's not. Consider an ordinary example. One day, I went down to the store and bought two high-tech products: a halogen light bulb and a database program for my computer. I brought those two products home, I walked over to the lamp, unscrewed the old incandescent bulb, and screwed in the halogen one. In an instant, and with hardly any thought, I transferred huge amounts of technology. It was transparent, because I already knew how to change a light bulb.

Then I went over to the database program sitting near my personal computer, took off the shrink-wrap, and pulled out the enclosed ten books, the smallest of which was 150 pages and titled *Getting Started*. I shoehorned the program onto my computer, but not before it ate up my entire hard drive. Then, for the next two weeks, I sat and stared. I couldn't even create a file. My response? I put as many of those disks and books back into the box as I could, took it down to my administrative assistant, and said: "Suzanne, look what the American hero just bought for you. I don't want to hear any more of those complaints that I don't buy things that improve your productivity." Well, it has been eighteen months and we do not use that database program. Never have. Never will.

What does this have to do with alliances? Alliances are about transferring knowledge, and if you are transferring your knowledge like that computer database company, you are not going to have a happy partner. But if you transfer knowledge like that halogen bulb maker, you are going to be thought of as a wonderful partner. To transfer something over to a partner as elegantly as that halogen light bulb, a company must learn how its partner operates and thinks. And then it must send the knowledge in an intelligent way.

Corporate camouflage can make this easier. Consider a hypothetical example: Company A and Company B have formed an alliance, agreeing that Company A will design the prototype and Company B will manufacture the product. Company A sends the prototype over, including all sorts of documentation. Company B doesn't do anything. Company A calls up and asks, "What's wrong?" And Company B says: "No documentation." What Company B meant was that the supplied documentation was not on their forms and they couldn't understand it. The lesson: when transferring information, make it look like it has been in the partner's organization the whole time.

Recognizing Cultural Differences

Culture clash is the invisible eight-hundred-pound gorilla in alliances. Managers don't know much about culture so they don't manage it. That neglect can tear a relationship apart. The president of a small company told me: "The corporate culture of [our large company partner] descended upon us like antibodies attacking a foreign substance."

A couple of tips on how to manage this coming clash. First, cultural differences cannot stand up to a relentless assault of trust and respect—the foundation stones of an alliance. Get people to know one another at an interpersonal level, and the cultural differences lose their power.

Second, have your company and your partner take an inventory of their cultural traits using one of the many standard tools in the organizational development repertoire. Share the results. Look for the alliance barriers and the leverage points. And now, all of a sudden, those cultural differences become something amusing to talk and think about. The gorilla is no longer invisible. After taking the test an alliance manager might end up in a partner dispute and just sit back, relax, and laugh, saying, "That's just the competitiveness of my partner's culture coming out."

Further Reading

Charles Handy. "Trust and the Virtual Corporation," *Harvard Business Review*, May-June 1995, pp. 2–8.

Rosabeth Moss Kanter. "Collaborative Advantage: The Art of Alliances," *Harvard Business Review*, July-Aug. 1994, pp. 96–108.

Source

This chapter is based on "Managing Alliances Effectively," *The Alliance Analyst* (May 1995). The article was edited for this book.

Leading the Relationship

13

Alliance Staffing

How should an alliance be staffed? Some ventures are extremely people-intensive: large consolidation and new business joint ventures can have a thousand or more employees; multibillion-dollar co-promotion alliances in the pharmaceuticals industry routinely involve several hundred people or more; and global airline alliances can "touch" almost every employee of a member-firm. Other alliances have far smaller staffs: early-stage research alliances in high-tech and co-brandings in the consumer products business, for example, often involve fewer than ten people, many of whom are less than 20 percent dedicated to the alliance.

Despite such variance, staffing is an essential element of successful alliances. A review of a large number of alliances suggests that six "alliance positions" are key: dealmaker, launch manager, governor, alliance chief or JV CEO, alliance operating staff, and corporate alliance manager. These positions correspond to three main tasks associated with alliance success: start-up, operations, and coordination (Exhibit 13.1).

Success depends on clearly defining these six roles, developing appropriate means for selecting and recruiting staff to fill them, and creating incentives and measures to drive individual and collective performance. The following sections explore issues across each of these roles.

EXHIBIT 13.1 Alliance Staff: Six Core Alliance Positions.

Start-Up	Operations	Coordination
1. Dealmaker • Develop and refine alliance strategy. • Screen partners. • Negotiate and structure contract. **2. Launch manager** • Plan launch (first 60–180 days). • Facilitate key launch meetings (such as the launch workshop). • Manage overall launch process (milestones, timelines, resource flows, and so on). • Help capture synergy and build alliance organization.	**3. Governor** • Set alliance's strategic direction. • Make key decisions (for example, approve annual budget, change scope). • Secure parent resources. • Monitor venture and alliance chief performance. • Identify opportunities to expand alliance scope. **4. Alliance chief or JV CEO** • Manage day-to-day alliance operations. • Make tactical decisions (for example, spot discounts to customers, non-extraordinary agreements). • Select and manage (or coordinate) core alliance staff. • Oversee communications with partner or parents. **5. Alliance operating staff** • Perform main work of the alliance. • Lead joint working teams or functional areas.	**6. Corporate alliance manager** • Shape and refine firm's overall approach to alliances. • Support key alliances (for example, as steering committee or board member). • Troubleshoot and help resolve relationship conflicts. • Maintain communication with partner. • Build corporate alliance infrastructure (tools, systems, processes). • Train alliance practitioners. • Help minimize conflicts and maximize synergies in portfolio.

Alliance Dealmaker

An alliance dealmaker is responsible for developing or refining the alliance strategy, screening partners, and negotiating and structuring the contract, including valuing partner contributions and overseeing the narrower work of functional specialists, including lawyers and financial experts. Although the role of dealmaker is quite familiar, a number of key questions are nonetheless instrumental to optimizing performance. For instance, should dealmakers specialize in alliances or handle the full range of business development options, including mergers and acquisitions, licenses, divestitures, and spinoffs? Likewise, how can the company provide dealmakers with the incentives to create alliances that are "operable" and successful over the long run—rather than those with a large net present value?

Leading companies are starting to answer these questions. For example, our discussions with more than fifty corporate business development units suggests that companies with alliance-intensive business models are often well served to create a subgroup of dealmakers specializing in alliances (for example, equity investments and joint ventures) leaving other dealmakers to focus on mergers and acquisitions and other deal structures. This division of labor allows alliance dealmakers to gain deep understanding of key alliance issues, including transfer pricing, governance and organizational design, and alliance launch.

Creating strong and balanced incentives is more challenging—but also possible. To encourage dealmakers to take a more operational orientation, some companies are experimenting with new roles and incentive structures. For example, one leading pharmaceutical company now expects its dealmakers to devote 10 percent of their time in Year One to helping operationalize each alliance formed. Although this means that each dealmaker completes fewer deals, it ensures that dealmakers truly understand critical operational issues and that essential "deal content" does not get lost in the transition from deal making to management. As one dealmaker points out: "One recent agreement contained twenty-six separate royalty payments—and I was the only one in our company who understood how this was supposed to work. Walking away at deal close would have put us at a considerable disadvantage." Other firms are considering using annual "partner satisfaction" surveys in Years 1 and 2 as partial basis for evaluating dealmaker performance and determining compensation.

Launch Manager

In contrast to deal making, few companies consider alliance launch management a distinct role. This is unfortunate, for there are strong indications that such a role is absolutely essential to success. At one leading technology company, for example, an internal study showed that alliances routinely stumbled during the first 100–180 days, losing critical time and momentum while failing to build the essential components of effective collaboration such as shared strategic intent and clear decision-making and working processes. By its own estimation, the firm was losing $500–$700 million per year as a result. To determine whether the company has sufficient focus on launch, it can be useful to ask a few diagnostic questions:

- Does the company make the same commitment to alliance launch as to post-merger integration?
- How long does the average alliance launch take—and how much value would the company create if it improved "launch speed" by 50 percent?
- Do managers routinely race out of the gate, focusing on operating plans without first building the basic understanding, processes, structures, and incentives for strong collaboration?

To ensure that an alliance gets off to a strong start during the first 100–180 days, companies should consider appointing a launch manager. A launch manager is responsible for such tasks as developing the launch plan (the detailed 100-day road map), orchestrating key launch activities (such as launch workshops), and translating and deepening the contract along a series of operational dimensions. This includes creating a detailed organizational blueprint and explicit strategies and plans for linking or combining partner resources such as brands, intellectual property, and customer data.

In some companies, the launch management job is a distinct and specialized position. One leading European pharmaceutical company, for instance, appointed launch managers to a key alliance for nine to twelve months, at which point they were rotated off and assigned to a new alliance. Another model is to include launch management as an element in another—broader—role. For example, it can be extremely effective to have the alliance chiefs (those responsible for day-to-day venture management) manage the launch. Of course, this requires the firm to appoint an alliance chief during the late stages of deal making (which can be difficult) and to have some institutionalized expertise around launch in order to ensure that the alliance chiefs have sufficient understanding of launch challenges and tasks. In other cases, firms have considered making launch management the responsibility of dealmakers or members of the corporate alliance unit.

Alliance Governor

Alliance governors are executives responsible for overseeing the alliance—that is, setting its strategic direction, making key decisions (for example, approving the annual plan and budget, changing contractual terms), monitoring venture performance, finding opportunities to expand the alliance scope, and championing the alliance within the company. Depending on deal structure, most governors will be members of either the alliance steering committee or JV board of directors.

Maximizing the impact of individual alliance governors hinges on an answering several questions: Other than showing up for meetings, what will be expected of each governor, and how will each be held accountable for performance? Should individual governors, for instance, have distinct roles and responsibilities, or even quasi employment contracts? How can companies avoid the overwhelming influence of "shadow governors"—that is, those individuals who are not members of the formal alliance governance system but nonetheless manipulate the alliance from behind the scenes?

Most companies need to sharpen their approach to the alliance governor role. All too often, governors float in and out of an alliance, with limited understanding of their role and limited opportunity or incentives to make a high-value contribution. To overcome this, it can be extremely helpful to create individual roles, rather than trying to treat all governors as equals. Our work reveals a number of such roles in use, including chair and co-chair, lead director, strategic coordinator, alliance advocate and functional lead and co-lead. Not all of these roles will be appropriate for each alliance, of course, but delineating responsibilities can create considerable added efficiency, accountability, and performance.

Consider one prominent U.S. chemical company. It routinely names one JV board member as "lead director"—and expects that governor to spend twenty to thirty days per year working to resolve issues with the JV CEO and management team and securing resources in the parent. In contrast, the non-lead directors are expected to spend five to ten days per year on the alliance, generally limiting their involvement to board meetings and basic oversight. By differentiating between these roles, board members have a much better understanding of what is expected of them—and the JV management team knows where to turn when problems arise.

Taking this thinking further, firms should consider creating a "quasi employment contract" for key governors. No more than one or two pages, this document should outline individual responsibilities and the basic metrics for success. For example, at one U.S. technology company, when a corporate dealmaker was invited to join the steering committee of a major non-equity alliance, he found that such a contract was instrumental in giving him the authority to play a strategic coordinator role—and to receive the credit he deserved for helping the partners better manage the alliance across key organizational and geographic gaps.

Alliance Chief

An alliance chief is responsible for the day-to-day operations of the alliance—that is, implementing the business plan, making tactical decisions, managing the alliance budget, communicating with the partner, and managing or coordinating key alliance operating staff. As such, the alliance chief serves as the critical linchpin between the alliance governors who are steering the venture and core and non-core operating alliance staff who are performing the work.

The profile and effectiveness of an alliance chief stems from a set of key choices around role definition, selection, incentives, and performance measures: Should there be one alliance chief from each partner, or a single alliance chief representing both? Should the alliance chief assignments be full- or part-time jobs? What operational power and resources should an alliance chief command—in other words, will the role be one of considerable authority or more focused on coordination? How will alliance chiefs be selected? For instance, will the partner have any influence over who is chosen for the position? Likewise, how will the parents evaluate alliance chief performance, and to what extent are incentives tied to overall alliance success? And, insofar as each parent has an alliance chief, how will the companies align their incentives?

To show how questions play out, we've created a key choices map (Exhibit 13.2). It contains a series of critical dimensions, each of which includes several discreet choices. There is no best answer to any of these choices, but we've found that top-performing alliance companies favor stronger alliance chief models—that is, give real power and resources to those in charge of the alliance—and to link individual metrics and incentives to the partner and to overall venture performance. Typically, such a model has been associated with JV CEOs—that is, executives running large joint venture companies with their own staff and resources. But such a model can also be constructed for non-equity alliances.

Consider one leading U.S. software company. For each of its hundred or so major sales and marketing alliances, it appoints a single

EXHIBIT 13.2 Alliance Chief—Key Choices Map.

Number of alliance chiefs	*Many* Partners each appoint multiple alliance chiefs.	*Cochiefs* Each parent appoints one alliance chief.	*Alliance CEO* Partners appoint one alliance chief to oversee alliance.
Dedication	*Part-timers* Alliance chiefs less than 50 percent dedicated to alliance.	*Ad hoc staff* Partners do not define alliance chief dedication—or expect it to vary depending on the needs of the alliance at a given time.	*Full-timers* Alliance chiefs more than 70 percent dedicated to alliance.
Power and resources	*Coordinator (weak)* Parents give alliance chief limited authority (mostly to coordinate meetings) and essentially no resources.	*Targeted manager* Parents grant alliance chief real authority in narrow and tightly defined alliance areas (such as spot discounts to customers, trade-show promotions).	*General manager (strong)* Parents grant significant power and resources to alliance chief, including large discretionary funds and power to hire, fire, and transfer alliance staff.
Partner influence on selection	*No say* Partner has no power to effect choice of alliance chief.	*Some influence* Partner has some influence over decision (for example, as part of limited number of "overrule" cards that can be played during overall governor and staff selection process).	*Veto power* Alliance chief must be approved by the partner.

Incentives: Links to alliance performance	*De-linked* Partners have not developed a system for assessing alliance performance—or make no effort to link alliance chief's performance to it.	*Partial connection* Partners link alliance chief's performance to a weak or high-level alliance scorecard—or only marginally tie performance to a strong scorecard.	*Strong ties* Partners have developed balanced scorecard or alliance P&L, and have based at least 50 percent of alliance chief's evaluation and compensation to it.
Incentives: Alignment between alliance chiefs (when each partner appoints one)	*Weak* Partners do not align individual incentives, in effect pushing each manager to maximize short- and long-term value for the parent.		*Strong* Partners make effort to create similar incentives for alliance chiefs, and to strongly reward collaborative behavior (for example, reviews are based on same scorecard and include partner success; collaborative behavior is called out on individual performance scorecards).

alliance chief (often a fresh recruit from a top MBA program), develops an alliance P&L that tracks alliance costs and revenues, and insists that the partners contribute to an "alliance market development fund" to ensure that the alliance chiefs do not have to go "tin cupping" across the organization in search of money or resources to execute their plan.

Alliance Operating Staff

"Alliance operating staff" refers to those individuals who perform the basic work of an alliance. In a joint venture, these are likely to be employees of the JV, whereas in non-equity alliances, they are typically members of the alliance working teams and committees. When thinking about alliance operating staff, it is useful to differentiate between core and non-core staff. *Core staff* is defined as those managers working closely with the partner or parents—and whose selection, role definition, location, and incentives have a strong bearing on alliance performance. Even in the largest alliances and joint ventures, core alliance staff rarely exceeds thirty people. On the other hand, *non-core alliance staff* is everyone else— essential and nonessential talent focused on non-partner activities.

Of the many interesting and difficult questions relating to core alliance staff, a few merit particular attention. For example, how will core alliance staff be selected, especially when the parents are not following a Noah's Ark model of human resource management (that is, creating "paired counterparts" at each key position)? One common model in JVs is for the partners to take turns filling slots, whereas another is for the JV CEO to be free to decide provided that some agreed-upon ratio is maintained between the partners. Other questions relate to the career path of alliance staff. For instance, how long will managers be expected to stay in the alliance, and what is the logical next career step? This is especially germane in JVs, where the parents need to determine whether staff members have a lifeline back to the parent and under what circumstances (for example, after two years).

In non-equity alliances, the issues can be quite different—or at least offer a different set of answers. For example, a common managerial decision in non-equity alliances relates to the overall size and composition of the core alliance team, specifically: How many people to include and how focused should each be on the alliance? In general terms, we've found that alliances with a small core alliance team (four to ten) with each member 50 percent or more dedicated to the alliance are much more effective than alliances with a larger but looser core group. These latter alliances simply lack the staff with the time or determination to get things done.

Corporate Alliance Managers

Corporate alliance managers are those managers within a corporate alliance unit who oversee and support the firm's portfolio of alliances. In most cases, these executives work with top management to refine the overall approach to alliances, support certain alliances within the portfolio, and build the infrastructure; these alliance managers typically do not run the alliance business itself—that is the job of the alliance chief and governor. The most prominent of these executives is the vice president of alliances—a title that many firms have created in recent years. Firms with a vice president of alliances often create the position of corporate alliance director as well—that is, one of that vice president's three to eight direct reports.

Our work identified a number of critical questions regarding corporate alliance managers. First and foremost: When should a company create a corporate unit containing such positions? As a general rule of thumb, such a unit and positions make sense when the portfolio contains more than twenty alliances representing 20 percent or more of corporate value, as measured in terms of revenues, corporate assets, research spending, or income (see Chapter Twenty-Five).

A second question: Which alliances should the corporate alliance manager focus on—and at what point in the alliance life cycle?

Many different approaches can be made to work, but we've found that most effective alliance managers do not cover the alliance landscape. Instead, they severely limit the number of alliances supported and narrowly define their role. For example, firms should segment their alliance portfolios according to strategic importance and complexity—and focus corporate alliance managers on the high-value, high-complexity deals. Moreover, the exact role of the corporate alliance manager in these alliances should be clearly defined—and often quite narrow. For example, Eli Lilly's corporate alliance managers were chartered as "alliance advocates"—that is, responsible for protecting and promoting the interests of the alliance (see Chapter Thirty-One). Other companies may give the alliance manager more operational responsibility, making them akin to an alliance chief or governor.

A third question: How will the performance of a corporate alliance manager be evaluated? Although this obviously depends on the nature of the role, a number of approaches can be helpful. For starters, the firm should develop a few broad benchmarks of alliance performance—for example, overall alliance reputation in the industry, number of unsolicited alliance proposals per year, and general partner and internal manager satisfaction ratings—and make these part of each corporate alliance manager's review criteria.

For example, in the pharmaceuticals industry, a consulting firm annually publishes a "partner of choice" ranking that rates pharmaceutical companies on their relative attractiveness to biotech partners. In addition to such general performance benchmarks, alliance managers should be evaluated according to the performance of specific alliances supported—and even more narrowly, their individual contribution to those alliances. Lilly used an annual fourteen-part survey to track individual alliance performance, for example. Going further, a corporate alliance manager who is supporting a specific alliance should develop a contract with the steering committee that defines the manager's role and attaches specific metrics to that role.

A final question relating to corporate alliance managers: What is their career path? Because the position of corporate alliance manager is new to most companies, defining the career path is essential to attracting top talent. In companies where the corporate alliance unit is small (that is, does not have line management responsibility for alliances), it is unrealistic to think that alliance managers will remain in place for more than three to five years. The reason: lack of advancement opportunity. As a result, the career path often has a number of possible routes: a return to the alliance manager's previous functional area (for example, marketing, corporate affairs, finance, research and development) or into the corporate business development group.

Alliance success hinges on people issues—in particular, defining roles and responsibilities and creating the incentives to drive individual performance. Although many talent-related questions remain, top-performing firms will focus significant energy on sharpening their views on the six roles outlined in this chapter and ensuring that those individuals who can determine the fate of an alliance are selected, positioned, and motivated in a manner that dramatically increases their chances of success.

Further Reading

Michael Y. Yoshino and U. Srinivasa Rangan. *Strategic Alliances: An Entrepreneurial Approach to Globalization*. Boston: Harvard Business School Press, 1995. Chapters 5–7.

14

Roles of the Alliance Manager

How should you select an alliance manager? Regardless of the well-documented importance of ongoing management to alliance success, few companies have developed a robust answer to this question. Even the best firms are not very good at selecting alliance managers, often treating alliances as the place where passed-over executives are sent to live out their careers. Or they use vague personality traits to pick alliance managers—they select people who are "diplomatic," "culturally sensitive," and so on.

And few firms consider how the evolution of an alliance affects the demands on the alliance manager—and indeed whether different people should be in that role at different phases of venture development. Research from the Darden School of Business at the University of Virginia shows that alliance evolution is important when making staffing decisions. According to Darden professor Robert Spekman: "An alliance lifestyle has seven distinct stages. The skill sets required from an alliance manager are different in each one of those stages—a visionary is called for at one stage and a facilitator at another."

To help companies improve their approach to selecting alliance managers, we examined three experienced firms—Lotus Development, Xerox, and Corning. The experiences of these companies show that choosing an alliance manager depends on many factors, including the scope, value, and duration of the alliance, and the culture and organization of the firm. We also compared these experiences with the findings of the Darden research on how the role of alliance managers changes across the alliance life cycle.

Career Paths: Three Models

Who is cut out to be an alliance manager? What professional background and individual skills are needed to promote venture success? What incentives should the firm offer to attract this talent? Should there be a defined career path for the alliance manager, and if so, what should it be? Xerox, Lotus, and Corning took different approaches to answering these questions. Although none offers the single solution, each provides a set of interesting responses that clearly worked within their specific context.

Xerox: The Marathon Man

The Xerox approach to staffing large joint ventures was to find a young manager who was resourceful and ambitious, and then link that manager's career to the long-term success of the alliance.

Jefferson Kennard was selected to manage the Fuji Xerox alliance in the 1970s and remained in this role for three decades. Kennard first became involved in the alliance when he was sent to Japan as Xerox's resident director. At the time, Fuji Xerox was barely out of the start-up stage, operating as a domestic marketer of American-designed copiers. By 2000, the joint venture was generating more than $8 billion in annual sales. It had also expanded far outside Japan, with a footprint across Asia and even into the United States. Its scope had advanced well past marketing into manufacturing and research. Indeed, the joint venture had become the company's worldwide center of excellence for low- to mid-range copiers and printer engines.

At the core of Fuji Xerox was an ongoing conversation between two individuals: Kennard and long-time Fuji Xerox CEO Tony Kobayashi. When Kennard went to Japan in the mid-1970s,

Kobayashi had just taken over the venture and took the unprece-dented step of asking Kennard to serve as his executive assistant as well as the Xerox resident director. This personal continuity and trust became a cornerstone of the venture's success. From the Fuji Xerox side, Kennard provided a steady face attached to an ever-changing Xerox—changing in terms of staff, strategic goals, and organizational structure. From the Xerox side, Kennard is the walk-ing storehouse of collected wisdom, the one person who can remem-ber what negotiations were like in the 1970s when Fuji Xerox wanted to design and manufacture its own low-end copiers.

Lotus Development: The Stepping-Stoners

"Many companies staff their alliances with washouts," according to Hemang Davé, who served as VP of alliances at Lotus Development from 1993 to 1996. "They are generally good people, but not good enough to be handed line responsibility." In 1993, Davé was brought to Lotus to take over worldwide responsibility for strategic alliances, and he worked furiously to create a different type of alli-ance organization. Faced with a choice between continuity and capability, he chose the latter. "I recruited from among the A-Team to be my alliance managers, the company's absolute best and bright-est," he says. "And I made it clear that if they proved themselves as an alliance manager, they would go off and run a business for Lotus."

Davé made membership in his fifty-person alliance organization a badge, arguing to new recruits that it was the best way to engage in regular conversations with senior management at both Lotus and a partner company such as HP or IBM. Develop alliance skills, the message implied, and you will be going places.

One problem for Lotus was staff turnover. While alliance man-agers were encouraged to stay for at least a few years, this hardly pro-vided the steadiness of a Jeff Kennard. "Potentially, it's a problem," Davé said. "While there is a lot of change at the alliance manager level, above it—at the director level and the vice president level—

we do our best to maintain continuity." It's still a tough task. Davé himself, two years after creating the Lotus alliance group, was reassigned to manage the Lotus-IBM integration, and soon thereafter left the company.

Corning: The Rotating Climbers

"We have seen it in almost every corporation: the bench is incredibly thin when it comes to good alliance managers," Darden's Robert Spekman says. Why? Because no one takes the time to develop the needed skills through training or by rotating good managers in and out of alliances. "The grand exception is Corning," Spekman notes. Tom MacAvoy, a former president and vice chairman of Corning and a member of the Darden research team, details this firm's approach:

> At Corning, there has long been a realization that alliances are both incredibly important to the company and pervasive throughout it. As a result, Corning needs a lot of people who are good at managing these things. Senior management, who has historically been responsible for staffing alliances, certainly knows this. Young, high-potential managers are often rotated into a joint venture very early in their career. At first, they are likely to be in a support role, learning the special dynamics of collaboration. If they prove themselves there, then they might get a little joint venture to run themselves. And if they continue to prove themselves, they could become the alliance manager representing Corning's interests on a billion-dollar alliance like Siecor, the joint venture with Siemens.

This is arguably the best approach to alliance staffing: it places an emphasis on continuity, it builds an organization full of managers with decades of alliance experience, and it attracts some of the most capable managers to alliances. But it is also the toughest to replicate.

Few firms have enough large joint ventures to accommodate this sort of career development.

Selecting the Right Model

What general lessons can be learned from these three leading companies? First and foremost is that the approach to staffing alliances depends on the firm's business model and the nature of alliances within it. Xerox was able to secure someone of Kennard's caliber—and managed to keep him involved in the alliance—because of the importance of the joint venture to Xerox and the venture's ongoing managerial complexity. Also, the fact that the alliance was based in Japan added to the importance of personal relationships and the desire for genuine continuity. Corning arrived at an alliance staffing model that reflected the fact that it had many large and independent joint ventures. Because of this, Corning was in a position to treat its alliances as a common variant of the classic business unit, where managing such ventures was seen as extremely valuable operational experience.

A second observation is the importance of making alliance management a defined role and creating a clear career path for alliance managers. Lotus did not offer its alliance managers the same level of operating experience as Corning, but it did elevate alliance management to a legitimate role in the company, something few firms did until years later. It also started to articulate a number of different career avenues for its alliance managers, including advancement within the corporate alliance unit.

A third observation is that the alliance manager role is not a generic one. Corning alliance managers were operating managers. Xerox appointed Kennard as a venture liaison—someone who connected the alliance to the corporate parent, but not someone who managed the operating alliance. Lotus alliance managers were relationship managers, in essence partner account executives who shared many responsibilities and traits with more traditional sales managers. Clearly, the precise role of the alliance manager must reflect the scope, potential value, and likely duration of the relationship that the firm needs to manage. Corning was building independent billion-dollar businesses. Lotus was managing fluid sales and marketing partners.

How strong is your company's performance in selecting alliance managers? Drawing on the lessons of these and other companies, we have created a simple diagnostic (Exhibit 14.1). Top-performing companies will answer yes far more often than no.

Alliance Management Skills

How do you know a good alliance manager when you see one? And when you find someone with the potential to grow in this job, how do you develop that potential? What skills can be acquired? What

---

EXHIBIT 14.1 Staffing Diagnostic: Alliance Managers.

---

1. Is alliance management a legitimate role in the company?
2. Does the firm have a defined career path (or paths) for alliance managers?
3. Does the firm attract top talent to alliance management? (Compare similar positions, for example, sales managers versus alliance managers; business-unit presidents versus JV presidents.)
4. Does the firm truly understand what skills and responsibilities make an alliance manager different from its relevant non-alliance counterpart?
5. As far as possible, has the firm taken steps to make alliances operate like true businesses (separate P&L, and so on)?
6. Does the firm differentiate between different alliance manager roles (for example, operating manager, venture liaison, relationship manager)?
7. Does the firm consider the alliance's developmental stage when selecting alliance managers?
8. Are alliance managers generally chosen and committed at least part time before the contract is signed?

---

skills need to be present at the hiring? Human resource managers in leading alliance companies have begun to struggle with these questions. Spekman and his colleagues have identified three levels of skills as being important for the would-be alliance manager.

Threshold skills, the must-have competencies, center around the ability to convey a sense of self-confidence and the ability to inspire others and urge them to novel ideas and new ways of thinking. Alliance managers must be respected, and they must respect the contributions of others. These skills form the foundation of the ability to build a cohesive team that can carry the alliance forward.

Distinguishing skills revolve around the depth and breadth of informal networks the alliance manager has developed, both internal and external to the alliance. These networks of business relationships are critical to the manager's ability to develop and nurture the alliance. The manager's network forms the base from which trust and commitment to the alliance can emerge. Confidence in the alliance manager's talent and judgment might let a skeptical alliance team member—or even a skeptical CEO—give an unproved alliance an opportunity, or even give people the patience to wait and see how a problem works out.

High-performance skills enable the alliance manager to help grow the alliance. Understanding the possible synergies between the partners and being able to articulate the mutual benefits are key high-performance skills. Credibility is an essential ingredient for the success of an alliance manager, and we found it to be a critical high-performance skill.

How are these skills developed? First, although many can be taught, several of the most critical skills must either be earned (for example, credibility) or form a natural part of the manager's personality (for example, people skills). Second, many alliance management skills build on each other and cannot easily be developed in isolation.

Some of these skills may be more or less useful during certain stages of an alliance's life. But the best alliance managers should have them all in reserve, perhaps to pull out when the alliance most needs it. Being an effective communicator and knowing how the parts of the business fit together are clearly important skills at all alliance life-cycle stages. Credibility appears to be most important earlier in the alliance; that is when it will facilitate corporate buy-in and trust, contributing momentum to the young alliance.

Alliance Manager Succession

Effective management of human resources requires more than identifying and training individual alliance managers. Succession planning is crucial, particularly because continuity and clarity of communication is central to good partner relationships. Just as firms plan for their next generation of senior managers, they should also plan for their next generation of alliance managers. Potential managers should be tested early on for the key attributes and competencies required to manage a successful alliance, then a pool of potential candidates should be identified.

The companies that have done this the best, such as Corning, then have newer alliance managers work with more experienced managers in a mentoring program, helping to ensure that values and corporate behaviors are passed on from generation to generation. If unexpected management transitions occur, new alliance managers are given enough time to become accustomed to the alliance and to meet all the members of the alliance family. A series of well-planned experiences can help ensure an alliance manager's development and can increase the organization's chances of success.

The corollary to these observations is that going out and hiring experienced alliance managers won't solve management problems in an alliance. External staff simply haven't earned the trust and respect of other members of an alliance or of the people in the organization; they probably won't have intimate knowledge of the aspects of the business that matter most to the alliance.

Choosing an alliance manager is one of the most important decisions that a company will make on the road to creating a successful alliance. But this selection is far from simple. Top-performing companies will take into account a whole series of factors, including the nature of the alliance and its stage of development. At the same time, firms must also ensure the existence of certain organizational components, including a recognition that alliance management is a legitimate role and a defined career path for alliance managers.

Further Reading

Robert E. Spekman, Lynn A. Isabella, and Thomas C. MacAvoy. *Alliance Competence: Maximizing the Value of Your Partnerships*. New York: Wiley, 2000. Chapter 8.

Source

This chapter is based on several articles in *The Alliance Analyst*, especially "The Ever-Evolving Alliance Manager" (October 1995) and "Darden's Alliance Guidebook" (August 1997). The articles were combined, edited, and updated for this book.

15

Life as an Alliance Manager

On a rare occasion, an executive will wax poetic on the role of alliance managers. "The goal of the alliance manager is not to create harmony but to create a sense of dynamic tension," said one CEO whose company was built around alliances. "Think of the cathedral at Notre Dame with its flying buttresses. It is the equal and opposing pressure that keeps it up. That is the basic architecture inside the alliance. An alliance manager must create a situation where all the different forces push inward and they are so strong that they create stability, provided, of course, they are all vectored in the right direction."

A beautiful image, but what does an alliance manager actually do? To find out, we talked to two alliance managers: Jim Burnham of Lotus Development and Dorine Hernandez of Baxter Healthcare. In the mid-1990s, Burnham managed Lotus's marketing and development alliances with Bull, Compaq, and AT&T. During broadly the same period, Hernandez was the full-time alliance manager for the alliance between Baxter and the American Red Cross that produced plasma.

Our aim was simple: rather than focus on strategic or structural issues of alliances, we wanted to understand the work patterns of successful alliance managers. What problems do alliance managers confront on an average day? What basic roles do they perform? With whom do they interact? And what sorts of skills and background are necessary to do the job well?

Three Roles of the Alliance Manager

Like other Lotus alliance managers in the mid-1990s, Jim Burnham was responsible for managing a few similar alliances. (In his case, he managed alliances with three computer hardware companies, while another alliance manager was responsible for, say, a few alliances with system integrators.) Burnham reported to a director who oversaw several alliance managers and in turn reported into the VP of alliances. Burnham performed three basic roles: internal advocate, external promoter, and relationship deepener.

Internal Advocate

Burnham spent a substantial portion of his time arguing the cause of his three alliances inside Lotus. Consider one Monday in December 1995, typical for Burnham. On that day, the Lotus team organizing Lotusphere, the firm's annual user conference, informed Burnham that a marketing workshop for one of his partners, Compaq, was to be canceled. They claimed that the Compaq workshop would conflict with Lotus's new corporate strategy. Months before, Compaq had received approval to hold a Lotusphere session to demonstrate how Notes servers functioned alongside Internet servers. But in early December, Lotus announced it was repositioning its hot-selling Notes software to become an integral part of the Internet rather than a competitor to it. "All of a sudden," Burnham recalled, "a Notes server was an Internet server. And thus Compaq's whole presentation . . . was outdated."

It fell on Burnham to determine how to keep both Compaq and Lotus happy. Compaq really wanted to host a session at Lotusphere: it was a chance to showcase its connection to Lotus and how well its products worked with Notes. Lotus wanted a consistent corporate message. Burnham's solution: submit a new proposal for a workshop that would focus on the performance and tuning of Compaq servers running Notes. "But the Lotusphere people said the session sounded too much like a Compaq sales pitch," Burnham recalled. "My reaction was, 'Of course it is! Compaq is going to Lotusphere to promote its products and get tangible benefits. They are a sponsor of the conference, they are paying money, and it should hardly be surprising that they want something back.'"

This was Burnham as internal alliance advocate—coordinating among various Lotus groups to ensure that his alliance partner was getting management attention, good treatment, and adequate resources. "I don't make any bones about it: I am the champion of that alliance. I am not some unbiased observer. I want Compaq to succeed within Lotus and, so long as I see that as in Lotus's interest as well, I am going to do everything I can to pull it off," Burnham said. "Often that makes me something of a gadfly around Lotus. But that is what it's like to be an alliance manager."

External Promoter

Burnham also promoted Lotus's cause within the partner firm. Witness the alliance with the computer unit of AT&T. Earlier that year Burnham and his counterpart at AT&T had identified ways to promote Lotus to AT&T sales reps. "I wanted them to know what Lotus Notes was capable of on their servers," Burnham remembered, "how we could support them as an organization, and how they could be our arms to the marketplace." Six months before, Burnham and his counterpart hosted a satellite broadcast to some five thousand AT&T sales reps across the world. "It was a couple of hours devoted exclusively to explaining the power of Notes," according to Burnham. "That took a tremendous amount of time to organize. We had to get the sign-off and resources from both companies, and we had to schedule it, set the agenda, and write our own scripts. It was a fairly complex process."

Burnham also promoted the alliances to customers. For instance, Lotus and AT&T were planning to cosponsor a road show in ten cities across the United States to demonstrate the new power of Notes. Lotus would fill the seats with potential users, AT&T would supply the new hardware, and both companies would manage the event.

Relationship Deepener

Burnham also spent time making sure that his partners had strong personal relationships across Lotus—in functions like development, marketing, sales, and support. Indeed, this desire for broad personal connections was one of Lotus's corporate guidelines in managing alliances (see Chapter Twenty-Nine).

The A&T alliance showed how successful Burnham had become. Although the alliance was mostly centered around sales and marketing, Burnham had organized engineers from both companies to participate in joint technical testing and benchmarking—meetings that further deepened the links between the development teams. For AT&T, those links went to the very top of the Lotus development pyramid: AT&T's alliance manager had personal ties to Lotus's Ray Ozzie, the software industry icon and lead developer of Notes.

Challenges Facing the Alliance Manager

Burnham came to alliances in a common way for Lotus. "We were looking for people with multifunctional backgrounds," recalled Hemang Davé, the executive who built and ran the Lotus alliance unit in the mid-1990s. "They need to be comfortable operating in all sorts of environments such as sales, marketing, management, and development. Experience in any three of those four is good."

Burnham had joined Lotus ten years before in a corporate staff position supporting field engineers. Over the next eight years he climbed his way through sales, sales management, and product marketing, before landing in 1993 in the still-forming alliances group. "Typically our relationship managers are among the more experienced people at Lotus," Davé explained. "In a company where the average age is thirty-two, a relationship manager today is likely to be thirty-five to forty-five, and has probably worked at another company or two." More important than experience or age was attitude. According to Davé, "I never hired because someone had a partnering background. I was looking for someone who could think like a CEO."

Thinking like a CEO meant dealing with ambiguity. "Ambiguity is a very prominent part of doing alliance work," Burnham said. "Straddling unclear situations between two organizations is one of my greatest challenges." As Burnham described it, a Lotus alliance manager faced three major challenges.

First was the need to advocate a partner's cause while treating all partners equally. A case in point was the AT&T road show. "We are excited to do this with AT&T, but that means another partner is not doing it with us. So what does that say?" Burnham asked. "We are looking into possibly developing similar programs with other partners." Does that argue that Lotus bends over backward to be utterly and always balanced? "Absolutely not," he maintained. "There are clearly some things which provide real benefit if they are exclusive. So the trick is to create some things for everyone and some exclusives for each partner."

The second challenge was knowing the best people to turn to within each organization. "There are so many people who can help each of my alliances—the support guys, the marketing guys, the development guys. Frankly, I need to sift through all those people and really focus on who can get things done for me and my partners."

The third challenge was measuring individual results. "Constantly we have to justify our existence to other parts of the company, and that is no easy task," Burnham explained. The problem was that most times a Lotus relationship manager did not produce direct revenue—but rather helped others make things happen. For example, if a customer purchased AT&T servers and a thousand Notes licenses, it probably would have been hard to determine to what extent Jim Burnham was responsible for bringing in the business. "There are a few occasions when my AT&T counterpart and

I clearly clinched a sale. But on most occasions I can really only argue that I did a good job of facilitating, coordinating, and behind-the-scenes promoting. That's enough for me in a day."

Tensions of Alliance Management

Imagine a car with two steering wheels—one on the left and one on the right—and with a different driver behind each. For more than two years, Dorine Hernandez's job was to sit on the hood whacking at overhanging brush and trying to get those two drivers going in the same direction. More often than not, though, she found herself reporting back on what they had bumped into and trying to get the two drivers back on track.

Dorine Hernandez was the contract administrator for the manufacturing alliance between the American Red Cross and Baxter Healthcare (for more details, see Chapter Ten). She was the sole alliance manager—and the first contact point between those who were actually collaborating and the senior management overseeing the relationship.

Late in her tenure, a fairly ordinary accident happened. Baxter employees operating the shared plasma manufacturing line threw away some intermediate paste belonging to the Red Cross. Under normal circumstances, the Red Cross would have generated added revenue by selling that paste to a third party. The question for the alliance—and more specifically for Hernandez—revolved around compensation. "One of the Red Cross's on-site staff came up to me and told me what happened, and asked what we should do," recalled Hernandez. "To me it was a question of whether the accident fell under the definition of normal business, or was it an extraordinary event requiring Baxter compensation of the Red Cross?"

Hernandez called for an investigation of the loss. She then made a recommendation to the alliance's governing body, the Contract Coordinating Group. Based on her understanding of the circumstances and the alliance agreement, she felt that Baxter ought to pay the Red Cross for the damage done. They agreed.

Requirements for Success

However mundane, the incident of the disappearing blood paste highlights some important characteristics and organizational positioning of successful alliance managers—and what companies need to think about when picking and nurturing these individuals.

Expert Skills. The manufacturing staff turned to Hernandez—and senior management listened to her—because of her position and proven understanding of the alliance. Prior to serving as the Baxter–Red Cross alliance manager, Hernandez had worked in Baxter's finance department, where she oversaw the financial aspects of the Red Cross contract and monitored the alliance's financial performance for the corporate parent. This experience gave her credibility.

On-Site Location. Hernandez was also within easy reach of the problem. The troubles on the manufacturing line did not have to wind their way through phone lines or e-mail. Hernandez was there to see the situation and talk to the participants.

Informal Power. Hernandez had also developed a lot of personal connections and informal power. "Over the three years as the alliance manager, I built a pretty strong network of people from the senior executives to the folks in research who were trying to find new ways to process plasma," she recalled. That informal power opened up several doors—including knowing who to talk to and the respect of the alliance's main governance committee, the Contract Coordinating Group (see Chapter Ten).

Governing Role. That respect from the Contract Coordinating Group grew, largely, from Hernandez's participation in the main workings of alliance governance. While she was never one of the four formal members of the CCG, she was in charge of setting the governing board's agenda, facilitating discussion, and adding insight into the day-to-day direction of the relationship. In fact, she was the only informal member of the CCG included in its executive sessions (usually held to resolve particularly sensitive issues).

Logical Career Path. After several years as Baxter–Red Cross alliance manager, Hernandez was promoted out of her role. Her new position, in Baxter's corporate development group working on new business initiatives, was a natural step for someone who had just spent years buried in the challenge of managing a single external relationship. Her career path—from Baxter's financial analyst of the alliance to full-time alliance manager to corporate dealmaker—sent a strong message to others looking at becoming alliance managers at Baxter. Such career movement is a powerful way to draw top talent to alliances and thus lift their chance of success.

One Problem

For all that Baxter did to make her role as alliance manager productive, one aspect of the situation created real challenges for Hernandez. She was a Baxter employee. And because she had no counterpart at the Red Cross, she was expected to act neutral. "I had to look out for the best interests of the alliance," Hernandez recalled. "But that was no easy task since I came from Baxter, since I reported into the vice president of manufacturing at Baxter, and since my future would depend on my next job at Baxter." Unfortunately, the surest solution to this problem—appointing a co-alliance manager from the Red Cross—was always seen as too costly to justify.

At Baxter, Lotus, and elsewhere, alliance managers play key roles in nurturing relationships with partners. Because of this, establishing the position of alliance manager has become the single most common step that companies take to improve the performance of their alliances.

Further Reading

Mitchell Marks and Phillip Mirvis. *Joining Forces: Making One Plus One Equal Three.* San Francisco: Jossey-Bass, 1998. Chapter 4.

Larraine Segil. *Intelligent Business Alliances*. New York: Random House, 1996. Chapter 2.

Source

This chapter is based on several articles in *The Alliance Analyst*, especially "A Day in the Life" (December 1995) and "More Than a Hood Ornament" (February 1996). The articles were combined, edited, and updated for this book.

Getting Out

16

Why Joint Ventures Die

Bruce Kogut

Joint ventures and alliances are often announced in the media with euphoria. Companies cite them as illustrations of their bold strategies; observers often interpret them as signaling new eras of cooperation in chaotic industries.

Yet the very pressures that typically give rise to alliances can also spell alliance failure. Not only does a joint venture face the usual competition of the market, it also is caught in the conflict between the partners. As a result, ventures are usually fragile.

Why do they die? This question is of more than actuarial interest. Understanding why and how joint ventures dissolve gives insight into how firms can make better use of them. The question of how to use alliances has been generally studied by examining the process of alliance formation. Here we focus on termination. But, before that, it is worth reviewing the fundamental conditions that give rise to alliances in the first place. These same fundamentals will help explain terminations.

Motivation for Joint Ventures

Narrowly defined, a joint venture occurs when two or more firms pool a portion of their resources within a common legal organization. This is done by selecting among alternative modes the ways by which two or more firms can transact business. Thus a theory of joint ventures must explain why a particular mode of transacting is chosen over other alternatives such as acquisition, supply contract, licensing, or spot market purchases.

Reasons given by CEOs for choosing joint ventures range from the benefits of sharing risk or exploiting economies of scale and size to the exchange of technologies and differential abilities. In many cases, these are promoted by governments who stipulate shared ownership as the only channel by which to invest in a country. The most common, however, are fear, profit, and learning.

Fear

Usually labeled "transaction cost theory," the fear motive can be boiled down to the following: whenever two firms transact on a long-term basis, problems arise from the difficulty of settling future prices, guaranteeing quality and delivery, and safeguarding technological and strategic decisions.

No matter how well contracts are designed, they may fail to provide effective guarantees. The necessity of stipulating contractual conditions increases, of course, with the complexity of the transaction and the difficulty of monitoring behavior. Contractual clauses regulating the development process are particularly troublesome to write and to enforce. A supplier that initially gives a low price, for example, may claim unexpected costs in developing a new process. The fears in relying on an outside supplier are heightened when the buyer must design around specific components and is thus precariously dependent upon the goodwill in the relationship.

A joint venture is frequently seen as the best alternative. By requiring mutual commitment of investment, it provides incentives for both parties to perform according to their obligations. This works rather like the principle of nuclear determent in East-West relations, whereby stability is maintained by holding both sides hostage. Similarly, a joint venture holds each side's investment vulnerable to loss in the case of breach of contract or poor performance.

Profit

Perhaps one of the strongest reasons for doing a joint venture is the pursuit of profit. Increased profitability can be gained by one of two ways: first, between firms in an oligopoly, joint ventures can stabilize competition and improve industry returns. Empirical research confirms that firms sometimes form alliances for this reason.

Second, enhanced profitability can be derived from the reduction of costs or the creation of new products and technologies that can influence the competitive positioning of the partners in their industries. For example, the tie-up between General Motors and its Korean partner (in which it has a minority investment) facilitated the export of low-cost vehicles from Korea through a well-entrenched distribution network in the United States. But the cooperation between the two companies also served to slow the penetration of untamed Japanese competitors, who were seeking to upgrade their auto lines into higher-priced levels on the basis of profits earned on their commodity vehicle sales.

Of course, fear and profit are not mutually exclusive. Many of the concerns noted earlier are also relevant when firms cooperate by contract, by merging, or by frequent launches between the top management in an effort to improve their strategic positioning. Yet if the cooperation entails the revelation of secrets, the transfer of technologies, or the sharing of brand labels, fear of the misuse of these assets will drive the partners to seek ways to enforce compliance with the agreement.

Organizational Learning

Amid the dour discussion of how fear motivates cooperation, it is important to balance this perspective by considering the role of joint ventures in creating and transferring knowledge among firms. This explanation views joint ventures as a means by which firms learn new, or seek to retain old, capabilities. Sharing knowledge is

especially important in ventures between firms from different industries who seek to pool their distinct competencies.

An example was the 1990s joint venture between Honeywell and
Ericsson to develop a telecommunications switch for the U.S. market.
Honeywell had considerable in-house expertise in software features
desired by the end user, as well as the ability to run a development
facility in the United States. Ericsson, in turn, had the switch technology and several years of experience in the international development and sales of the product. The development efforts resulted in a
product that is fully adapted to the target market.

Of course, knowledge can be transferred by other means than a
joint venture, such as through a license or outright sale. Again, we
are confronted with understanding why a joint venture is a better
way to transfer some kinds of knowledge. However, the choice in
this case may not be driven by fear but by the difficulty of transferring knowledge that is organizational in character. One reason why
joint ventures are commonly used among firms in international
markets is, in fact, to exchange the distinctive managerial skills of
countries.

Causes of Termination of Joint Ventures

To gain insight into joint venture termination, I studied a sample of
ninety-two manufacturing joint ventures formed in the United
States in the late 1980s and early 1990s. For each venture, I tracked
whether and when it was terminated, and what form termination
took—either complete dissolution of the venture or the acquisition
of one partner's share by the other, or of one or both shares by a third
party. Dissolution may represent a business failure on one hand, but
can also reflect a fundamental conflict among the partners. Acquisitions suggest that one of the parties, or an outside party, places a
higher value on the venture than the other does, regardless of the
reasons for the differences in valuation.

From these data, I compared the share of joint ventures that
died in each year, as a share of total ventures still existing in that

year. The overall results are shown in Figure 16.1. On average, about 13 percent of joint ventures existing at a given moment tend to die within the year—roughly half of them by dissolution and half by acquisition. The data in this sample suggests that the third year of a joint venture is particularly hazardous, but much depends, of course, on external circumstances in the industry.

Deeper analysis revealed other interesting patterns. Acquisitions of joint ventures were more likely to occur under two kinds of industry conditions: few competitors and unexpected growth. In concentrated businesses (that is, industries where a few firms dominate), joint ventures often serve two functions: one is to restrict output and thus avoid price wars; the other is to extend the life span of a firm that can no longer go at it alone in the industry but is unwilling to divest abruptly.

The 1990s joint venture between Asea Brown Boveri (ABB) and Westinghouse is a good example. The industry was concentrated and mature. Therefore, in the case of termination of the venture, it benefited the industry that one of the parties acquire the operation rather than leaving both parties to invest separately in further plant capacity. As a result, the venture contract gave ABB a call option to buy the venture and Westinghouse a put option to sell. One way to see this joint venture, therefore, was as a staged divestiture on the part of Westinghouse. The firm might prefer this way of divesting

FIGURE 16.1 Rates of Termination of Joint Ventures.

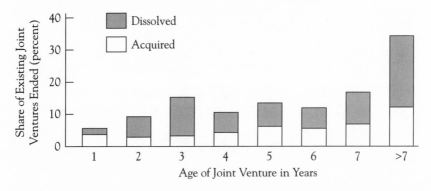

the business either because it could not commit to divest it fully right away, or because the arrangement provided a hand-holding service until ABB could run the U.S. operations alone.

The analysis of dissolutions presents a radically different profile. A primary factor in dissolution is whether or not the parties have other business agreements. Like the mutual hostage positions described earlier, ventures turn out to be more stable if the threat of dissolution is deterred by its possible impact on other relationships. Stability, in other words, is stronger between partners who have a history of partnership.

The study of joint venture termination provides two fundamental findings: first, ventures are often options to divest or to expand depending on the market; second, their stability is strongly affected by the familiarity and commitment of the partners.

Lessons for the Design of Joint Ventures

An understanding of the reasons why joint ventures end provides a few sound rules on how they should be designed. There is no fail-safe method of designing any business plan and its implementation. But a joint venture is especially difficult for one simple reason: it is under the ownership of more than one firm. Joint venture contracts do not make good reading. It is unlikely that any advice can make these contracts slimmer, but the following considerations might eliminate the need to reread the terms as often.

Design the Venture to Guarantee Your Sleep

Participants in every venture worry about the loss of control over technologies and brand labels. One way to eliminate the problem of technology leakage is to begin with the assumption that a leak will occur. What is it worth to you? If there is a price at which the technology can be sold, then sell it as part of the capital contribution of your firm to the venture. If it is, in a sense, priceless, then do not share it.

The questionable quality of a joint venture's products can cause serious damage to brand reputations. In their venture, GM and Toyota simply agreed not to share or create a common brand label. Nor did Honeywell and Ericsson share a brand label. Market reputations are hard and expensive to establish. Sharing brand labels is often necessary, but some loss of sleep can be expected.

Do Not Burden the Joint Venture

Cooperative arrangements frequently devolve into each member trying to do the least amount of work; it is logical that partners will try to make sure they are getting something out of the venture. Therefore, both generally suffer the temptation to burden the venture with excessive channels of remuneration, such as transfer prices on goods sold or bought from the venture, or licensing fees and royalties.

Such a policy has a fundamental problem: the financial evaluation of the venture will look very different to each partner. Unless the venture is healthy, not only will one partner be more upset than the other but the management of the venture itself will be jeopardized.

Design the venture so that both partners are equally interested in the profitability of the concern. The only way to structure such an outcome is to let dividends be the primary channel by which profits are divided. Backdoor channels should be encouraged only when governments impose rules on how equity is shared at different rates, for example, on dividends and licensing fees.

Choose the Right Benchmark for Evaluation

Joint ventures are often not popular decisions. Engineers are upset that technology is "given away" or bought from the outside; business managers worry about the effect on competitive positioning. Thus negotiators face a second negotiation at home. The common temptation is to oversell the venture, a temptation especially appealing when someone else will be assigned to manage the cooperation. No wonder that one joint venture president said the first thing one should do before starting the job is to tear up the business plan and start again.

Unreasonable expectations will also plague the long-term evaluation of the venture. It is essential that the joint venture managers remember why they did the deal in the first place. Consider all the heat and discussion of whether American firms have been robbed blind by Japanese partners. The agreements signed by Honeywell in computers, Firestone in tires, Dresser in trucks, and Westinghouse in power generation suggest another interpretation: were these firms no longer willing to go at it alone? In this case, the benchmark should be how the return on the venture compares to an outright divestment.

Build for the Future

No rule will ensure the success of a joint venture. As in a business, the working out of conflict and challenges requires the participation of effective managers. It is important that the venture be supported by a wider relationship among the partners.

A harder task is to work out how the relationships of each partner—with other players (and potential, or existing, competitors) in the industry—affect cooperation. But as many firms have learned to their dismay, the growing number of joint ventures leads to unusual patterns of coalitions in an industry.

In a time of industry redefinition, it is not surprising that the spate of joint ventures should lead to competitors who, if not directly cooperating, are only once-removed in their kinship. No joint venture should be accomplished without an analysis of the wider industry cooperative relationships as they stand today—and as they may evolve tomorrow.

No organization is forever. Joint ventures in particular are often stepping-stones to something else. As tools of transition, they must be designed for success, but also with the flexibility for change. Sometimes, change means dissolution or acquisition. Managers should thus enter and manage these ventures with an understanding of how and why alliances die.

Further Reading

Bruce Kogut. "Joint Ventures: Theoretical and Empirical Perspectives," *Strategic Management Journal*, 1988, 9, 319–332.

Ashish Nanda and Peter J. Williamson. "Use Joint Ventures to Ease the Pain of Restructuring," *Harvard Business Review*, Nov.-Dec. 1995, pp. 119–128.

Source

This chapter is based on Bruce Kogut's "Why Joint Ventures Die So Quickly," *Chief Executive* (December 1989). Rights reserved. Used with the permission of *Chief Executive* magazine. The article was edited for this book.

17

Graceful Exit

All alliances end eventually. The average joint venture lasts seven years, according to a McKinsey study, with almost 80 percent ending up in a sale to one of the partners. (See also Chapter Sixteen.) Merck sold its stake in Astra Merck after nine years and its interest in DuPont Merck after five. British Petroleum and Mobil terminated a pair of European downstream oil JVs three years after forming them.

Non-equity alliances often have shorter life spans. In high-tech and retail, for example, marketing alliances often last no more than a year or two, with some measuring their existence in months. Even the highest-profile alliances come undone. Delta Air Lines ended Global Excellence Alliance, its pioneering global partnership with Swissair and Singapore Airlines, after the Star Alliance changed the nature of industry competition. And after eighty years, Firestone announced the end of its supplier alliance with Ford Motor following a bitter dispute over safety issues.

Termination is a natural part of the alliance life cycle, yet most companies do not adequately plan for it. Some firms pay no attention to exit, preferring instead to believe their own press releases that proclaim the alliance is a marriage that will last forever. Other firms do think about termination, but do so in incomplete ways. Some spend their time assessing and working to prevent the common causes of alliance termination, rather than maximizing termination success. Others focus on a limited number of contractual provisions around termination without addressing important strategic considerations.

How do companies improve the termination process? We believe that companies need to take a broader—and more strategic—view of alliance termination, and do so during the initial phases of venture creation. Indeed, just as companies should preplan the initial integration of assets, companies must also carefully prepare up front for termination. And this demands a careful assessment of both strategic and contractual considerations.

Strategies to Shape Termination

Strategic considerations are those factors outside the detailed legal language of the alliance contract that determine the path of termination, including the firm's overall ability to end the alliance and the cost and speed of doing so. Although many strategic considerations shape termination success, five merit special attention:

- Set clear termination goals.
- Make appropriate contributions to the alliance.
- Keep the deal structure flexible.
- Institute effective human resource policies.
- Develop a portfolio of options.

Clear Termination Goals

A critical but rarely asked question about termination is: What are our termination goals in this alliance? In many cases, firms focus on one termination goal—avoiding termination, or at least premature termination by the partner. Although this is a reasonable ambition, it is almost never the complete answer. Before entering an alliance, the deal-making team should generate a list of perhaps three to ten termination goals. These may include maintaining control over contributed assets, receiving a fair market price for those assets, preserving positive relations with this partner in the future, and terminating the alliance quickly. This list will help shape important decisions around contributions, deal structure, human resource policies, and options for alternative ways of achieving the alliance's purpose, all of which have enormous influence on termination success.

Appropriate Alliance Contributions

When companies enter into an alliance, they agree to make certain contributions available to the partner or to the venture. The nature of these contributions has important effects on exit. At the most general level, the more deeply the partners integrate their contributions, the more difficult exit becomes. For example, consolidation joint ventures like those formed in telecommunications and energy in recent years are usually a true combination of assets where the firms integrate staff, brands, customers, technologies, and other assets in their international businesses. Undoing such an alliance is a substantial operational challenge.

When the firm is concerned about termination costs, it may want to consider ways to provide contributions that are *coordinated* rather than combined. By coordination, we mean the partners position themselves to provide essentially separate contributions to the alliance, often at different points in the value chain.

Firms should also consider the complexity of contributions—especially when there are worries that the partner will prematurely terminate the alliance. As a general rule, when firms contribute complex bundles of inputs—or competencies—it can make termination much less attractive to the partner. The reason: competencies are typically much harder for partners to learn over the course of the alliance and thus replicate on their own. Therefore, for a company looking to prevent premature termination, it is best to ensure that at least some contributions to the alliance are complete competencies (retail site selection, financial management, deep water drilling, and so on) rather than disaggregated elements.

Flexible Deal Structure

Some ways of structuring an alliance facilitate exit more than others. For example, BP and Mobil structured their European downstream oil consolidation as two separate JVs—one focused on refining and marketing, the other on lubricants. BP became the operating partner for the refining and marketing venture, while Mobil managed the lubricants business. The partners had other reasons for creating two separate JVs with separate management teams and assets, but this structure also made it easier for the partners to exit the alliance if needed. Indeed, when larger forces in the oil business made these alliances less attractive, BP simply bought out Mobil in the first venture, while the partners divided up the assets in the second.

Other structural moves facilitate exit. One of the most common in the high-tech field is to structure alliances as a series of short-term renewable contracts, often with a trial period up front. Yahoo! has said that it almost never formed an alliance that didn't come up for renewal in a year or less. Mapquest, a leading provider of online directions and travel information, formed a series of short-term alliances as it was experimenting with ways to bring its content to wireless devices such as cellular phones and personal digital assistants. Such deal structures obviously do not make sense in all circumstances, but they can be powerful ways to smooth the exit process in highly uncertain environments that do not demand deep asset integration between the partners.

Forming broad, multifaceted relationships can also improve exit performance. This runs counter to conventional wisdom, which holds that deeper relationships will entangle the firm and make exit harder. Our discussions with executives suggest this may not be the case. When two firms have many operational initiatives (or even separate alliances) in place, it is often easier to sever an underperforming piece of the relationship. In part, this is because the alliance champions and managers are less committed to defending individual elements than they are to supporting the total relationship. In addition, it is often possible to easily transfer people and other corporate resources from one initiative to another with the same partner, thereby reducing the termination costs.

Other structural issues may also be considered. For instance, managers should ask questions such as these: Would a joint venture best serve our exit goals, or is a non-equity alliance best? Would a direct investment in or from the partner have a material effect? Would the number of partners in the alliance in any way alter the context for exit? Although many of these questions may not lead to decisions different from those the firm would otherwise have taken, they are nonetheless worth asking. We believe that the best firms do make structural decisions based on overall exit goals.

Effective Human Resource Policies

Human resource policies can also shape termination process and performance. Of the many ways to make this happen, three are worth mentioning. First is to appoint an executive sponsor, a move that increases the chances that the alliance will not die too soon or linger on too long. As a general rule, executive sponsors provide the strategic perspective to terminate the alliance at an appropriate time. Second is to rotate alliance managers, or find other ways to keep the blood fresh. An underappreciated risk in alliances is that the alliance manager will become too connected to the partner and lose focus on the company's own best interests. Rotating alliance managers every two years or so can help overcome this problem. Third and related is to create a clear career path for alliance management. When managers see alliances as a profession where current skills can be applied to future relationships, they are less prone to defend an alliance at all costs.

Portfolio of Options

It can also be useful to create alternatives—or options—in case the alliance fails. Consider Microsoft, a firm that over the years has been extremely skilled in creating alternatives to its alliances, positioning itself to win even if an individual alliance does not. This was clearly the case in the late 1980s in the operating system market. At that time, the company used alliances (and internal initiatives) to generate options as it was trying to understand what would replace the aging MS-DOS. Microsoft not only allied with IBM and its OS/2 initiative, it also entered into alliances that gave it a role in the Apple Macintosh and Unix operating systems. At the same time, Microsoft continued to invest in DOS while also pouring money into the eventual winner, Windows. The point is that an alliance can fail for many reasons—many of which are outside the firm's control. Therefore, termination success can hinge on having other alternatives in the water.

A winning exit depends on many strategic considerations, of course. But in focusing on the nature of contributions, the structure of the deal, human resource policies, and options, the chances for a successful end noticeably improve.

Contractual Terms Governing Termination

Termination success is also contingent on the details in the alliance contract. As an intellectual model, we recommend that firms focus on four contractual dimensions: trigger events, future ownership rights, valuation methods, and post-termination demands. More than merely knowing that these dimensions exist, managers need to understand the many different choices and implications within each.

Trigger Events

The first step in assuring that the alliance contract deals sufficiently with termination is to determine what events will trigger termination—that is, allow the corporate parents to end the alliance. A review of numerous alliance contracts reveals seven broad categories of triggering events, each containing many different options:

- Alliance completion
- Alliance performance failure
- Change in external environment
- Change in parent status
- Parent breach
- Parent deadlock
- Termination at will

We recommend that firms consider each in some detail.

Alliance Completion. It often makes sense to indicate that the partners have the right to terminate the alliance when the venture crosses certain time, technological, financial, or market thresholds. For example, a biotech research alliance could set a three- or five-year milestone, after which the partners must agree to end, extend, or revise the agreement. Likewise, the partners may want to stipulate that termination rights are activated as soon as a certain chemical compound enters Phase II trials.

Alliance Performance Failure. The partners may want to have the option to end the alliance if the venture or one of the partners fails to achieve some predetermined performance milestone. For example, a cross-Atlantic airline alliance might allow the partners to exit if antitrust immunity is not secured within a certain period. A marketing alliance or new business JV might automatically trigger termination rights if a certain market share is not reached, or one partner fails to make a certain number of sales calls per month.

Change in External Environment. Since changes in the external environment can have materially adverse effects on the future of the alliance, the partners may want to indicate which of these events will trigger termination rights. An oil industry alliance might specify that a drop in the per barrel price of crude oil below $10 would do this, whereas a consumer products JV in Indonesia may want to link continuation to certain indicators of political stability.

Change in Parent Status. Firms should also consider whether certain changes in the status of the corporate parents should prompt termination rights. At a macro level, these could relate to such ownership issues as the sale of one partner to another firm or the transfer of a substantial portion of the firm's assets (say, above 35 percent). These changes may also relate to financial health, including the bankruptcy or financial insolvency of either corporate parent. At a micro level, it may make sense to indicate that some material change in the employment status of members of the management team, board of directors, or other staff who are essential to the functioning of the alliance (for example, scientists, alliance managers) would trigger termination.

Parent Breach. The most common exit trigger is breach of contract—that one partner fails to meet its basic obligations to the agreement.

Parent Deadlock. An alliance contract should indicate what will happen if the partners deadlock on critical decisions. The best agreements tend to include dispute resolution mechanisms, including a process for appealing the decision to incrementally higher levels within the parent companies, and ultimately to external arbitration. Even with a clear dispute resolution process in place, however, the firms may still want to indicate that termination rights are triggered in the event of a sustained deadlock.

Termination at Will. In some situations, it is in the strategic interest of the parents to simply allow the partners to terminate the alliance whenever desired. As a general rule, this tends to make sense only when the alliance entails very limited resource integration between the firms (and hence limited termination costs) and when the business context is extremely fluid and uncertain, putting a high value on the resulting flexibility.

In determining what sorts of events trigger termination rights, the firms should think about balance—that is, to what extent the partners have similar rights. Although no law mandates that partners must have identical rights, the relative balance does affect the tone and tenor of the relationship. For instance, when a contract makes the alliance contingent on one partner (but not the other) hitting all sorts of milestones, or gives one partner (but not the other) termination-at-will rights, then such a relationship starts to feel much more like a classic customer or vendor relationship.

Future Ownership Rights

The alliance contract needs to spell out who will own the alliance-related assets in the future once termination rights have been triggered and closure is the chosen course. In non-equity alliances, this can be a straightforward exercise: each partner simply retains the assets it lent to the alliance. When a pharmaceutical company and a biotech company shut down a research alliance, for example, each firm would expect to bring its scientists and equipment back home. When two e-tailers terminate a co-marketing alliance, each firm would retain its own brands, customers, and other assets.

In some non-equity alliances, however, the contract will also need to address the ownership of ideas and other intellectual assets created in the course of the alliance. Typically, alliance contracts deal with this in one of two ways. One is to allow the partners to share the rights. The other approach is for one partner—usually the one funding the alliance—to control most or all of the intellectual assets coming out of the alliance. This is often the model in biotech alliances and other forms of funded research.

Joint ventures raise more complex ownership questions. In almost all cases, it is impossible or undesirable to return the contributions to the corporate parents. Within a few years, most joint ventures have so fully integrated and built on the initial parent contributions that it is no longer possible to determine who owns what. Even if such a determination could be made, chances are that the partners would destroy substantial value in reclaiming their contributions. Presumably, the joint venture as a functioning and unified business is worth more than the assets held separately. As a result, when firms decide to terminate a joint venture, the contract needs to address who will take ownership of the business and how the exiting partner's stake will be valued.

Valuation Methods

The contract should indicate how the firms will value the business in the event of termination. It is essential to make this determination up front, for otherwise a firm can be led to unwanted outcomes, such as assets valued at below-market prices or protracted legal battles with its partner. There are three basic models for valuing assets in joint ventures.

Perhaps the most common valuation model is *roulette*. Here, one firm (usually the one that exercises the right to terminate) places a dollar value on the total business, and the other partner then determines whether it wants to buy or sell its interest based on that price. This approach is appealing on many levels: it is simple, fast, and seems fair. After all, the partner setting the price has strong incentives to set a reasonable valuation since it does not know whether it will be the ultimate buyer or seller of the assets.

However, as the McKinsey study showed, this is often not the case. In JVs, one partner is usually the natural buyer. In most cases, the natural buyer will set a low price for the assets since it can reasonably assume that its partner is less attracted to the business. (Indeed, if the natural seller is the one setting the price, it too will often set a below-market price since it does not want to get stuck with the business.) Therefore, appealing as the roulette model may be at first glance, firms need to think twice before depending on it alone as a valuation method.

Another model is to allow an *independent assessor* such as an investment bank to set a price on the assets. When this is the chosen approach, it also makes sense to stipulate in the alliance agreement what guidelines or criteria the assessor should use to determine valuation (for example, multiple of earnings or revenue). A third and related valuation model is to set a *predetermined price or pricing formula* for the business.

It is often useful to link different triggering events to different valuation methods. Consider the U.S. refining and marketing JVs formed in the 1990s between Shell Oil and Texaco. The venture contracts reportedly stated that if one partner decided to terminate at will, the other partner could buy its share back at a 10 percent discount on a fair-market assessment of the firm's interest. This provision shaped the exit terms when Texaco decided to get out of the JVs so as to gain antitrust approval for its merger with Chevron.

Post-Termination Demands

The alliance contract also needs to indicate whether the partners will have any future demands placed upon them after the alliance terminates. Such demands can be divided into future relationships, restrictions, and responsibilities.

Future Relationships. Depending on the nature of the alliance, the firms may decide that some continued links are needed after the alliance has ended. For example, a new business JV may depend on some or all corporate parents for ongoing access to certain brand names, technological know-how, or material supplies. In such a case, the firms may want to stipulate in the formation documents that these resource flows continue for some period after termination, as well as indicate the terms and conditions for future use.

Future Restrictions. It is common for the partners to have at least some restrictions placed upon them following the unwinding of the alliance. Such restrictions may include noncompete provisions that block some or all the partners from competing in a certain product or geographic area for a period. Other restrictions may prevent poaching staff from the former partner.

Future Responsibilities. Sometimes, terminated alliances have remaining obligations to customers, suppliers, or other parties. Although it can be difficult to anticipate precisely what these responsibilities will be, the firms should attempt to think them through up front and deal with them as best they can in the contract.

Alone, contractual considerations do not guarantee a successful termination. But when managers have a framework for thinking about these provisions and do so within the context of broader strategic understanding, such considerations can well make the difference between success and failure.

Think Ahead, Work Backward

To get started, members of the deal team can pose some basic questions about the potential alliance. By answering these questions before entering detailed structural discussions, managers will gain a new appreciation for the timing, path, and tasks of alliance termination. These questions include

- What is the realistic (versus stated) life span of the alliance?
- What are the ten most likely reasons that the alliance will end?
- Are there natural decision points for terminating or recommitting to the alliance?
- On a scale of 1 to 10, how large are the termination risks? (1 = no material effect on our firm; 10 = threatens our very survival.)
- What are the main termination goals in this alliance?
- Will certain alliance structures or asset contributions make it much easier for us to exit the alliance, or harder for the partner to do so?
- Is it in our interest to make it harder for our partner to exit the alliance?

- What will be the five hardest tasks in closing down the alliance? (For example, valuing assets or determining future ownership.)
- Are there ways to create options today in case this alliance fails tomorrow?

The point in asking these questions is not to generate precise answers. Rather, it is to spark a general discussion among team members and to gain a deeper appreciation of termination issues. Depending on the value and complexity of the alliance, it may be best to approach these questions with some discipline. For a billion-dollar joint venture spanning multiple business functions, for example, a member of the deal team could separately canvass other leading participants for their opinions on these questions, then facilitate a half-day discussion on termination issues. This would be overkill for most short-term marketing alliances. Here the deal team may want to use these questions as simple thought-starters when conceiving and structuring the deal.

It is a paradox that successful termination depends on actions taken well before the alliance even starts. But we have found that the best firms anticipate the tasks, challenges, and risks of termination with great care before entering an alliance. After all, all alliances end eventually.

Further Reading

Joel Bleeke and David Ernst. "Is Your Strategic Alliance Really a Sale?" *Harvard Business Review*, Jan.-Feb. 1995, pp. 97–105.
Charles Roussel. "The Science of Alliances: Making an Exit," *Accenture Outlook Point of View*, 2001.

Source

This chapter is based on several articles in *The Alliance Analyst*, especially "Graceful Exit" (February 2000). The articles were combined, edited, and updated for this book.

PART THREE

Competing in Constellations

Managing Networks

18

Constellation Strategy

A few years ago, Cable & Wireless ran a series of glossy advertisements that proclaimed: "The corporation is dead. Long live the federation." It was a catchy slogan that seemed to contain a compelling vision for a global alliance constellation. The C&W federation would unite fifty-plus firms from around the world into a new supercorporation. The partners were local operators in markets ranging from Britain and Bahrain to Hong Kong and Jamaica, and many had been C&W partners for decades. In uniting them into a federation, Cable & Wireless hoped to leverage their diverse skills and assets and offer seamless global service to multinational customers. The firm also aimed to raise its own reputation as a partner of choice in the telecom industry, a business that was moving toward alliance-based competition.

But the C&W federation dissolved in public view. Despite the pronouncements, the partners found few benefits in multilateral cooperation, or perhaps the cooperation never got going properly. Within a year of the bold advertising campaign, Cable & Wireless changed its tune at the same time that it changed CEOs. The federation strategy was replaced by more modest goals.

Strategic Goals

Despite this failure, companies can compete—and win—by using a constellation of allied firms. Airbus competed with great success against Boeing. The Star Alliance with its dozen or so members altered the nature of competition in the airline industry. Sprint built its wireless business through a multipartner alliance with three leading cable companies. And BP Amoco revolutionized elements of the upstream oil business through an alliance with suppliers and service companies in the North Sea's Andrew Field.

How do companies ensure that their constellation is among the winners? For starters, it is useful to have an intellectual construct—a framework—for understanding constellations. We define *constellation* as a set of firms linked through alliances and competing in a specific business domain. Constellations share many traits with bilateral alliances, but managing them also presents important new issues and accentuates others. The most important issue is increased complexity; as one pharmaceuticals executive said: "Every time another partner is added to an alliance, the challenge increases exponentially."

To be sure, not all constellations are the same. In examining a hundred prominent constellations formed between 1990 and 2001, we found five basic motivations behind constellations, each of which often conditioned the design of the group:

- Linking markets
- Combining skills
- Building momentum
- Reducing costs
- Sharing risk

Few alliance constellations are a pure form of any of these models. Most constellations have multiple goals, and often add goals over time. For example, Advanced Photo Systems had three main goals: to share risks, to set standards, and to combine skills (it contained both film and camera companies). The Star Alliance also has multiple goals: its main goal is still to link markets, but the partners have also used the alliance to reduce costs, forming a purchasing cooperative and combining assets like ticket counters and passenger lounges. Nonetheless, it is useful to look at the models individually.

Linking Markets

Companies sometimes form constellations to connect local markets and, in the process, provide customers with broader geographic coverage. Consider Star and oneworld in the airline industry. Both constellations united a number of national airlines, each with a limited geographic footprint, into a global brand with integrated services such as frequent flier programs. Market-linking constellations are common in industries such as telecommunications, professional services, and airlines where regulations or other market conditions make it hard for firms to expand outside the local market but where customers are more global.

Combining Skills

Companies also form constellations to assemble a diverse basket of skills, sometimes to launch a totally new business. Consider the market for personal digital assistants—handheld devices that combine the computing power of a simple PC, the communications capability of a cellular phone, and the size, styling, and durability of consumer electronics. Not surprisingly, constellations emerged that each contained at least one firm from each of these industries.

Building Momentum

Constellations are also used to create market momentum—that is, to persuade customers, suppliers, or competitors to adopt a new technology or business protocol. General Motors, Ford Motor, and

DaimlerChrysler formed a joint venture to launch a Web-based components exchange, expecting their combined market power would attract suppliers to join. Although constellations are not the sole means to create market momentum, multipartner alliances can be a fast and effective way to persuade the market to move in a new direction.

Reducing Costs

On occasion, companies form constellations to reduce costs. Some of these constellations are three- or four-way joint ventures that serve the parent firms. In the mid-1990s, for example, three Japanese chemical companies folded together the manufacturing and sale of resin for plastic bottles in a bid to reduce costs and improve operating efficiencies. A more common form of cost-reduction constellation is the purchasing cooperative. In health care and other fragmented industries, it is not unusual for firms to form multipartner alliances to exert pressure on suppliers to generate larger discounts.

Sharing Risk

Companies also assemble multiple partners to share large investments or risks. Oil companies long formed multipartner joint ventures for decades to spread the uncertainty in oil exploration. More recently, semiconductor manufacturers, pharmaceutical companies, and photographic firms have used constellations with the same goal. For example, Eastman Kodak was one of five firms that formed Advanced Photo Systems, a ten-year research alliance that invested $1 billion to develop a revolutionary new photo technology.

Design Dimensions

Given a set of goals and the basic logic of a constellation, how do you make it work? Of the many design elements that enter the equation, our work suggests that firms must pay careful attention to four—group size, membership mix, internal rivalry, and governance.

Group Size

The total size of a constellation, that is, the number of member firms, is a key design criterion. For some of the five goals, the more the merrier—for example, many partners help build momentum and may share risk or reach markets better than few partners. But for other goals, such as combining skills or even reaching scale economies, the number of partners is less important than the type and size of each partner. And, in all cases, the more partners are involved, the more separate interests will be represented, and so the more challenging will be the governance of the constellation.

The strategy behind the Cable & Wireless global telecommunications constellation seemed to be to assemble as many partners from as many countries as possible. Yet neither of these features mattered much to global customers, except perhaps C&W's stake in Hong Kong Telecom, which offered substantial regional advantages. AT&T, too, pursued many partners in the early constellation it called Worldpartners. Even so, in the battle for global telecommunication services, Concert, British Telecom's joint venture first with MCI and later with AT&T, became a market leader with just two partners. BT understood that in the battle to provide voice, video, and data services to multinational corporations, the competitive advantage of a group of allied firms hinged on the size and reputation of the lead firms as well as on the nimbleness of the alliance itself, not on the sheer number of partners.

Several lessons flow from this and other cases. First, managers must realize that the ideal size and scope of a constellation depends critically on its goal and competitive context—different business strategies require different collections of players. Second, they should not increase the size of a constellation without good reason, as in itself large size imposes management costs. Third, in setting the size and scope of a prospective constellation, focus on the elements that are important for competitive success—sometimes success will indeed stem from having many sponsors, but more often than not it stems from having large, leading, and capable partners, even if not many of them. And fourth, in developing the constellation, consider introducing partners in phases—often an early partnership will attract others; just as often an overgrown constellation will sometimes need later trimming.

Membership Mix

At times, advantage for a group comes from its ability to assemble a diverse set of capabilities. What matters then is not the size or number of the pieces but rather getting the right pieces assembled snugly together. Determining the ideal membership mix is an exercise akin to selecting a partner in simpler, bilateral alliances. Good partner matches are those that combine complementary capabilities in a way that creates value in the marketplace (see Chapter Five).

By extension, a good membership mix in a constellation is one that combines multiple skills and capabilities. Doing this requires, again, a keen sense for the success factors in a competitive domain, that is, a good understanding of the value chain and an estimate of who has strong capabilities in each key part of the value chain.

Membership mix has been important in constellations in the market for personal digital assistants (PDAs) from the very start of this industry segment. From the first, a PDA needed to combine the processing capabilities of at least a simple computer, the communications capability of a cellular phone, and the size, styling, and durability needed to appeal to the consumer electronics market. To compete in this environment, early entrants thus knew that they had to force the convergence of elements from at least four industries—computer hardware, computer software, telecommunications, and consumer electronics. Major companies in each of these industries entered the field, each arriving with their own particular strengths. IBM, Apple, and Hewlett-Packard approached the business from their experience in computer hardware; Microsoft and Lotus, from computer software; AT&T, Motorola, and BellSouth, from telecommunications; and Sharp, Casio, Tandy, and Amstrad, from consumer electronics. Even so, they each assembled constellations that gave them access to the technical capabilities they lacked.

In other businesses, the key criterion driving membership mix might be geographic diversity. Consider the case of Asia Link, a constellation in the Asian advertising business. Asia Link was composed of firms with similar sets of capabilities: each had a diverse range of industry experience, $10–$80 million in annual revenue, and a staff of fifty to a hundred professionals. Yet in terms of geographies, the members were distinct, focusing almost exclusively on their own local markets, which ranged from Japan to India. By creating a grouping that spanned these geographies, Asia Link tried to defend itself against such encroaching global giants as Ogilvy & Mather and Saatchi & Saatchi.

The lessons are clear. First, managers must examine carefully what elements are needed to mount a credible strategy in a given business. This means thinking outside the constraints of your own firm. Don't start by asking what you have that helps you compete—ask what a hypothetical competitor would need to succeed. Only after that should you consider precisely which of these critical elements you have, which ones are only weakly present in your firm, and which you lack completely. The third step is then to identify which other firms might have the elements that, if added to yours, would create a potentially winning combination. And, as with partner selection in bilateral alliances, be careful in this last step to consider not only what the other firm might add but also how easy or difficult it might be to work with that firm.

Internal Rivalry

Key among the factors that determine how firms work together in an alliance is the degree to which they compete with each other. This is well known for the case of bilateral alliances (see Chapter Six), and it holds in spades for multifirm constellations.

But it is increasingly rare to find partner pairs that are totally devoid of competitive friction. And, again, this problem increases exponentially as you add members to a group. So most alliance constellations cannot avoid some degree of internal rivalry; the key to success lies in minimizing this rivalry by careful choice of partners and then managing the rivalry by careful design of the structure and governance of the group.

Asia Link was also designed to restrict competition among member firms. Each member was the constellation's only representative in a given national market. One member would make a referral across boundaries, receiving a royalty fee while continuing to retain that portion of the business left back home. This is not dissimilar to the practice of Japanese keiretsu, where a more or less formal "exclusion rule" often stipulated that there should be no duplication of activities among members.

But is exclusion always best? No. Some internal duplication—and thus rivalry—may, in fact, encourage innovation, increase flexibility, and protect against uncertainties through diversification. Because of this, the lead firms in a constellation may choose to involve multiple partners in specific areas, even if it leads to a certain amount of internal friction. The point is to do so consciously and to weigh the pros and cons of internal rivalry. For whereas some internal rivalry can spark innovation and limit dependencies, it also usually introduces tension and slows down collective decision making.

The microprocessor industry offers an interesting case. In the early 1990s, four constellations had appeared to challenge the preeminence of Intel. The groups were led by HP, IBM, Sun, and Mips, and each was betting that Intel could be challenged by group momentum and a more advanced processing technology, called reduced instruction set computing or RISC. While the groups had this goal in common, they took radically different approaches to the question of how much internal rivalry to tolerate.

HP explicitly limited internal rivalry by choosing members for their unique capabilities or markets, following an informal exclusion rule. Sun Microsystems, on the other hand, promoted competition within its group, and especially encouraged members to compete for the design of each next-generation chip. By pitting chip designers against one another, it would spur innovation. Sun also promoted many resellers and, to some extent, clones of its machines, believing that this would facilitate the spread of its architecture.

Mips chose a line somewhere between HP and Sun. It encouraged competition but also contained and managed it consciously. Its constellation could be envisioned as rings around a core, with rivalry among members intensifying as one moved outward (Figure 18.1). That core was Mips, which vowed not to compete with its allies and prevented any from competing with it. Mips was the constellation's only chip designer.

The chip manufacturers—the next ring of the constellation— would be limited to a maximum of six licensed firms. Competition in this area was compartmentalized, because the semiconductor partners were chosen according to their geographic market strengths. According to Mips president Robert Miller, the aim was to sign on

FIGURE 18.1 The Mips Constellation, ca. 1995.

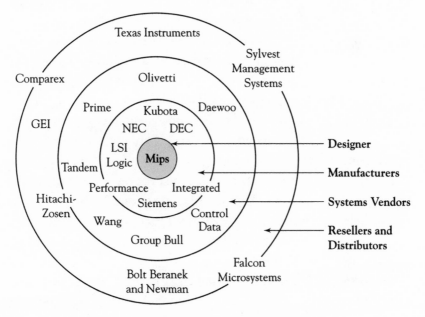

"one of the three semiconductor firms in the United States, one of the top three in Japan, and one of the top three in Europe."

The outermost rings of the constellation were for sales and marketing partners. Here competition flourished. Mips developed relationships with OEMs, distributors, value-added resellers, and systems integrators, and let them create and divide the market.

Which one of these three approaches worked best? All—and none. Mips proved itself too small to lead a constellation with so many powerful members and ended up being acquired by a partner and later spun off again. Still, the Mips technology was spread widely by this alliance strategy and became one of the most popular RISC architectures, used in computer game consoles. Sun perhaps had the most success with its model, but only because it held such a strong position at the center of its group. In addition, Sun too found itself needing to reduce internal competition among chip suppliers, and it practically killed the clone business when this threatened to encroach on its own sales. HP's model never really took off and, in the end, HP abandoned its own RISC design in favor of a major alliance with Intel.

The main lesson from these cases is thus again conditional: how much internal rivalry you allow in your constellation depends on your strategy, your position in the constellation, and the nature of the business. An effective constellation must create an organizational structure that promotes collaboration rather than competition. But, under certain conditions, some internal competition can be useful—if not to all members, then certainly to the most powerful lead members. Also, internal competition is less damaging when it does not involve the lead firm—a clarity of purpose is gained from having the leader above the fray, able to arbitrate in the best interest of the group. However the level of internal rivalry is determined, it should be consciously tuned, not the result of ad hoc growth of the constellation.

Another lesson is that internal rivalry can be managed by design of the roles and responsibilities of member firms. Mips did this by limiting the scope of its various alliances clearly and avoiding too many broad, across-the-board alliances. Narrow-scope alliances often live side by side more effectively than do broad ones. This means that firms developing a new constellation must look ahead and not sign away broad rights to the first partners too quickly; doing so may well preempt the addition of new partners or create internal conflicts when new partners do join.

A final lesson is that members of a constellation often benefit from creating separate organizational structures that can transcend the individual interests of the members. Not every constellation should be managed in this way; Sun and Mips didn't use this model. But the Star Alliance did, and so do many companies joining forces to create "shared utilities" (see Chapter Nineteen).

Governance Structure

Creating a separate organization is but one form of governing a constellation. Whether or not this model is used, a key issue in constellation design is how group decisions will be made and how member strategies will be coordinated and aligned. As with bilateral alliances, governance is key (see Chapters Ten, Eleven, and Twelve).

A governance structure does not necessarily mean a formal, separate organization or consortium office. With one strong firm at the center of a constellation, governance is usually managed by that firm as part of managing its alliance portfolio. Many firms have no separate stand-alone organization for managing their supplier networks or networks of marketing allies.

However, a formal and separate organization is often useful when a constellation is large and when it has a high degree of internal competition. Such an organization gives partners a more or less neutral way to establish common goals and rules of behavior. Broadly, three types of governance structures are common in alliance constellations: general assembly, core and periphery, and lead firm.

The General Assembly. The first model is the United Nations approach to alliance governance. It may be appropriate when the number of partners is large, when multiple capabilities are being assembled, when there is no clearly dominant firm, or when the dominant firm wants to downplay its leadership role. The first and last of these were the primary reasons behind the construction of the AT&T global telecom group in the late 1990s. WorldPartners developed an intricate web of staff, committees, and meetings, all of which encouraged information exchange among members. Despite these advantages, the general assembly model can be slow, lack an aggressive edge, and require much energy to manage. In AT&T's case, the general assembly approach did not work as well as intended. This was one reason why AT&T left its own constellation to join BT's Concert joint venture when MCI, BT's former partner, was acquired by Worldcom.

The Core and Periphery. A wholly different model is one that features a core group of tightly allied members with a larger number of loosely allied members orbiting this core. Such an approach is often used when there is, in fact, a small set of partners that want to tie themselves tightly to each other. United Airlines and Lufthansa were the lead members at the core of Star, with other partners tied more or less tightly to them. In addition, Star also used a separate organization to manage the large number of partners in the group. In this way, United and Lufthansa tried to avoid one of the common drawbacks to this model, which is that it may tend to grow wild beyond the organized core.

The Lead Firm. The most common constellation structure is a variant on the core-and-periphery model: the core consists only of one firm. This model requires the least amount of conscious organization, as the lead firm manages the group in the course of its normal alliance management. But this firm must indeed be a leader in the group and not be overwhelmed by its partners, as Mips was. So, typically, this model is used by a large firm like GM, Boeing, or IBM. These lead firms often offer other members some important advantages to joining, such as large and guaranteed volumes, adjudication of disputes, and discipline of uncooperative members.

Conclusion

Whatever the formal governance structure, the collective has to have some way of coordinating actions. Without leadership or an agreed-upon process for making joint decisions, a constellation cannot be expected to formulate and execute a consistent strategy. Instead, internal divisions and differences in perspectives among members will most likely pull the constellation in different directions. An analogy from the American Wild West is apt: out in the barren plains, cowboys would tie their horses to each other at night, knowing that each horse would pull in a different direction and the group would go nowhere. An alliance group without leadership and collective governance will be no different—but the resulting immobility is unlikely to serve its members' interests.

Further Reading

Henry W. Chesbrough and David J. Teece. "When Is Virtual Virtuous: Organizing for Innovation," *Harvard Business Review*, Jan.-Feb. 1996, pp. 66–73.

Benjamin Gomes-Casseres. "Group Versus Group: How Alliance Networks Compete," *Harvard Business Review*, July-Aug. 1994, pp. 62–74.

Benjamin Gomes-Casseres. *The Alliance Revolution: The New Shape of Business Rivalry.* Cambridge, Mass.: Harvard University Press, 1996. Paperback reprint, 1998. Chapters 3–5.

Source

This chapter is based on "The Corporation Is Dead . . . Long Live the Constellation," *The Alliance Analyst* (June 1996). The article was edited and updated for this book.

19

Constellation Governance

How do companies govern alliance constellations? To start to answer this question, we focused on shared utilities, one of the most common constellation forms. We define a *shared utility* as an organization with a large number of member firms (often ten or more) who are also customers, and in which the venture is operated as a more-or-less independent business. Firms tend to form shared utilities as a way to gain scale and lower costs in performing some non-core functional task, such as transaction processing or network management. But the purpose might also be to share risk and increase market momentum in a core process such as research and development.

Governance in these situations revolves around the management of resource flows and other strategic interactions between the constellation and the corporate parents. At the most basic level, this governance is shaped by the structure, workings, and membership of various decision-making bodies. These bodies include, but are not limited to, the organization's board of directors and its management committee. Although this is a somewhat narrow definition of governance, and one that focuses on formal governance bodies, it allows us to examine the practical elements of collective decision making.

Our interviews with many leaders and managers of shared utilities suggest that firms should think about four organizational elements: overall governance structure, the board of directors, the CEO, and the alliance managers in member firms.

Drawing on discussions with the CEOs of WorldPartners, the World Insurance Network, and other multipartner constellations, we describe here the workings of these elements. Their experiences in these constellations, both good and bad, offer important insights and lessons to the next generation of constellation designers.

Overall Governance Structure

By the *overall governance structure* of a shared utility we mean the system of formal and strategic linkages between the alliance and the corporate parents. How do companies create structures that foster good governance? WorldPartners shows the importance of building multiple components of governance, and how these structures may need to change over time.

Govern at Multiple Levels

WorldPartners was formed in 1993 to provide seamless telecom services to multinational companies operating across multiple local markets. Over the years, the alliance contained nineteen members covering thirty-four countries serving eleven hundred multinational companies, with AT&T, KDD, Singapore Telecom, and Unisource as the lead partners. Within a few years of forming the venture, the partners had created four levels of constellation governance.

The main level was the *Executive Forum*. Held once a year, it typically assembled two senior executives from each member firm to meet with top management of the joint venture, the WorldPartners Company. According to then WorldPartners CEO Simon Krieger, the purpose was to "talk about where we are, what we are doing right and what we are doing wrong, and how we plan for the future."

Two or three times a year, the constellation held a *General Forum* to discuss more operational issues. Perhaps 125 people would attend, most of whom were responsible for implementation at such functional levels as billing, operations, engineering, marketing, and sales.

Below the general forum were *Mini Forums*. Here, managers from the member firms and WorldPartners staff focused on a different constellation issue, such as promotions. Held five or six times a year, the mini forums were a platform for operating managers to discuss issues in depth and build a network of practitioners across the global constellation.

WorldPartners also had a *Governing Board*. During the mid-1990s, it contained two directors from each of the four equity partners: AT&T, KDD, Singapore Telecom, and Unisource. It met once a month, generally for one or two days. Half the meetings were face to face, with the remainder done via conference call.

Involve Different Members Differently

A consortium formed by several electronics firms took a different tack. It also found that multiple governance bodies were important to smooth operation of the constellation—though it took more time to build these governance structures. The business model of this grouping depended on a large number of partners, including telecom service companies and hardware manufacturers. The group itself developed and licensed software that linked these firms.

Initially, this constellation's main governance mechanism was its board of directors. The board contained the CEOs of the company's first equity partners, plus representatives from new partner-owners as they joined the constellation. But as more partners were added, management decided to create a smaller and more traditional corporate board without its alliance member-owners. Part of the reason was to avoid inherent conflicts. According to the group's CEO at the time: "Fifteen members on my board of directors would have been a cauldron of conflicting interest. I had felt tremendous conflicts of interests in the air in the early years when I had just six members. Every time executives spoke I didn't know whether they were speaking on the best interest of the alliance as a whole or were speaking on the best interest of their own company."

To replace the board as the main platform of constellation governance, the group formed the Founding Partners Council. Meeting three times a year with each of the fifteen or so corporate partners holding two seats, the Founding Partners Council operated as something between a board of directors and an advanced users group. At council meetings, management would present a ten-year vision of its overall strategy, plus near-term product and technical details. The partners were asked to provide blunt feedback, and to share observations with the company and with one another.

Over time, the consortium added select layers of governance. The Founding Partners Council formed committees to address particular functional or industry issues, such as manufacturing or telecommunications. It also formed regional committees, allowing, for example, partners from Japan or Europe to discuss issues germane to their business environments.

Govern Strategy and Operations Separately

What wider lessons can be drawn from the experiences of these constellations? One lesson is that when designing an overall governance structure, firms should differentiate between constellation governance and operations.

Governance relates to solving strategic issues: that is, making strategic decisions (capital expenditures, changes in product or geographic scope, and so on) and managing the overall relationship with the member firms. In contrast, operations relates to the more tactical matters of the business, including developing products and services and managing people and administrative functions.

In almost all shared utilities, constellation operations will involve the member firms—that is, it is not something that the venture performs alone. As a result, shared utilities often need to develop formal communication channels (committees, forums, task forces, workshops, and so on) to facilitate these operational interactions. One shared utility in the electric power industry conducted over two hundred workshops per year to develop and disseminate innovation with its member firms.

Minimize Bureaucracy . . .

These organizational structures can be extremely important to constellation success, and some of the most successful shared utilities have found that developing these structures is essential for the member firms to extract value from the alliance. But they are not governance structures. As a simple rule, firms should promote the active development of operational structures but keep true governance structures to a minimum. As in all alliances, having a large number of governing bodies promotes slow and inefficient decision making.

This does not mean depending on one governance body. Constellations with ten or more members are almost impossible to govern through one committee—there are simply too many interactions and decisions. This is especially true when the members are also customers, and thus responsible for defining technology standards and operating interfaces. It is possible to have fewer governance bodies when membership size is smaller, as with the World Insurance Network described later in this chapter.

When member firms create two or three governance bodies, care must be taken in defining the role and composition of each group. Critical questions:

- What decisions will each group be responsible for?
- How often will each group meet?
- How many members will each have?
- What levels of executive personnel will participate in each?
- What is the executives' expected level of commitment?
- How will the different governance bodies relate to one another?

Failure to answer these questions can lead to a complex and unclear overall governance structure that produces poor and extraordinarily slow decisions.

And Keep It Flexible

Firms should expect the overall governance structure to evolve with time. WorldPartners did not launch with a fully formed governance structure, nor did the electronics constellation discussed in this chapter. In both cases, the member firms and venture management saw a need to expand or otherwise alter the governance system, and did so once these needs were clear. As Simon Krieger noted: "The unique nature of the WorldPartners model makes it necessary for us to constantly evolve—to meet the challenges as they come up. We don't have rules and models for everything. As we go along, we deal with it."

The Board of Directors

When a shared utility is structured as a corporation with multiple owners (that is, a formal joint venture), the main component of governance is usually the corporation's board of directors. This board has the fiduciary responsibility to protect the interests of the shareholders, to oversee venture management, and approve certain venture decisions.

But unlike the usual corporate board, this board often assumes an extensive operating role, as it is the main link back to the members that provide resources and derive services from the utility. Given this focus, how do firms determine the membership composition and role of the board of directors? The World Insurance Network offers some answers.

The World Insurance Network (WIN) was established in 1997 to create an online platform that would allow insurance brokers and underwriters to share information and dramatically reduce transaction costs. WIN was formed by the six largest insurance brokers in the world, including Aon Group, Marsh & McLennan, Sedgwick, and Willis Corroon, representing more than 70 percent of the world-wide market.

Committing Member Resources

The WIN partners wanted to create a board of directors where the members had both real control over parent resources and a personal commitment to work with the venture on an ongoing basis.

To meet these two distinct goals, the partners recruited two different sorts of board members. The first were top company executives—the chairman or chief executive from each corporate parent. According to David Evans, who served as co-CEO of WIN soon after its launch: "This is absolutely critical. You would never get these changes through the industry unless it was the senior executives, or the equivalent, making the decisions."

Each shareholder also had an operating member on the board, someone who was focused on the day-to-day activity of the venture. These operating members provided the ongoing links between the corporate parents and WIN's full-time management, as well as guiding WIN along the path to shareholder goals.

Making Decisions

Unlike traditional public companies, WIN drew on and communicated with its board members extensively between formal meetings. For example, before each board meeting, WIN management visited the chairman or chief executive at each corporate parent, explaining the agenda and goals of the upcoming board meeting. These discussions were "extraordinarily time-consuming but absolutely essential," according to Evans. As co-CEO, Evans wanted no surprises: "One of the things we've learned is that there is no point in having a board meeting unless we've taken all the decisions outside."

The aim was also to tease out the true aims of each shareholder—something that the directors did not always make explicit in the formal board meeting. These discussions were also used to reassure the corporate parents that the venture was acting responsibly. As Evans noted a year into WIN's existence: "As we grow up from being a little baby—we are probably now at the advanced infant stage, still in mother's arms—it's essential to recognize that we need to continuously assure the shareholder that we are not off with the fairies."

Designing a Board Structure

Because the board of directors is the main structure of constellation governance it deserves considerable attention. When thinking about a constellation board, we've found it useful to think in terms of four topics: overall role and context of the board, its membership, the roles of individual directors, and the evolution of the board.

Overall Role and Context. The overall role and context of a constellation board may be compared to those of a standard corporate board. An alliance board differs from a traditional corporate board in a number of regards, and these differences can have a material effect on the board's overall role. One important difference is that in constellations, the board's mandate is not only to oversee the top management of the venture but also to manage resource flows between the corporate parents and the venture. This gives the constellation board much greater influence than a corporate board, and a much more extensive role in decision making.

A second difference is that individual directors do not represent all the shareholders, but the specific interests of a subset of shareholders, where the directors themselves are also employed. This means that constellation directors will pursue goals that are more complex than those of corporate directors, where shareholder interests must be reduced to the lowest common denominator (for example, maximize profits, increase share price). Also, because constellation directors represent different shareholder interests, there is a real potential for conflict within the board itself. These differences mean that firms must expect to take more time to define which decisions the board has influence over, as well as to create devices to manage conflicts within the board.

Board Membership. Board membership—that is, which member firms will sit on the board—is also an important issue in constellations. Smaller alliances can accommodate all the member firms, but this is not the case in larger constellations. Other research has shown that in larger constellations, board composition may be limited to some group of core members. For example, at the Semiconductor Research Consortium, a constellation with more than sixty members, ten of the nineteen board seats were reserved for the ten largest fee contributors.

Below overall board role and membership, firms need to determine the *responsibilities of the individual directors.* Will each director perform the same role, or will there be differences? At WIN, the chair was a distinct position, rotating between the member firms from year to year. The WIN chair was expected to spend a great deal of time outside board meetings talking to the other directors and the venture co-CEOs, shaping the shared constellation vision. It can also be helpful to differentiate between different directors from the same company. WIN did this by thinking in terms of strategic and operational board members. In another alliance, a firm differentiated between lead and non-lead directors. The lead director was expected to spend twenty to thirty days per year working with the alliance, while the non-lead director spent far less, primarily involved in approving major budget and strategy decisions. This approach, which made one director more available to the alliance, helped to considerably smooth and accelerate decision making.

Finally, boards too *evolve over time.* Of the many potential evolutionary paths, the most common is for the board to become less interventionist with time, not unlike the board of a venture-backed start-up. At WIN, venture management expected that it would need to communicate less with board members between meetings. As Evans noted: "Progressively, as we get positive cash flow, as we begin to get a profit, as we begin to develop a management structure that is mature, shareholder involvement will wane and we will become a trusted citizen in our own right."

The CEO

The CEO of the shared utility is another linchpin in the overall governance structure. How should members choose this executive, and what role will the job entail? Again, the World Insurance Network offers some guidance.

Roles of the CEO

The World Insurance Network operated with two co-CEOs during its formative period. One of these co-CEOs was David Evans, who also served as chief information officer at Aon. The other CEO was a full-time employee of the joint venture, which he ran on a day-by-day basis. According to Evans, "He is there to keep the internals of the organization ticking over. You have to have management on the ground running these things. . . . I spend a lot of my time massaging, stroking, and calming [the board members] down, assuring them that we are not up there to spend their money in an uncontrolled manner. The reason we have two CEOs was shareholder competitiveness—they would not have a CEO from just one of the shareholders. We are supposed to counterbalance each other and keep each other from making self-interested decisions."

Operating the alliance with co-CEOs was not intended as a permanent solution—and indeed it was not even the initial vision. In fact, WIN first went through a difficult period without clear leadership before settling on this solution. Evans explained: "The shareholders' sense of ownership made them reluctant to allow this little bird to fly the coop and they were protective about the venture's strategies. So we marked time for several months on this issue—several months that we did not go forward. The delay caused confusion with our technology vendor, who by this time was wondering what on earth was going on. It was resolved by putting in a management team from the shareholders. I found myself bundled in, kicking, screaming, and unwilling, along with the other CEO who was more willing."

Selecting a CEO

The CEO thus serves as the main connection point between the venture and the member firms. Because of this, it is important to choose someone with good knowledge of the businesses of the member firms. Consider SEMATECH. Its founding CEO was Robert Noyce, co-founder of Fairchild Semiconductor and Intel and a founding member of the semiconductor industry association. His background as industry statesman gave Noyce tremendous credibility among SEMATECH members, as well as a real understanding of their interests and decision making processes. It also allowed the constellation to attract top scientific talent.

Similar characteristics can be found in other constellation CEOs. This can also be said of Leonard Schrank, CEO of SWIFT, a successful financial services constellation; Schrank had been an executive at Chase/International Data. Prior to becoming president of WorldPartners, Simon Krieger was an AT&T international executive with significant Asia/Pacific business relationships. These CEOs were both familiar with and independent from the member firms.

The downside of selecting a CEO with good member connections is the risk that the CEO will not be independent, or will not be viewed as such. To help reduce this concern, firms can take a number of steps. One is to ensure that the CEO's individual compensation is strongly linked to constellation performance and determined by the board rather than the one corporate parent. A more aggressive approach is to establish "no lifeline back" hiring policy, whereby the CEO cannot return to the member firm where he or she worked.

Alliance Managers in Member Firms

The last critical element in constellation governance is the alliance manager who manages the day-to-day link between member firms and the shared utility. These managers can be crucial in understanding the interests and goals of member firms, as well as in managing conflicts. The constellations discussed in this chapter took different approaches to locating these individuals.

Role and Location

The electronics consortium assigned three people to each member firm. The *alliance manager* was the overall guardian of the relationship—and indeed was often the one responsible for bringing the firm into the alliance in the first place. The *technical coordinator* ensured compatible interfaces. And the *project coordinator* arranged specific ongoing activities, such as conducting product tests or coordinating work between different partners.

The group's alliance management resources were spelled out in its partnership contracts. Upon signing on to the shared utility, firms each committed contractually to provide certain types of staff and support. Although the member firms did not get directly involved in selecting the alliance managers, the firms did contribute money to defray some of the associated costs.

WorldPartners did not appoint alliance managers to oversee operational communications with its member firms. Rather, the constellation managed its members either through the various forums or on an issue-by-issue basis within the functional departments of the joint venture company. For example, if a member had a question about billing procedures, then the billing development unit within WorldPartners would respond.

WorldPartners also required member firms to devote resources to alliance management, but left these staff in the member organizations. These "member-designated resources" were responsible for handling the three WorldPartners services areas—private line, frame relay, and virtual network. Some member firms had separate individuals responsible for each of these areas, whereas others had one manager responsible for all.

Interdependence and Routine

As a general rule, shared utilities need alliance managers to ensure smooth relations with the member firms. The appropriate number and level of alliance managers will depend on the degree of inter- action between the venture and its members, which is often a func- tion of the venture's age.

For highly independent and well-established shared utilities such as Visa International or MasterCard, it is often possible to standardize many of the interactions between the venture and its members, and thus reduce the per-firm management resources. However, when the constellation exhibits a high degree of inter- dependence with its members, something common in the earliest stages of venture formation, then alliance managers are critical. In fact, one shared utility in the financial services business found that managing the relationship with one member consumed an esti- mated 50 percent of total management time for three to six months.

This carries several implications. One is that shared utilities often need alliance management resources at the time when they are least likely to exist: at the very beginning. It is at this point in the business life cycle when the constellation will be working most closely with its member firms. As a result, it may make sense for the constellation to depend on the member firms to contribute to the expense of these managers or, as WorldPartners did, to require members to designate an alliance manager within their own com- panies to relieve some of the managerial burden.

Constellation governance is not limited to formal structures. In almost all constellations, at least some interaction and decision making take place outside the formal channels of governance. Nonetheless, these structures are the building blocks of good governance, and firms should start here when designing governance processes for shared utilities.

Further Reading

Raymond E. Corey. *Technology Fountainheads: The Management Challenge of R&D Consortia.* Boston: Harvard Business School Press, 1997.

Gianni Lorenzoni and Charles Baden-Fuller. "Creating a Strategic Center to Manage a Web of Alliances," *California Management Review,* Spring 1995, *37,* 146–163.

Source

This chapter is a synthesis of material from several articles in *The Alliance Analyst,* especially "Confessions of a Constellation Designer," an interview with Simon Krieger (June 1996); and "The Brokers Respond," an interview with David Evans (February 1998). All quotes are from those interviews, and reflect thinking of the interviewees at that time.

20

Constellation Dynamics

Alliances spread like wildfire. Once key players in an industry begin to use alliances for one reason or another, their rivals often are not far behind. Take the growth of alliances in the airline industry, shown in Figure 20.1. Through the early 1990s, a few new alliances were formed every year, leading to early constellations that remained limited in membership. But a number of important players continued to compete more or less as single entities. By the late 1990s, the pace of alliance formation picked up to a frenzy—new constellations were formed and grew rapidly. After 2000, almost all large airlines had joined a constellation, and the largest groupings counted over ten members.

The pattern in airlines is by no means unique. In the early 1990s, there were alliance waves in the telecommunications, health care, and commercial real estate industries as well. Biotechnology alliances took off in the mid-1980s. Earlier, the late 1970s and early 1980s saw alliance waves in the automobile, aircraft, and chemicals industries. Often, these waves were followed by periods in which alliance formation declined or at least slowed down. To some, these cycles of booms and busts suggest that alliances are a passing fad, subject to the ebb and flow of management fashion. We believe this view to be mistaken. Instead, we see a distinct logic to alliance cycles. Understanding the logic of this cycle in your industry is key to using constellations for effective competition.

FIGURE 20.1 Spread of Alliances in Airlines, 1980–2000.

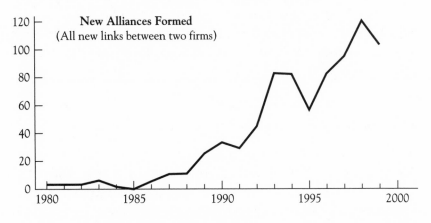

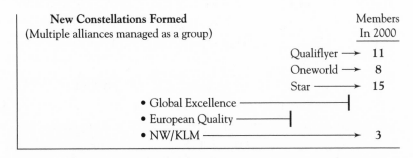

Source: Compiled from data in Wilma Suen, "Firm Power and Interdependence in International Strategic Alliances," Ph.D. thesis, Tufts University, 2001. Includes only alliances of major airlines and constellations.

Why do firms in one industry often increase their use of alliances at about the same time? Why does the spread of alliances often come to a halt and even decline after a few years? And how are constellations restructured when the growth spurt subsides? We will explore here the leading explanations for these patterns.

Drivers of Growth of Constellations

Three types of factors can drive the spread of alliances and the growth of constellations. The first is *change in the business environment,* such as in technology, regulation, or demand. The second is *imitation*, in which managers follow organizational fashions, including those thought of as best practices at the time. The third is *competitive rivalry*, in which companies react to each other's strategic moves.

Change in the Business Environment

The simplest explanation of an alliance wave is that firms are reacting to common changes in their business environment. For example, when the emergence of a new technology favors the formation of alliances, most firms in the industry will seek partners. Thus when the oil crisis of the 1970s created new demand for energy-efficient small cars, all the U.S. carmakers headed to Asia to seek allies that could help them build and sell small cars.

But often the firms in an industry do not face exactly the same environmental forces and certainly do not interpret these forces in identical ways. And there is always more than one possible response to a given environmental change, leading some firms to choose alliances and others not. For example, faced with similar competitive pressures in the 1990s, some airlines chose to use alliances to attract global travelers, while others preferred instead to focus on regional markets, a strategy that did not require as many alliances.

In addition, the nature of an environmental change is seldom clear-cut from the start; more often, change evolves from competing trends that only become clarified in time. Alliances are attractive tools for managing risk in such conditions (see Chapter Three), because they help firms experiment with new strategies. After this early wave, such experimentation may no longer be needed, because the nature of the environmental change has been clarified and other long-run responses may have been found. This is a good explanation for the rise and decline of alliances in the PDA business—first, all major firms used alliances to form PDA constellations; later, they dissolved these in favor of more focused approaches involving fewer partnerships.

Imitation and Management Fads

Another popular explanation of why alliances spread rapidly is management fashion. Certainly, alliance strategies are not immune to the hype common to other management trends.

Imitation sometimes can be a reflection of how companies learn. Followers will imitate successful leaders when the leaders have demonstrated that a new strategy is useful. This kind of imitation is common when a strategy has been dubbed "best practice" by industry players. In the 1990s, as more and more leading firms formed alliances, others began to study their methods in the hope of discovering keys to success. All too often, the results of these best-practice studies were disappointing, as the tactics of one company failed to fit the circumstances of other companies. Yet there is little doubt that the positive example of successful alliance practitioners, some of which are featured in this book, have helped educate others and encouraged them to form new alliances.

More cynical observers see management imitation as a much less rational process. In this view, following the trend offers protection in numbers. Management gurus and consulting firms may unwittingly promote this process by raising one strategy or another as a model. The Internet boom of the late 1990s was replete with this kind of imitation; venture capital investors pursued one fad after another, including the rampant use of alliances. Driven by investor expectations, many dot-com start-ups created large constellations of allies just to show how popular they were.

There is thus at least some truth to the view that alliance waves are driven by fashion. But even in the case of the dot-com start-ups, the tendency to follow fashion was a managerial response to competition in securing capital and customers. Rivalry of this kind often lies at the root of constellation dynamics.

Competitive Reaction to Rivals

Economists have long noticed that close rivals in an industry often follow each other's strategic moves—whether it is entering a new market, offering new products, or using a new organizational form such as a constellation. In the case of alliances, firms tend to react to each other in this way for three strategic reasons: to match the capabilities of rival groups, to pursue first-mover advantages, and to preempt rivals in new markets.

Matching Capabilities. Firms often follow each other's strategic moves to avoid falling behind. The reasoning in alliance formation is as follows. Assume that constellations A and B are rivals, and that A expands its group by adding members that bring new capabilities to the group. If B decides not to follow and A's new strategy generates advantages, then B falls behind. But if B follows by expanding its own group, then the two rivals are likely to stay close competitors, regardless of how the strategy turns out. When competitors are averse to risk, they are likely to choose this follow-the-leader strategy, which lowers their chances of either moving ahead or—more important—falling behind their rivals.

The tit-for-tat imitation implied by this process is illustrated by the growth of constellations in airlines, telecommunications, and automobiles. In each case, leading firms or constellations have used alliances to span the globe with common services and products—Star, oneworld, and Qualiflyer in airlines; Concert and Global One in telecommunications; and GM, Ford, and DaimlerChrysler in autos.

The Pursuit of First-Mover Advantages. Sometimes, being first is the key to success. When an industry has high economies of scale, high customer switching costs, or steep experience curves, competitors can be expected to try to establish a dominant market share early. Firms can use alliances to shorten the time needed to establish a lead position. Or, if they are latecomers, they can band together in an effort to erode the position of the lead firm. Alliances may thus quicken the race for first-mover advantages.

The early history of the personal computer industry provides a famous example. In 1979, Apple was the first vendor with a professional desktop computer, the Apple II. IBM countered in 1981 with the IBM PC, but could not get to market quickly enough on its own—it depended on Microsoft for the operating system software and Intel for the microprocessor. This three-part alliance was able to wrest market leadership from Apple in the early 1980s, particularly after Compaq and others joined with clones of the IBM machine.

Preemptive Alliance Strategies. In alliance formation, preemptive strikes often offer substantial advantages because of the finite set of opportunities for collaboration that exist at any point in time. Tying up early gives you the best choice of partners and preempts rivals from tying up with an attractive partner. Much more than imitation is at work here. A constellation may execute a preemptive alliance not because it is in a rush to match the capabilities of a rival but because it wants to keep the rival from assembling this set of capabilities.

A firm's incentive to form alliances preemptively is thus likely to depend on its expectations about its rivals' moves. The more likely it appears that a rival will form an alliance, the greater the incentive to preempt. This tendency, too, can accelerate the spread of alliances: the formation of alliances breeds the expectation of further alliances, which leads to preemptive alliances by firms that would otherwise remain single.

Limits to the Growth of Constellations

Just as several factors drive the growth of constellations, a variety of limits may inhibit their expansion beyond a certain point and usher in a phase of slower growth in alliances. The airline industry did not encounter these limits before 2000, but there were indications that some of the larger constellations were beginning to face constraints on growth.

The simplest of these constraints is overcrowding of the field. The pool of eligible partners will diminish because of the boom in alliance formation itself. Or, including the still-available partners into an existing constellation may threaten to increase conflicts of interest among group members. This form of saturation in the industry has been called "strategic gridlock," because it tends to limit the strategic flexibility that alliances typically offer a firm.

Other limits to growth of constellations stem not from the external environment but from internal constraints. Managers often cite scarcity of management capacity as a constraint on alliance formation. Negotiating each agreement requires great effort, and major alliances require the continual, direct, and personal involvement of top management. These demands on management increase with the size of the group and the complexity of member interactions.

In addition, cooperation becomes increasingly difficult as the number of members in a constellation rises (see Chapter Eighteen). Conflicts may also arise when one of the partners has another alliance that influences the goals of the first alliance. Whatever the root causes, such conflicts of interest will add to the coordination costs of the group and limit the degree to which the group can be integrated to implement a common strategy.

When such frictions arise, constellation leaders often respond by restructuring the group. In fact, just as for single alliances, it is common for constellations with multiple members to be reshaped in response to new challenges.

Restructuring of Constellations

The frictions that may lead a constellation to be restructured can express themselves in different ways. Sometimes a constellation is challenged from the outside, that is, it is unable to keep up with rivals competitively. At other times, the constellation may be challenged from the inside, that is, one or more members may be unhappy with their lot in the group. Often, these two forces combine and internal strife goes hand in hand with competitive challenges. These pressures commonly result in one of four patterns of restructuring: member revolt, leadership consolidation, structural reform, or death.

Member Revolt

Sometimes the restructuring of a constellation leads to a dramatic redistribution of power away from the dominant firm. Visa International underwent a major restructuring following member-bank demands seven years after its formation. Visa International was initially launched as the BankAmericard consortium, where member banks licensed the BankAmericard name and issued credit cards to their customers. As the constellation struggled to compete against new entrants in the credit-card field, members forced a change in structure that gave them more power and benefits. (See Chapter Twenty-Two.)

Such transformations tend to happen when two circumstances exist: a dominant constellation leader without truly differentiated assets, and a large block of similar members. Both conditions existed inside the BankAmericard consortium. Bank of America had a brand, but it was not essential to the success of the network. Likewise, the hundred or so member-bank licensees were effectively a single interest group with similar assets, economic circumstances, and concerns. In time firms formed a block within the constellation and ultimately exercised their considerable collective leverage to redistribute returns.

Leadership Consolidation

On other occasions, change comes from a dominant firm that sees an opportunity to gain greater control over the constellation. Consider Coca-Cola. In 1919, some twenty years after creating a constellation of bottling partners, the Coca-Cola Company embarked on an eighty-year consolidation drive to purchase the parent bottlers and certain frontline bottlers. It also started to exercise control over communications within the constellation. (See Chapter Twenty-One.)

Why could Coca-Cola consolidate its position in this way? First, Coca-Cola controlled differentiated assets, notably the secret formula and brand name. Second, Coca-Cola was playing a distinct role within the constellation, and was not competing with others in the group. These distinct assets and roles, combined with strong financial resources, made it extremely difficult for other constellation members (that is, the bottlers) to overthrow the constellation leader. Third, the members had much less incentive to do so: the Coca-Cola constellation created substantial economic opportunities for all involved in the network.

Structural Reform

Firms may also restructure a constellation with the goal of improving operating efficiencies. Airbus Industrie did just that in 2000, after twenty-nine years of success under its original structure. From its inception, Airbus was a joint venture between four European aerospace firms that operated as a sales and marketing consortium. The partners would agree on aircraft designs but then separately manufacture different sections. These sections would then be transported from the partners' factories to those of Airbus in France for final assembly. Airbus was then responsible for marketing and sales.

Although this structure did not prevent Airbus from becoming a rival to Boeing, it did produce operating inefficiencies. Because the main source of value for the partners was the price and volume of sales to Airbus—not the overall performance of the JV—the partners had incentives to conceal their true financial and manufacturing data from one another.

To correct these problems, Airbus converted its loose constellation structure into a more conventional corporate model, with a single balance sheet, a centralized procurement system, and full disclosure of manufacturing costs. For the first time, the joint venture would own all its production assets, and could figure out the full costs of producing an aircraft. Managers predicted that the new, tighter structure would allow it to compete more effectively and raise capital on private equity markets.

When they are first formed, constellations typically have organizational arrangements that are less than optimal for the long run. Over time, as conditions in the market or inside member-firms change, the partners may come to understand these inefficiencies or gain the will to address them. In many cases, as with Airbus, the solution lies in deeper integration of the members. In other cases, looser integration may be a better solution. The personal-computer constellation around IBM, Microsoft, and Intel is one that over time grew looser and in which the center of power shifted from IBM to Microsoft and Intel. Finally, some constellations that grew rapidly at first often decided later to curtail membership and to allocate clearer roles to existing members. Colliers International is an example of this pattern (Chapter Twenty-Three).

Erosion, Collapse, and Death

Constellations do not always evolve—sometimes they die. They can die slowly as membership erodes, or quickly, when members decide to end the grouping. When capabilities change and markets shift partners may be left wondering whether it is useful to maintain the multipartner alliance. Termination or sale might then be the only way out.

Bellcore went down the sale path. Founded in the 1950s inside AT&T, Bellcore had long been one of the world's great technology wellsprings. In the early 1980s, following the breakup of AT&T, Bellcore was transformed into a multipartner joint venture with the seven local Bell operating companies, including Bell Atlantic, Bell-South, and Southwestern Bell, as owners. For many years, Bellcore operated as a successful multipartner constellation, with the member firms using the venture as a means to pool research funds. During this time, the owners did not compete with one another in their core local telephone business.

But as the 1990s progressed, the partners increasingly found themselves competing on the frontiers of telecommunications: in cellular systems, digital communication, multimedia, and overseas markets. This changed the nature of partner interaction. By 1995, joint research had virtually dried up, leaving Bellcore with seven separate research teams, each working individually with one owner. A year later, the owners had had enough, and agreed to sell Bellcore for $700 million to a defense technology firm with a growing interest in telecom consulting.

Other constellations break up for different reasons, or they just erode and fade away. The telecommunications industry has seen much rivalry among global constellations that sought to provide integrated services across continents. In the early 1990s, Concert was a joint venture between British Telecom and MCI; it competed against WorldPartners, owned by AT&T and a number of European and Asian companies, and Global One, owned by Deutsche Telekom, France Telecom, and Sprint. When WorldCom acquired MCI in the late 1990s, the latter pulled out of Concert. AT&T then left WorldPartners to replace MCI in Concert. This implied the breakup of WorldPartners. Global One then faded away for reasons of its own, and Concert itself was disbanded a few years later. Constellations in global telecom were a useful experiment and a strategy few players could avoid, but in the end they were replaced by other strategies, including looser affiliations and wholesale acquisitions.

Managing Change in Constellations

The ways in which constellations grow and change over time are still not completely understood. Practitioners are continually experimenting with new approaches, and researchers are always trying to draw conclusions from industry trends. The best thinking and experience to date suggests the following guidelines for managers:

- *Map your constellation and those of your rivals.* All too often, key decision makers in a company do not have a clear mental image of their own constellations, and of the various constellations in their industry. Here a picture is truly worth a thousand words: Create a diagram and update it regularly. Do that for your constellations and for those of your rivals—analyzing the alliance strategy of rivals is now a key element in competitive intelligence. Evaluate the strengths and weaknesses of your constellation compared to theirs.

- *Be clear about why you follow your rivals, or why you don't.* Imitation among constellations is common, as noted earlier. But this does not mean that you should follow blindly. Rather, understand what drives imitation in your industry, who might be worth learning from, and when you should desist from following an example. One senior executive was fond of sending little notes to subordinates, attached to the latest news of a rival's move: "Why are we not doing this too?" he would ask. His point was not to encourage his managers to copy, but rather to get them to evaluate and fashion a response to rivals' actions.

- *Plan the growth of your constellation as much as you can.* No constellation is ever thought out fully in advance. But it is worth thinking systematically about which partners should be courted first, which new members might bring in additional members, which allies in fact might repel future allies, and so on. Sometimes, to get a leading firm to join, you may first need to tie up with its allies; at other times, a dominant firm will join only when it senses that second-tier players may beat it to the game. Either way, it is better to think in advance about these reactions.

- *Adjust constellation structure to respond to new conditions.* Just as with the single alliance, a group of partners can never stand still—it must be flexible to pursue new opportunities and fix problems. In a constellation with many members, this can be difficult because of the multitude of interests involved. This is one reason why leadership from one or a few firms is critical to good constellation design (see Chapter Eighteen).

Further Reading

Shona L. Brown and Kathleen M. Eisenhardt. *Competing on the Edge: Strategy as Structured Chaos.* Boston: Harvard Business School Press, 1998.

Benjamin Gomes-Casseres. *The Alliance Revolution: The New Shape of Business Rivalry.* Cambridge, Mass.: Harvard University Press, 1996. Paperback reprint, 1998. Chapter 4.

Wilma W. Suen. "Alliance Strategy and the Fall of Swissair," *Journal of Air Transport Management,* forthcoming.

Source

This chapter is based on "The Logic of Alliance Fads: Why Collective Competition Spreads," by Benjamin Gomes-Casseres, in Mitchell P. Koza and Arie Y. Lewin, eds., *Strategic Alliances and Firm Adaptation* (forthcoming), as well as "Midlife Migration" and "When the Hub Spoke" from *The Alliance Analyst* (October and December 1996).

Veterans and Pioneers

21

Reaching Every Pocket

Coca-Cola

Current wisdom holds that there is no benchmark for multi-partner alliances. The perception is that such ventures are so novel and untested that launching one is a leap into the managerial dark. This is patently untrue. Consider Coca-Cola. This company built its entire business as a constellation—a global network of marketing and bottling partners. In 1999, Coca-Cola's executives noted that 100 percent of its business depended on alliances.

This is not a tale of mere franchising of a brand. Since 1900, the Coca-Cola alliance constellation has involved a blend of equity stakes and joint ventures, as well as more conventional licensing agreements. It has also experimented with vastly different sets of alliance structural configurations—from two tiers of partners to four, from a loose leader to a dominant one, from three partners to three thousand. There are sharp and counterintuitive lessons here for the modern executive. The Coca-Cola constellation argues for dominance at the center. It points to the need to manage competition within the constellation. It counsels for clear definition of scope and partner roles. And it shows that firms must prune their constellations to adapt to new conditions.

Building the Coca-Cola Constellation

The Coca-Cola constellation was launched on a hot July afternoon in 1899. On that day Asa Candler, owner of the Coca-Cola Company, agreed to grant Coca-Cola bottling rights in perpetuity to a pair of portly Tennessee lawyers named Benjamin Thomas and Joseph Whitehead. In return, Candler received his partners' commitment to buy syrup for $1 a gallon, to meet demand (which Candler thought would be minimal), and to open a bottling plant in Candler's home town of Atlanta. The agreement reflected Candler's low expectations of bottling; he viewed it as a great distraction from his core business of selling syrup to pharmacies and soda fountains. Candler reckoned that bottling was a high-risk venture, especially since attempts a decade earlier had led to exploding containers, injured workers, and a product that often contained putrid and murky substances.

But Thomas and Whitehead were obsessed with the idea of bottling Coca-Cola. They loved two things—baseball and Coca-Cola— and wanted to enjoy both together. To make this happen, they needed some way to transport or store the drink. A year earlier, the two had enlisted a runner to carry glasses of Coca-Cola from a local soda fountain to the ballpark. But they found the drink had lost its fizzle before it reached them. Thomas and Whitehead then switched their attention to bottling and headed off to see Candler in Atlanta. Although bottling promised to open up a whole new market for Coca-Cola (one that stretched far beyond ballparks), Candler had a word of caution as Thomas and Whitehead headed out the door with their new contract in hand: "If you boys fail in this undertaking, don't come back to cry on my shoulder, because I have very little confidence in this bottling business" (Allen, 1994, p. 106).

The Network of Bottlers

Thomas and Whitehead knew a huge opportunity had landed in their laps—and that, short of cash, they were in danger of losing it. Their contract with Candler was to meet demand across the entire

United States, minus New England, Mississippi, and a piece of Texas. If they failed to fulfill this obligation, the rights to bottle Coca-Cola would revert back to Candler and the Coca-Cola Company.

Thomas and Whitehead plotted an alliance strategy of their own. Their six-hundred-word contract with Candler was a study in simplicity—and omission. It did not bar the bottlers from signing subfranchise agreements, nor did it specify any terms of such agreements. Thomas and Whitehead planned to turn an army of Tennessee friends into partners, and scatter them across the country to open bottling plants in every American town of consequence. They would plant partners at fifty-mile intervals and ensure each had some training, some cash, and a properly equipped horse and buggy.

This was a different alliance approach from that of Candler, who had embarked on the licensing decision as a way, in modern parlance, to pursue a non-core opportunity. Thomas and Whitehead, however, viewed bottling as their core business, and used alliances as a means to race their product across all available markets. Differences in the motives behind the alliances of these partners (for example, maintaining focus versus reaching markets) are reflected in the types of contracts they signed, their desire for equity, and their tactics for ongoing management. Candler sought short-term revenue and was unwilling to invest time or resources in developing or managing the alliances. He signed a blanket agreement for perpetuity—the ultimate don't-bother-me alliance contract. Thomas and Whitehead, although in a hurry, were looking to nurse a long-term opportunity. This made them quick to dirty their hands in network management, customizing contracts, revisiting the terms and progress, and seeking equity wherever they possibly could.

Early Divorce

But before Thomas and Whitehead started signing their external alliances, their own relationship started to rupture. The partners had a series of disagreements over such issues as bottle size, bottle color, cancellation provisions with underperforming front-line bottlers, contract duration, and risk-sharing provisions. Their differences ultimately drove Thomas and Whitehead to end their partnership just a year after forming it.

In their restructuring agreement, the partners divided the U.S. market. Thomas took the bottling rights in the North, the Mid-Atlantic, Midwest, and West. Whitehead held the South, where the hot, humid weather generated the greatest demand for the drink. Thomas set out to conquer his territory alone, while Whitehead decided to bring in a new partner, a wealthy Chattanooga businessman named J.T. Lupton, who had made his money in patent medicine.

Despite their product and pricing differences, Thomas and Whitehead pursued remarkably similar alliance strategies in the ensuing decades—and strategies that were quite different from Candler's. Unlike Candler, they both formed alliances with friends and acquaintances, rather than strangers knocking at the door. Unlike Candler, they both linked their financial success to partner profits rather than per-unit royalty payments. And, unlike Candler, they took equity positions in as many partners as they could. Indeed, the wealthy Lupton often financed half the needed start-up capital for bottlers in the Southeast, receiving equity in exchange.

Early bottling subagreements called for Thomas or Whitehead and Lupton to provide a franchisee with syrup, bottle caps, advertising, and an in-plant supervisor. In return, they would take half the profits. This structure had several implications. Not surprisingly, it meant the original franchisers quickly lost interest in bottling Coke themselves; they concentrated most of their energies on accessing the greater returns of acting as parent bottlers to a mass of frontline bottlers.

The contract terms soon proved onerous on several fronts. Many bottlers, particularly those signing on in the early years before Coca-Cola took off with American consumers, were going bankrupt. To stay afloat, they demanded a greater share of profits. Meanwhile, the parent bottlers were finding it impractical and expensive to station a supervisor (read: alliance manager) at each bottling plant. The parent bottlers also came to understand that placing one of their employees inside a bottler's plant created suspicion and distrust.

In 1901, the parties amended their contract. The parent bottlers would take a straight royalty of 6 cents per case, or 0.25 cents per bottle, rather than half the profits. They backed away from their obligation to provide a plant supervisor. But, in most cases, they retained their equity positions in their frontline bottlers.

Consolidating the Constellation

The Coca-Cola constellation continued to evolve. By 1919, the relationships were producing tremendous returns for the partners. But there were pressures for change. In particular, the Coca-Cola Company wanted control of the parent bottlers—firms it believed no longer served a useful role. The push for consolidation started when Asa Candler sold his interest in the Coca-Cola Company to a syndicate of banks in 1919. The two original parent bottlers, Thomas and Whitehead, were dead. Their companies had proved enormously effective in searching for, training, and coordinating new constellation partners. But the era was over. Having integrated the new partners, the parent bottlers ceased to play a meaningful role. Nonetheless, these firms were collecting royalties of $1 million a year.

Between 1923 and 1942, the Coca-Cola Company acquired five of the six parent bottlers, most of which were corporate spin-offs of the original Thomas and Whitehead partnership. The major coup came in 1933 when the company convinced J.T. Lupton and the Whitehead heirs to sell their Southern parent bottling company in exchange for Coca-Cola stock and cash. The sole holdout was the Thomas Company, which controlled territory covering one-third of the U.S. population.

Coca-Cola hoped these acquisitions would ease resentment within its constellation. The large riches and low work demands of the parent bottlers had stirred trouble in the ranks, both among front-line bottlers and Coca-Cola employees. Coca-Cola's president in the 1910s claimed J.T. Lupton had spent "his entire business life . . . getting all he could put his hands on" (Pendergrast, 1993, p. 78). Coca-Cola was in a mood to start owning as much of its constellation as it could. With greater control of the network, the firm focused on two main changes in the constellation structure: overseas expansion and creating an authority structure within the constellation.

Overseas Alliances. Having gained control of Coca-Cola in 1919, the syndicate of banks announced their intention to extend the operations not only in the United States but also in foreign countries. Two years later, the company's annual report admitted that eager would-be foreign bottling partners had deluged the company, but that it had decided that "the foreign field should be occupied by direct representation, owning plants, manufacturing, and bottling our own product."

Coca-Cola's international expansion started in earnest in the early 1930s. Much to the company's chagrin, it often ran into pressures to find local partners. In most cases, Coca-Cola either signed limited-term franchising agreements or, taking a page from the old Thomas and Whitehead playbook, formed joint ventures with local players.

Authority Structure. Back at home, new distinctions and divisions were emerging within the constellation. Some observers described the bottler network as a hierarchy of different-sized bottlers. Some bottlers were large, operating in several states, others were larger still, and some ran giant networks that operated across whole regions of the country. Some of the largest of these bottler networks were owned by single families in which management and ownership passed from father to son to grandson. Such large multiunit franchisees were by no means unique to Coca-Cola. Professor Jeffrey Bradach of the Harvard Business School analyzed how common this model was in modern franchising networks, including those of KFC, Pizza Hut, Hardee's, and others. "Multi-unit franchising not only transformed the internal operating dynamics of the franchise arrangement," he explained, "but it also reconfigured the relationship between the chain operator and the franchise community" (Bradach, 1998, p. 54). In other words, the balance of power within the constellation was shaped in part by the relative sizes of the members.

As a general matter, some sort of hierarchy—or, more accurately, partner categorization—is often an important component of constellation design. Lotus created a simple yet powerful pyramid to classify its corporate partners (see Chapter Twenty-Nine). A classification system such as this can help the firm allocate management resources to its alliances, with top alliances getting the most attention. It may also help the firm recognize the different needs of different types of alliances, such as the role of different contractual terms.

Improving the Constellation

By the 1940s, the Coca-Cola bottling constellation was stabilized, and it began to experiment with new forms of alliances and ways to leverage existing collaborative infrastructure. For instance, Coca-Cola and Delta Air Lines launched a co-branding alliance in the 1940s and 1950s, remarkably parallel to the late 1990s Starbucks Coffee/United Airlines alliance where the airline promoted its partner's beverage on board as a way to differentiate itself from competitors. The bottlers also searched for other innovative alliance-based promotions. In the 1950s, a group of bottlers underwrote a national radio show aimed at teens. They also made Coke a named sponsor of the *Mickey Mouse Club*, further developing what would become a profound relationship with the Walt Disney Company.

The bottlers wanted more, however. They argued that the rise of vending machines demanded new products from Coca-Cola. Coke drinkers occasionally longed for a root beer, ginger ale, orange soda, or even a low-calorie version of their old favorite. One bottler grew so weary of the Coca-Cola Company's refusal to come up with new flavors that he created Veep, a lemon-lime drink distributed for a short time in New York. In 1960, the Coca-Cola Company finally understood it could use its constellation infrastructure to promote new products. Over the next decade and a half it launched, in succession, Sprite, Fanta, Tab, Mr. Pibb, and, in 1975, Diet Coke.

By that time, the Coca-Cola Company had completed the acquisition of the last remaining parent bottler, the Thomas Company. It took it fifty years to complete the consolidation, but the company had at last maneuvered an obsolete rung in its constellation into extinction.

The Push Ahead

By the 1980s, the Coca-Cola Company was on a deliberate march to seize equity stakes in, or outright ownership of, its frontline bottlers. Some consolidation was necessary in a world that had, three-quarters of a century before, planted Coca-Cola bottlers every fifty miles. Eighteen-wheeler trucks had replaced horse-drawn wagons; supermarkets had supplanted corner stores; scale economies had overrun personal connections. Further consolidation was inevitable.

That Coca-Cola spent much of the 1980s buying up small, scattered bottlers is testament to its desire to tip the balance in its constellation. It did not need domestic partners to take its product to market; sales of Coca-Cola were not as dependent on the personal rapport of the bottler and the local retailers as they once were. The prize acquisition came in 1986 when Coca-Cola paid $1.4 billion for JTL Corporation, a large frontline bottler. By 1988, Coca-Cola owned equity in five of the top ten U.S. bottlers, which accounted for 78 percent of nationwide volume.

The company created a holding company structure to manage its new frontline bottling interests. It founded Coca-Cola Enterprises, now the largest bottling business in the world. To keep the debt off its balance sheet, Coca-Cola took a 49 percent stake in the venture and issued the remaining shares in a public auction. The company pursued a near-identical strategy in Canada.

Coca-Cola Enterprises joined a new class of bottler, the "anchor bottler." Coca-Cola later explained in its annual report that it would designate certain bottling operations as an anchor bottler due to their level of responsibility and performance in the network; the company was then likely to invest equity in these bottlers. Anchor bottlers would be strongly committed to Coca-Cola's strategic goals and to expanding the company's worldwide production, distribution, and marketing systems. They tended to be large and geographically diverse and have strong financial and management resources.

Once again, Coca-Cola was creating hierarchy within its constellation. And once again, it continued to buy stakes in frontline bottlers. In 1995, for instance, the company invested $160 million in the Coca-Cola Bottling Company of New York, raising its interest to 49 percent. By 1996, Coca-Cola had substantial equity positions in approximately thirty-two unconsolidated bottling, canning, and distribution operations worldwide, including bottlers representing 43 percent of the total U.S. unit case volume. It was at last in control of its core bottling constellation.

Lessons: Four Elements of Constellation Design

What can the history of the Coca-Cola constellation teach us? Once the contract was amended, the Coca-Cola constellation was poised for explosive growth. By 1920, more than a thousand local bottlers were members of the constellation, many of whom would become millionaires, and Asa Candler would retire the richest man in Georgia and become the mayor of Atlanta. During those two decades, Coca-Cola and its partners achieved growth rates, profitability, and market share that would leave today's most ambitious constellation designers agape. Though savvy marketing and technological breakthroughs played an undeniable role, the success was tied to four design features embedded in the constellation.

Dominant Leader

The Coca-Cola Company has always stood at the center of the network of relationships. It demanded exclusivity from its bottling partners. It retained full control over the product. It designed the packaging, set the advertising agenda, and developed and launched new products.

Defined Roles

Despite the dominance of the Coca-Cola Company, the constellation depended on all three levels of partners (constellation leader, parent bottlers, and frontline bottlers), each of which had a clearly defined role. Coca-Cola controlled the formula; its thriving fountain trade gave a huge boost of public awareness to the burgeoning bottling business. The parent bottlers, despite later claims that they were useless bloodsuckers, played a crucial role in recruiting, coordinating, and training an expanse of local bottlers. And the local bottlers were the link to the customer, distributing the product across the country, and putting it "within an arm's reach of desire," as a later company advertisement would claim.

Constellation Infrastructure

"Coca-Cola, when you come right down to it," an Atlanta city official once remarked, "is just a bunch of cousins tied together by financial arrangements." An exaggeration, but the comment underlines the kin-like behavior of the Coca-Cola partners, forever battling among themselves but always sticking together. But unlike most families, the Coca-Cola network built an infrastructure to manage communications and cooperation.

In 1909, the 397 Coca-Cola bottlers agreed to hold their first annual convention in Atlanta. In the same year, Josiah Willard, a nephew of Asa Candler, launched the *Coca-Coca Bottler*, a magazine for the bottlers and affiliated trades. It was full of profiles and how-to tips for the bottling partners. Then in 1913 the bottlers cre-ated the Coca-Cola Bottlers Association. Its mission was to defend members from a torrent of lawsuits, most by fast-buck freddies claiming to have dug out dangerous substances (for example, poi-son, glass, and frogs) from their bottled Coke. In time, the bottlers association worked outside the courtroom, taking on the role of standard setter. For instance, it commissioned the design of the now famous curvaceous bottle, agreed on common bottler trucks and driver uniforms, and pushed for minimum levels of quality in bot-tler plants.

Self-Organization and Expansion

Many bottlers found the demand for Coca-Cola so strong they divided their territories and assigned rights to a new genus of sub-bottlers who built smaller, more modern plants. Although the Coca-Cola Company and the parent bottlers had an interest in see-ing the constellation spread (and generate more royalties), they had no involvement in searching for, signing on, or managing these new partners. To Asa Candler and the parent bottlers, it may have seemed that the bottling constellation was spinning out of their control. It was. But the freedom to spawn new partners prevented decision making from bogging down and greatly facilitated Coca-Cola's market penetration.

Modern Applications

Are these four design elements applicable to all modern constella-tions? Certainly not. The idea of having clearly defined roles does seem to be applicable in many, if not most, modern constellations. But the other elements are best applied in limited situations. For instance, having a dominant partner is especially well suited to two constellation structures—system integrators (for example, Ford, Boeing) and product marketers (for example, Coca-Cola, Oracle). In both situations, the dominant company develops a product and employs partners to either build components or sell to hard-to-reach markets. Other constellation structures, however, such as shared utilities and research consortia, may be best run more like democracies or independent companies free from the overwhelming influence of any partner (see Chapter Nineteen).

Nor is it always wise to have an extensive and complex constellation infrastructure. Firms must assess the risks associated with partners' sharing technology, pricing information, or complaints against other constellation members. Indeed, many leading alliance practitioners have concluded that pulling partners into multilateral meetings actually weakens the overall constellation structure. For Coca-Cola, three features of its network made infrastructure building safe. One was its ownership of the secret formula and trademark, which prevented the bottlers from encroaching on Coca-Cola's sacred turf. Second were exclusive territorial licenses, which made the bottlers colleagues rather than competitors and promoted open dialogue. Third was the perpetual, fixed-price syrup contract between Coca-Cola and the bottlers, which eliminated an area of emotional negotiation normally associated with such relationships. But these tactics do not always work or are not always possible to implement (see Chapter Twenty-Three).

And what of the idea of relying on self-organization and spontaneous expansion? The prudence of this approach hinges on where the constellation is in its life cycle. Constellations still in formative development stages may be an inappropriate place for such freedom. Early-stage constellations may be better served concentrating efforts on defining the product and business model; turning partners loose to simultaneously recruit new partners is a dangerous distraction. However, constellations focused on marketing may want to consider such liberties.

Further Reading

Jeffrey Bradach. *Franchise Organizations*. Boston: Harvard Business School Press, 1998.

Source

This chapter is based on "Coca-Cola, Classic Constellation" and "Coca-Cola's Wrestle for Control," *The Alliance Analyst* (November and December 1996). The articles were combined, edited, and updated for this book. The historial information of Coca-Cola is drawn from two outstanding books: Frederick Allen, *Secret Formula* (New York: HarperBusiness, 1994); Mark Pendergrast, *For God, Country, and Coca-Cola* (New York: Macmillan, 1993).

22

Network Effects

Visa International

Visa International, the credit card consortium, is one of the most successful alliance constellations ever. Over a period of thirty years, Visa took a business teetering on collapse and transformed it into one of the most successful enterprises in the financial services industry, creating hundreds of billions of dollars in value for its member-owners. The Visa organizational model has also been widely emulated.

An alliance of more than thirty thousand banks, Visa is what we call a *shared utility*. A shared utility is an organization established by multiple firms with the purpose of performing certain common tasks that, if the owners performed alone, would lack the essential scale or scope. Visa performs a number of roles for its members. It manages the Visa brand name, one of the most recognized in the world. It establishes and maintains the processes and standards by which member-banks and other system participants interact with one another. To be sure, Visa is not the only successful shared utility. MasterCard is another example; another would be Sabre in airline reservation systems. (See also Chapter Nineteen.)

The Growth of Visa International

How did Visa International achieve such success? And what lessons does it offer today's constellation designers and managers? To an-

swer these questions, we examine Visa's evolution over three distinct phases of organizational development (Exhibit 22.1).

The Failure of Proprietary Bankcards

Visa International started out as a wholly owned operation inside
Bank of America. In 1958, Bank of America offered its first credit
card, the BankAmericard, with a simple business premise: the bank
would distribute cards through its extensive California retail branch
network to customers who then would use it to make purchases at
accepting retailers. Bank of America would make money by taking 2
percent to 6 percent of sales (depending on volume) from retailers and
a small annual fee from cardholders, plus interest on unpaid balances.

This business model was a slight modification of an idea first
tried at the Flatbush National Bank of Brooklyn. In 1947 Flatbush
National persuaded a network of local retailers in a two-block
radius to accept its card as a form of customer payment. Flatbush
National earned its fees from the retailers, who paid a percentage
of sales to the bank. Consumers were charged nothing, but were
expected to pay their bill within thirty days. Flatbush's business
soon attracted followers.

By 1955 more than a hundred banks had established similar
community credit plans, though most were finding the going rather
difficult, lacking the transaction volume to offset the large fixed
overhead. Eager for another income stream, many banks began to
offer revolving credit on balances carried past thirty days.

Whereas many smaller banks were turning in lackluster perfor-
mances, Bank of America brought some strengths to the credit card
business that few others possessed—brand and reach. Bank of America was the nation's largest bank, an industry icon, and it operated in
California, the nation's most populous and prosperous state. If any
bank possessed the assets to convince a still skeptical public that
credit cards were both safe and useful, it was Bank of America. The
idea was that once its brand name and contacts started to attract
cardholders and merchants the bank would start to benefit from

EXHIBIT 22.1. Three Waves in the Development of Visa, 1958–2002.

Wave 1 Proprietary Bankcard *1958–1965*	*Wave 2 Licensing* *1966–1970*	*Wave 3 Alliance Constellation* *1970–Present*
Cooperation: Nonexistent	*Cooperation: Lopsided*	*Cooperation: Egalitarian*
Bank of America offers its own bankcard, joining the fray among hundreds of banks with proprietary systems.	Bank of America, facing coming competition, begins to license its bankcard.	Licensees buy out Bank of America and establish what will be renamed Visa.
• Local acceptance	• National acceptance	• Nonthreatening national brandname
• High overheads difficult to offset due to low volumes	• Begins to offset overheads with jump in usage volume	• Strict enforcement of alliance structure and risks
• Chicken-and-egg dilemma of signing up cardholders and merchants	• Dramatically increases cardholders through nationwide mass mailing	• Widely distributed profits
• Limited difficulty in coordination since all transactions performed by Bank of America	• Troubles with interfirm coordination	• Continued climb in number of members
	• Growing dissatisfaction among licensees	

network effects. More cardholders would attract more merchants, and more merchants would attract more cardholders. The result would be ever-greater scale and operating efficiency. Between 1958 and 1965, Bank of America (BA) was making progress toward this end. But it was not enough.

Licensing: Creating a Network

Bank of America could have attempted to build a national presence on its own. But it chose not to, preferring instead to license the BankAmericard name to other banks. It took this first step toward a constellation for two reasons. First, BA lacked a convenient way to sign up merchants and customers. In those days, conventional wisdom held that banks should directly market credit cards to their own customers, not through unsolicited mail campaigns to targeted but unknown customers, as is current practice. Yet BA did not have, and indeed was prevented by federal regulation from having, branches outside the state of California. It needed local representatives.

The second reason was time. Word was spreading that Citibank (then known as First National City Bank of New York) wanted to buy Diners Club, a travel and entertainment card. If acquired, Diners Club would give Citibank a national network of its own from which to attack BA. So Bank of America felt it had to act soon.

In response to these pressures, Bank of America signed its first BankAmericard licensee in 1966. As an alliance structure, the agreements were rather hierarchical and one-sided. Bank of America charged each bank a $25,000 entry fee, and forced each to issue a branded BankAmericard—that is, a product emblazoned with a fierce competitor's name. Some in the licensing banks at the time felt that this payment and operating structure made them subservient to Bank of America.

Competing Alliance Constellations

Throughout the late 1960s, BankAmericard tried to survive under such a licensing system. Yet it suffered from two major economic ills. First, it no longer had the market to itself. In 1966 four other California banks formed an alliance and, after linking with several other regional networks, formed Master Charge. Second, and of much graver concern, was the looming financial collapse of the whole credit card industry. Losses—from operations, credit, and fraud—were believed to be in the tens of millions of dollars.

And it was only getting worse. Although Bank of America had been able to process its own credit card transactions, its interchange system had a hard time handling the expanded demands of hundreds of member-banks. There were widespread reports that transaction receipts were regularly lost or kept in bank drawers for weeks before being sent off for processing. At the same time, in an effort to boost the number of cardholders, both the BankAmericard and Master Charge constellations launched aggressive and unsolicited mass mail campaigns. Ready-to-use credit cards were sent out pell-mell, landing in the mailboxes of people who were poor credit risks, or, at best, unlikely users of the cards. Such moves raised public concerns. In the midst of it all, *Life* magazine ran a cover story depicting the credit card industry as Icarus flying toward the sun on wings of plastic, one of which was labeled BankAmericard and the other Master Charge.

With Icarus's wings melting, Bank of America called a meeting of its licensees. While the plan was to discuss operating problems, the meeting quickly ignited a vigorous debate. Dee Hock, then a vice president at the National Bank of Commerce in Seattle, stepped forward to develop a new plan for the organization. Hock soon was huddled with three colleagues in a Sausalito hotel, considering the most fundamental questions about constellation design and structure. There, they sketched the outlines of what would become Visa, a much more democratic constellation structure that was not dominated by Bank of America. Hock and his colleagues created an inside-out holding company owned equally by all the members—a structure that would lead Visa into unprecedented growth.

Bank of America ultimately agreed to the restructuring. The new structure was somewhat unpalatable to bank executives, but the alternative appeared far worse. Without dramatic change, the system was unstable. And that was a dim prospect for Bank of America, the only member of the constellation that was then profiting. The restructuring reduced—but did not eliminate—Bank of America's special status. The BankAmericard name was retained for several years; the bankcard operations continued to be housed in Bank of America's San Francisco headquarters, and Bank of America was awarded five seats on the new organization's board of directors. In time, the card's name was changed to Visa, headquarters were moved down the road, and Bank of America's number of board seats declined to one.

In 1970, with Hock at the helm, the licensees created a new company to oversee the credit card business. Over the next few years, this independent, non-stock corporation purchased the entire bankcard operation from Bank of America and established the mechanisms for hundreds of members to interact and to annually process billions of transactions. Hock thought it was impossible to design an organization to manage and control such complexity, so instead he built a structure that was mostly self-regulating.

Visa emerged as a simple and sustainable constellation model. The new organization was run by a group of directors, deemed to represent the diverse interests of the member-banks. It had a system of fines and other penalties for members that did not abide by the requirements of the system, something Bank of America had earlier found impossible to enforce. And it created a defined and predictable set of rules for its interchange system. At the center, the full-time Visa organization and staff carried out such constellation-wide tasks as developing operating regulations, coordinating interchange between members, developing system innovations, promoting the brand name through advertising, and coordinating other systemwide tasks such as fraud control. With this new structure in place, Visa was poised for rapid growth.

Membership started to mushroom in the 1970s and now includes more than thirty thousand members.

Lessons: The Power and Challenge of the Network

What can modern constellation designers and managers learn from Visa? For one, there is the confidence in using alliances as a long-term, sustainable strategy. And, as it turns out, there is quite a lot more.

Lesson 1: Network Businesses Require Network Organizations

The computer industry, and particularly the rise of the Internet, has spawned a rash of businesses with strategies that revolve around "network effects"—the idea that value to consumers and thus profits to producers increase with the number of users in a market. The fax machine, telephone system, and the Internet itself are prime examples: the more users there are in each system, the more attractive the system becomes to new users, and so the faster the growth of the community of users.

Credit card systems also benefit from such network effects; more users lead to more card acceptance, which leads to more users, and so on. The lesson of Visa is that in such businesses, a single, closed, proprietary strategy rarely works. It was only after Bank of America opened its system to licensees that the model took off. And, later, rivalry between card networks revolved around who could attract more members and offer the most open access.

Lesson 2: Cooperation Is Often a Learned Behavior, Not a "Natural" One

The role of network effects is easy to state with hindsight, but Bank of America initially pursued a proprietary approach and then gradually opened up the business to partners. With competition coming from the rival Master Charge constellation and Citibank's bid to buy Diners Club, plus the need to secure greater scale economies, Bank of America decided to license its card. And only when this licensing system was challenged by members did BA finally let go and allow a more egalitarian constellation structure to form. In other words, regardless of the value of cooperation, it is often not a first choice; companies, especially industry-leading players, will often come to the alliance strategy only after failing at other approaches.

Lesson 3: Good Management Can Loosen the Constraint on Constellation Size

Do alliance constellations have a natural size limit? Many managers and consultants seem to think so. A senior executive at Ameritech told the *Wall Street Journal* that "seven partners was just too many" and decided not to combine its four-member cable television joint venture with a similar three-member alliance. Likewise, the computer consortium of Mips Computer Systems fell apart when its membership edged over a hundred firms.

Yet Visa is made up of more than thirty thousand partners. How did the credit card consortium achieve such size where other constellations have not? The answer comes down to constellation strategy and structure. Visa is a shared utility: its member-owners created the venture to perform a few distinct business tasks. At the same time, the members had standard demands placed on them and were entitled to similar benefits. In short, these traits reduce the overall coordination demands and allow the constellation to add new members with limited marginal costs.

Lesson 4: Rivalry Pits Constellation Against Constellation

Banks were the first to apply the Visa constellation model to other businesses. For example, the automated teller machine (ATM) business followed a similar evolutionary path to that of the credit card:

from proprietary systems to regional networks to national and international constellations. This cooperation was in fact part of industry tradition, as banks had to work with each other to clear checks.

The unnamed driver behind the growth of this and other constellations is rivalry. In the credit card industry, the rivalry between Visa and MasterCard drove both organizations to grow and open their systems more and more. In airlines, alliance constellations formed and broke in fits and starts until the Star and oneworld constellations began a tit-for-tat growth process that threatened to stretch each to grow beyond its management capabilities. In the computer industry, Microsoft and Intel were successful in both opening their systems to rival PC makers and simultaneously maintaining a strong grip on the proprietary elements they make. Later, another threat to Microsoft's grip would come from systems that offered users more openness, such as the Linux operating system and Internet-based applications.

Even New Economy constellations thus have something to learn from a pioneer such as Visa International. Visa's financial network depended on the same kind of network economies as did technology businesses in the Internet era. The more members in the network, the more attractive it would be to become a member, and so the more members would join. As a result, leading companies in such businesses depended on help from a constellation of allies to grow and create value. But just recognizing this strategic logic is not enough; Visa International stands out as an industry leader because it was able to organize its constellation to exploit this logic.

Further Reading

Dee Hock. *Birth of the Chaordic Age*. San Francisco: Berrett-Koehler, 1999.

Lewis Mandell. *The Credit Card Industry: A History*. Boston: Twayne, 1990.

Joseph Nocera. *A Piece of the Action: How the Middle Class Joined the Money Class*. New York: Simon & Schuster, 1994.

Source

This chapter is based on "The Chase of Visa" and "Visa's Lessons," *The Alliance Analyst* (September 1995). The articles were combined, edited, and updated for this book.

23

From Local to Global

Colliers International

Professional service firms traditionally have been local businesses, whether in law, real estate, financial advice, or advertising. The reason: success depended on close personal relationships with customers and an intimate understanding of local markets. As a rule, the further a professional service firm wandered from its local market, the more elusive success proved to be.

But in the 1990s all this changed. As customers expanded overseas, professional service firms came under intense pressure to follow them. Firms like Grubb & Ellis in real estate, WPP in advertising, and Clifford Chance in law started to transform themselves into global enterprises. Many did so through acquisitions—purchasing existing local players and assembling them under a global corporate umbrella. Compared to internal growth, acquisitions offered a number of advantages: they were faster to do and, because the purchased firms were proven local businesses, they tended to produce a stronger indigenous flavor.

Alliances were another option. In professional services, alliance-based globalization often meant building a constellation—a network of perhaps ten to fifty local firms. In some cases, these constellations were no more than simple referral networks, loose affiliations where members merely referred business to one another, making no attempt to integrate assets or business processes. In other cases, these constellations enabled deeper bonds, encouraging member-firms to combine assets and capabilities in a manner that allowed them to reduce costs, gain new skills, and provide a seamless global service to customers.

One prominent example of this model was Colliers International, a global constellation in the commercial real estate business. In this chapter, we examine the Colliers strategy and organization in about 1995, a time when its members were struggling to deepen their cooperation. Since then, Colliers has changed substantially and in ways not covered here; even so, the historical case contains enduring lessons about the promise—and the pain—of launching a global constellation in professional services.

Colliers Strategy, Structure, and Philosophy in the 1990s

Colliers International was formed in 1985, the result of a merger between two smaller real estate networks, each of which had existed for a decade or so. As of 1995, Colliers contained forty-five member-firms operating in more than 180 offices around the world with combined annual revenue of $450 million. Its first CEO and the driver behind its early growth was Stewart Forbes, a real estate industry veteran and long-time friend of many of the member-firm owners. Although Colliers was an alliance between separate companies, its headquarters in Boston commanded resources with which to help orchestrate cooperation between the partners.

By the mid-1990s, the Colliers headquarters maintained an eleven-person staff, including an operations manager, an information systems manager, and a research department. To pay for this overhead, the member-firms contributed annual dues of between $10,000 and $40,000 (depending on firm size) plus 5 percent of referral-generated commissions.

Two committees governed the Colliers global constellation: the U.S. Executive Committee and the International Council, both of which Forbes chaired. In the United States, the twenty-eight member-firms each held one seat on the committee. The role of the committee was to evaluate prospective members, conduct periodic recertification of existing members, and, on rare occasions, expel members that were not performing to the constellation's standards. "We were all carrots and no sticks," Forbes explained. Through cajoling and convincing, Forbes could influence the direction of the network—notably the pace and path of its growth.

The Colliers alliance philosophy emerged gradually, but by the mid-1990s was characterized by three tenets: voluntary cooperation, exclusivity, and selective membership. In each area, Colliers faced challenges. Its success in implementing the philosophy was often constrained by the tradition of local self-reliance of its members.

Encourage Cooperation, Don't Legislate It

The Colliers of the 1990s did not tell its members what to do or when to work together. For example, if the Colliers member-firm in New York had a client looking to lease a factory in North Carolina, it could refer the business to the existing Colliers member in Charlotte. It could work in tandem with that member. But it did not have to do either. The network imposed no demand that members work with one another. "However," added Forbes, "that broker had to inform headquarters and had to inform that Charlotte agent. We did this for quality control, and to ensure that the Colliers firm being skipped over was not lacking needed capabilities. If the member was found lacking, we would either address these shortcomings or reconsider their membership."

Demand Exclusivity as Much as Possible

The one area in which Colliers was more insistent was in membership exclusivity. Member-firms were expected to not join competing industry alliance constellations such as Encore. "We gave our members an exclusive and we expected them to give us one in return," explained Forbes. "We didn't have any written rule on this, but in my gut I just didn't think you can have two wives." In the early days of Colliers—when the alliance was less confident—it allowed one particular member to join another network. After a few years of conflicting loyalties, Forbes finally asked the owner to choose a single affiliation. Forbes explained: "I wasn't asking members to keep all of their options open," he noted. "I was saying, 'Close some of your options and help build this organization.'"

Such exclusivity was reflected in the territorial divisions within the Colliers constellation. From the beginning, there was an overarching belief that there should be only one Colliers firm in a given market. In all but one case, markets were defined by country. So, for example, Colliers Erdman Lewis was the sole U.K. member-firm, and Colliers Jardine was the exclusive Hong Kong representative. In the United States, where the depth and breadth of the market did not allow for a single national player, informal boundary lines were drawn around regions and cities.

Yet avoiding conflict and potential overlap was not simple. Consider a situation the group faced in 1995. The Colliers member-firm in Cincinnati had decided to merge with a Columbus-based firm that had operations in Indianapolis, a city where Colliers already had a member-firm. While Forbes wanted to encourage the growth of members and was not prepared to block the merger, he would not allow the new Indianapolis affiliate to fly the Colliers flag. And he did not believe the firm's office in Columbus—where there was no Colliers member—should be allowed to fly the Colliers flag either. He explained his thinking in these terms: "We did not want to recognize Columbus as a Colliers city. It was a little hard for their Indianapolis affiliate to come to a Colliers meeting and share its operating details and discuss strategies when one of the people sitting there was a direct competitor of theirs in their own market."

Add New Members Selectively

A final tenet of the Colliers philosophy in the 1990s was methodical expansion. "I didn't think we were losing any business because we were too small," Forbes observed. "The real danger lay in bringing in members too fast and not paying attention to creating real links between the members."

But Colliers did need to expand its footprint and become a truly global constellation. Rather than adding new members, Forbes favored the expansion of existing members into bordering markets. This had happened in Asia and Europe. Hong Kong member-firm Colliers Jardine, for instance, expanded on its own across Asia. Colliers Erdman Lewis and Colliers Auguste-Thouard, the constellation's British and French member-firms, were leading the charge into new European markets. Colliers did not always subscribe to such an expansion strategy. "In 1990 we thought we could link ourselves to existing firms in the smaller markets—more of a boutique approach," Forbes said. "But we found that the relationships were too many to manage."

Strategies for Deepening Cooperation

Forbes had long envisioned Colliers as an alliance network with deep connections between the member-firms—connections that meant more than sharing corporate letterheads. Forbes wanted members to share know-how, create expertise that none could develop alone, and, in the process, create substantial competitive advantage for all the members. But the deeper cooperation, which depended on new technology and new organizational structures, was not easy to engineer.

For many years, Forbes's calls for knowledge sharing and communication technology did not resonate with real estate brokers, a group that tended to focus on the short-run demands of doing deals. The brokers who ran the member-firms in the early days wanted two simple things from the alliance: to be able to tell a client that they were part of a global network and to recoup their $10,000–$40,000 annual Colliers membership fee though commissions generated by network referrals. But in the early 1990s, this started to change as the Colliers member-firm owners saw tangible benefits in their global alliance. The head of marketing at one member-firm recalled what happened at the 1993 Colliers annual sales meeting: "It was a watershed. Up until that point, the Colliers firms had been saying, 'Leave us alone. Our business is really local. Yes, we are members of Colliers, but don't call us, we'll call you.' Then whammo! Stewart must have felt like he walked into a barn and stepped on the wrong end of a rake. All of a sudden member-firms were saying, 'We want leadership. We want coordinated programs. We want more unity. We want a whole laundry list.'"

What caused the shift? Increased comfort with technology was one explanation. A second explanation was the realization that the role of the real estate broker was changing from being a simple deal-maker to more of a consultant, similar in many ways to Britain's chartered surveyor. This higher-value-added role brought new competition. Now, not only were other real estate firms trying to lift their profile and skills, but other professionals—notably investment bankers, accountants, and management consultants who already had the ear of top-level corporate decision makers—were edging over to advise on real estate strategy. Colliers brokers believed that if they were going to outcompete these other players, it would be by leveraging the full know-how and power of the Colliers alliance.

In response to these demands for deeper cooperation, Forbes began to rethink the communications lines and structure of the Colliers constellation. Because he had so few resources at his direct disposal, he faced a challenge in convincing member-firms, and in particular the individual brokers, to devote their own time and money to the joint efforts. To do so, Forbes battled to build and nurture three new communication vehicles: Colliers managers, peer groups, and an electronic community. These were at the core of his new vision of Colliers as an information federation.

Colliers Managers

Since the network's earliest days, member-firms designated a Colliers representative to act as the link between the firm and the network. In the early to mid-1990s, Forbes and the owners took steps to tighten this connection.

First, individual owners were blocked from serving as Colliers alliance managers, as was originally the common practice. Forbes explained: "There had to be an advocate for the Colliers business within the firm—someone who stood up at a sales meeting, pitched the cause, and distributed Colliers news and information. Someone needed to explain what was going on, and to listen to those people that had a problem with the organization or who saw an opportunity we ought to exploit. Our previous experience had shown that an owner or a company sales manager inevitably had other priorities—not necessarily conflicting priorities, but other priorities—that tended to make Colliers tenth on their 'To Do' list."

Second, office managers were to be compensated for their work. Again, this was something that did not often happen through the 1980s and was still not universal as of 1995. "It may have taken just a few hours per week to fill out the surveys and answer requests, but to someone who was commission-orientated, this represented a significant opportunity cost," Forbes said. Not all the brokers and Colliers managers saw it that way, however. Many saw the chance to talk to other brokers and clients as a way to generate contacts and develop their own business.

Third, member-firms were asked to designate a Colliers administrator within each office. "It may have been the information-systems manager, or someone's secretary, or maybe someone in accounting; but someone had to input all the information that the Colliers network needed," explained one Colliers executive.

Fourth, to ensure continuity, Colliers recommended that office managers and administrators keep their posts for a minimum of three years. While executives at headquarters were pleased with the progress of the role of the Colliers manager, they were not fully satisfied. One explained: "We created this Colliers manager position, but it was a mixed bag. We had someone to pass paper through but they did not have enough weight in their firm to tell people what to do. We decided we needed someone who could fly around and communicate the benefits of Colliers, someone to rev the troops up and go on sales calls to really show people how to pitch the benefits of the network. We essentially needed someone to coordinate all the Colliers office managers. Someone who could walk their walk, and talk their talk."

Responding to these shortcomings, Forbes promoted an enterprising marketing manager from one of the member-firms to become national coordinator. The new Colliers executive later described his role as follows:

I went around and visited all the local firms and told them about the resources of the Colliers network. I explained this to the owners, to the Colliers manager, and to the brokers. I went on client calls and showed the local brokers how to pitch the benefits of Colliers to the client.

What I was really doing was trying to transfer the confidence that I had in the entire organization to the local manager. Real estate is such a local business that I would say 20 to 25 percent of our best firms' business was outside their local market. So the typical local broker was hesitant to ask a client something like, "How can I help you in Singapore?" for fear that the answer might be "You can help me by doing a property valuation for me in Singapore."

The local brokers didn't ask the question because they did not have the same confidence in their ability to deliver abroad as they did in their backyard. The best job I could do was to transfer my confidence in the organization to the local manager.

Peer Groups

Peer groups also deepened the connections within the Colliers network. In the early 1990s, a dozen or so property managers independently formed a roundtable to discuss issues facing their corner of the real estate business. Forbes saw some lessons: "A dozen people is, roughly, the size of group which breeds intimacy. The lessons to me was to stick with your peers—you have got to work off a tight group who see each other as equals who can help build each other's businesses."

Soon there was a movement afoot to create other similar round-tables; a like-sized group of investment sales specialists began to meet, and Forbes started to incubate a group of retail leasing brokers. At the International Council of Shopping Centers, a large convention of real estate developers and retailers, Forbes organized a gathering of Colliers brokers in attendance, and started to explore ways to turn them into an ongoing peer group.

Success of these peer groups hinged on support. The investment sales group went dormant for eight months because, according to Forbes, "the brokers didn't have the time to handle the group administration, coordinate the next gathering, or articulate the upcoming agenda." Soon thereafter, the Colliers head office agreed to handle the backroom duties.

Another issue with the potential to be divisive was rules for admittance into these peer groups. Forbes insisted the number remain small and participants be equals. He explained:

We were not saying, "Okay, anyone interested in investment sales sign up here." Within Colliers, there was a huge divergence of talent. I believed it was best to start with a couple of people who were strong in their field and who viewed themselves as equals and then Colliers could help find other similarly qualified people. Making additions to that group had to be selective.

But there was a limit to how much you could keep people away who were beating on the door. My approach was that I wanted to see something work first, and once we got it working, we might regionalize it, we might fragment it in various ways, or we might form a totally new group in the same function area.

Electronic Community

Forbes's last frontier was cyberspace: "What I was really trying to do was to create an electronic sales meeting," he later said. His ideal was to put a laptop in the hands of every Colliers broker and plug them into an open electronic community for queries and discussions. He wanted to support this electronic community with a database of case histories, lessons learned, profiles of member-firm skills, and client and transaction details.

This vision took shape slowly; it was tough going. Member-firms in developed markets like Britain, Japan, and the United States were connected to e-mail. But the technology was slower to reach most emerging market offices, which still had to rely on the phone or the fax to access the Colliers system. It was also slow to reach the individual broker. E-mail connected Colliers offices but not individuals, leading to a situation where queries from other member-firms came into one main computer. The process was for the Colliers office manager to read the e-mail and then decide whether to have someone in the office answer the question.

Then there was the database. From its inception in the mid-1980s, Colliers had maintained an ongoing record of member-firm deals: the client, the property, the terms, and the broker. The database also included a profile of member-firms, their key corporate relationships, and their skill levels. This information often proved critical to a broker's search for someone in the Colliers network with past experience or connections relevant to a current transaction or sales pitch. In the early days, the database was accessed by a phone call to the Colliers network office in Boston, where staff then conducted a search. In the late 1980s, Colliers made the database accessible online through CompuServe. A few years later it supplemented the online access by sending the database out on disk to each Colliers office.

The approach had several problems. First, brokers remained uncomfortable with an online database, the result of generally low levels of technological expertise. Second, the disks contained out-dated information; limited resources prevented Colliers from sending out the disks more than once a year. The first two problems caused a third: lack of comprehensiveness. One Colliers executive explained: "It was garbage in, garbage out. No one reported everything, not even close. Firms were very selective. They didn't make it a priority to enter or give us this information. I figured that if every firm had reported every transaction in 1994 we would have had 100,000 new entries. We had a fraction of that for a ten-year period."

To overcome some of these problems, Colliers hired a case-writer to develop one-page descriptions of key transactions. By the summer of 1995, for example, 230 Colliers cases were available on the database; but these cases were more descriptive than analytical. The Colliers team at headquarters then decided to redirect the effort toward "value statements"—detailed case studies that focused on an innovative approach that a member-firm had taken and on the value delivered to the client. One Colliers executive explained:

> The real estate industry works a little bit like stock brokerage. A firm might take out a tombstone ad after it took Boston Chicken public, saying, we sold five million shares for the undersigned. Well, the real estate industry ads would say that we leased a million square feet and made a million dollars for the client. That's what our case studies are like.
>
> But what did that really tell the client? Nothing, if you ask me. What we were trying to do to distinguish ourselves in the marketplace was to explain our services from a client's perspective, answering the questions they cared about. Did we save them money? Did we increase the value of the property? Did we increase their operating efficiencies? Did we put their employees under one roof and make them more productive? Our value statements tried to do this.

The trick was getting the Colliers brokers to believe there was value in the more detailed case studies. According to one Colliers manager this was not easy: "We were trying to get the brokers to shift their thinking, but it was difficult. We were dragging them kicking and screaming—it was just alien to their nature."

Lessons: Pacing the Growth of a Constellation

Colliers in 1995 was a work in progress—a global constellation producing benefits for its members but also falling short of its CEO's vision. Yet there are lessons that can be drawn from this history.

Lesson 1: Don't Assume That Deeper Cooperation Is Always Better

In many constellations, firms may be able to create more benefits with less cost and more flexibility through less, not more, integration. In service industries like law, medicine, and banking, relationships develop informally over time and produce tremendous gains. A lawyer in Charlotte may get to know someone in Memphis and start to send business their way. The lawyers develop greater trust as more business is passed back and forth. But these referrals don't have to be formalized through a formal alliance with overhead costs and national dues.

To be sure, sometimes deeper cooperation is preferred—and more elaborate structures are needed. When an alliance aims to be more than a marketing tool or referral mechanism, for instance, then the partners should consider integrating assets, formalizing the relationship, and investing in alliance-specific staff and resources. Colliers created many of these elements of integration—but did not fully explain the reason for the deeper integration. Too many constellation designers suffer from a *Field of Dreams* syndrome: "Build it and they will come." Success depends on identifying, targeting, and explaining the benefits of cooperation to all members.

Lesson 2: Create an Integration Road Map

In situations where deeper integration is needed, firms should develop a road map to make it happen. In the very least, this means isolating a few spots where cooperation will produce quick and clear benefits, and putting resources behind these.

Even better, firms should develop a more formal process, developing a road map for cooperation that develops capabilities that build on each other. John Harbison, an alliance expert with Booz-Allen & Hamilton during the 1990s, recommended that firms think in five levels, from shallow to deep integration. For Colliers, Level One could be for brokers to record standard transaction details: price per square foot, lease term, and so on. This information could provide clients with all sorts of information about the local market. Level Two could involve using that same format across geographies. This way, the partners could start to share trends across offices; once that process starts to show benefits they will begin to make simple referrals. Level Three might be to create some cross-regional service like cost of office property figures that could really distinguish Colliers in the market. Levels Four and Five would take the cooperation deeper. The point, according to Harbison, was to develop a road map for deepening the cooperation, and then to create new capabilities and momentum as you go.

Lesson 3: Tap into Partners' Areas of Expertise

Global constellations often have tremendous variance in member-firm skills. The best constellations will find a way to leverage these differences. Harvard Business School professor Michael Porter published a well-known framework in 1990 that explained differences in competitive advantage between nations. Porter argued that nations developed an advantage based on their local environment and the competitive pressures within that. As a result of this, countries became good at a few things—the Swedes were good at trucks and furniture; the Japanese at electronics and miniaturization, and so on.

The same thing happens in global alliance constellations. Within the Colliers alliance, different members—because of individual location and industry mix—became good at certain types of transactions and clients. The Bostonians might be skilled in serving law firms and financial service firms, while the member-firm in Detroit probably had deep expertise in understanding the requirements of large manufacturing companies. The local market dictated these specialties. Successful constellations work to transfer such skills across the network.

Lesson 4: Experiment with Innovative Structures

No one ever said that constellations—no matter how deep—must operate under one multilateral structure. Large networks may be well served to supplement the multilateral agreement with separate bilateral deals. Take trade agreements among national governments as an example. Major global agreements under the auspices of the United Nations or the World Trade Organization are multilateral—they inch along at a snail's pace, often settling for solutions that represent the lowest common denominator among members. But there are also regional trade agreements that are signed by only two or a subset of like-minded countries. This group within the constellation decides to bind itself a little more tightly on some topic like, say, agricultural subsidies. Not all corporate constellations will benefit from this approach, but firms should look at innovative structures to speed decisions and create partner value.

Conclusion

In sum, alliance constellations may promise to bring a wider market reach and broader expertise to independent firms that otherwise would be fragmented along geographic or functional lines. With such enhanced capabilities, these networks may compete more effectively against larger multinational players. But getting such a network of independent firms to coalesce around a common strategy and mode of operation is not trivial. Often, the leadership of the global organization has to battle against the entrenched local interests of its members. Once the local firms see the value of the global network, however, they will be more interested in participating actively.

Further Reading

Yair Aharoni, ed. *Coalitions and Competition: The Globalization of Professional Business Services*. New York: Routledge, 1993.

Peter Hwang and Willem P. Bergers. "The Many Faces of Multi-Firm Alliances: Lessons for Managers," *California Management Review*, Spring 1997, pp. 101–117.

Nitin Nohria and others. "Colliers International Property Consultants, Inc.: Managing a Virtual Organization." Harvard Business School Case, No. 396–080.

Source

This chapter is based on "Colliers: Background, Structure, and Three Rules to Live By," "Service Networks: Hearing the Hoofbeat of History," and "Three Perspectives on Colliers," *The Alliance Analyst* (May and June 1995). The articles were combined, edited, and updated for this book.

24

Leading Wagon Trains

Western Wisdom

Independence is an ironic name for a town that was the launching point of unprecedented acts of cooperation. A century and a half ago, Independence, Missouri, was the beginning of the Santa Fe Trail, the California Trail, and the Oregon Trail, the routes that opened the American West during the period 1820–1860. Americans who had come to Independence from the East Coast more or less alone, and who had never before seen one another, banded together here to overcome the grave danger of the trek to the West Coast.

Yet collaboration did not come easily. Traveling with a party of more than 160, Lansford Hastings recorded his impressions of how, as his wagon train rolled out of Independence, his earlier vision of cooperation met with the reality of the task: "The harmony of feeling, the sameness of purpose, and the identity of interest seemed to indicate nothing but continued order, harmony and peace, amid all the trying scenes incident to our long and toilsome journey. But we had proceeded only a few days travel when the 'American character' was fully exhibited. All appeared to be determined to govern, but not to be governed. Here we were, without law, without order, and without restraint; in a state of nature, amid the confused, revolving fragments of elementary society."

In many ways, modern business left Independence in the last decades of the twentieth century. After a century of striking out alone, many companies came to a spot where solo travel became inadvisable. It was not the fear of Indian attack, sick oxen, or shattered wagon wheels that drove them together. Instead, today's business pioneers were joining to combat the rising cost of technology, the shortening lives of products, and the convergence of skills and markets with which they were vastly unacquainted.

Fortunately, earlier expeditions left us their wisdom in *The Prairie Traveler: A Hand-book for Overland Expeditions*, by Randolph Marcy. A U.S. Army captain, Marcy put pen to paper in 1859, assembling "those minor details of prairie-craft which, however apparently unimportant in the abstract, are sure, upon the plains, to turn the balance of success for or against an enterprise." A copy of his manual should belong dog-eared and riffled-through in the breast pocket of every alliance manager. Here we review the wagon train wisdom that is still valuable in a different time and place.

Reasons to Join a Collective

> The advantages of an association . . . are manifestly numerous. It is the only way to resist depredations of the Indians, and to prevent their stampeding and driving off of animals.

By combining forces, Marcy wrote, prairie travelers not only stood effective watch against adjacent danger, they also attained significant new efficiencies. To those coming from the East, Marcy recommended waiting until Independence to purchase mules and oxen, then bidding as a group to gain better prices. And once on the trail, a group of pioneers could cross rivers, repair impassable roads, and efficiently hunt for buffalo and other game—acts unimaginable to the lone traveler.

Association, then, had its clear benefits. But for Marcy, that realization was not enough: there was a right way and a wrong way to go about it and, fortunately, he was happy to spell it all out.

Optimal Size of the Party

The company should be of sufficient magnitude to herd and guard animals, and for the protection against Indians.

Marcy thought fifty to seventy men, properly armed and equipped, would suffice. Any more only made a party's movement cumbersome and tardy. Any fewer would prevent a proper circling of wagons, and would stretch the men too thin to have a meaningful front and rear guard.

Undersized wagon trains often hitched themselves to other groups, effectively forming a network of wagon trains. These groups stuck together through the prairie's toughest stretches and, once the acute danger had passed, or the novelty of massive collaboration wore off, they splintered. Such was the experience of James Pritchard. Out on the prairie, Pritchard and his seven men came across Captain Fash and his party of seventeen wagons and sixty men. "We temporarily attached ourselves to his train until we could make further arrangements," Pritchard wrote in his diary. Within a week, however, the disadvantages of a large alliance were starting to sting. Deciding the progress was too slow and, after convincing a few wagons from Fash's own party to join them, they sped off ahead to test the dangers of the prairie in a more nimble enterprise.

Alliance Leadership

After a particular route has been selected to make the journey across the plains, and the requisite number have arrived at the eastern terminus, their first business should be to elect a commander.

A clearly defined leader was critical to successful prairie crossing. That leader made such day-to-day decisions as how to cross a stream or where to camp for the night, thereby avoiding wagon-train–wide committees to handle routine matters. Commanders were generally chosen by democratic vote, and it was tempting for naive members of the company to assume that a buckskin-clad trapper or expert marksman would be a good man at their helm.

In fact, the best wagon train commanders (like alliance managers) were great organizers of people. They ran a transient community without set social rank—and without significant resources at their direct command. Wagon train commanders had to inspire, cajole, stomp, and browbeat others into action as they stormed across the unfamiliar landscape.

The Need for a Collective Agreement

> Unless a systematic organization be adopted it is impossible for a party of any magnitude to travel in company for any great length of time, and for all the members to agree upon the same arrangements in marching, camping, etc. . . .
>
> An obligation should be drawn up and signed by all the members of the association . . . [obligating] themselves to aid each other, so as to make the individual interest of each member the common concern of the whole company.

Marcy offered specific advice for drafting such a document. He suggested the company create a separate pool of funds to purchase oxen, mules, and food. These collective assets would be distributed as members ran into unexpected happenstance. In the event that a wagon had to be abandoned, a company's code should require each member to shed belongings to make room for the luggage of their disabled colleague.

The document should also be short and pointed: covering perhaps no more than four or five pages. Brevity made the message more powerful, and encouraged all to know the rules. It was not a legal treatise, and was almost never written by a lawyer. The American pioneer knew that it was not laws but understanding and trust that would guarantee safe passage.

The company's code usually designated certain leadership positions such as captain, assistant captain, treasurer, and secretary. Each post was accompanied by a defined set of responsibilities and terms (say twenty or thirty days for the captain, and three or four months for a treasurer). Prairie travelers were great bootstrappers of governance—not waiting for some rules of community to come limping across from Washington.

Planning and Budgets

> The allowance of provisions for each grown person, to make the journey from the Missouri River to California, should suffice 110 days.

A prairie traveler had to know not just the requisite food to bring, but also the amount of water, clothing, bedding, and, of course, arms. (Marcy was a big fan of revolvers and breech-loading rifles, and suggested each man carry one of each through Indian country.) Travelers needed a clear resource budget—from 150 pounds of flour all the way down to four pairs of socks and a bit of beeswax. Overloading was a real danger, as Marcy recollects:

"I once traveled with a party of New Yorkers en route to California. They were perfectly ignorant of everything relating to this kind of campaigning, and had overloaded their wagons with almost everything except the very articles most important and necessary; the consequence was, that they exhausted their teams, and were obliged to throw away the greater part of their loading. They soon learned that champagne, East India sweetmeats, olives, etc, etc, were not the most useful articles for a prairie tour."

Poor up-front planning left many pioneers dead on the prairie—starved, frozen, or, more likely, unable to recover from minor sickness or injury. Though not always fatal, poor planning was always inefficient. If supplies were available at outposts such as Fort Dodge or Council Grove, the desperate traveler was almost sure to face exorbitant prices.

Advice of Consultants

Bear in mind that there are several different routes which may be traveled with wagons, each having its advocates in persons directly or interested in attracting the tide of emigration or travel over them.

Unfamiliar with the process of putting together wagon trains and with the best route to take to the Pacific, pioneers often fell victim to the whim and bias of those claiming deep experience. While many such consultants *did* know better, the uninitiated pioneer was best served by taking the counsel of many and, above all, sticking to the established trails.

Some listened to the wrong adviser—and paid the price. The Donner Party listened in 1846 to a man whose counsel proved monstrously inadequate. The Donners were a little concerned that they were getting a late start to the season, thus pushing perilously close to winter. Their guide suggested that the Donners leave the well-trodden trails and take a shortcut through the Rockies. And it was in the Sierra Nevada, in what is now known as the Donner Pass, that a blizzard paralyzed the ill-advised party, leaving it to engage in one of history's best-known episodes of cannibalism.

Yet Marcy spoke highly of local people who could help guide the traveler:

> It is highly important that parties making expeditions through unexplored country should secure the services of the best guides and hunters, and I know of none who are superior to the Delawares and Shawnee Indians.

Manage Expectations

On such a journey as this, there is much to interest and amuse one who is fond of picturesque scenery and wildlife in its utmost primitive aspect, yet no one should attempt it without anticipating many rough knocks and much hard work.

Despite the growing number of Americans who had made the jour-ney west by the 1840s and 1850s, many still romanticized the vision. From their homes in Virginia or Massachusetts they could rarely grasp the discomfort of a wagon without springs, the heat of the Kansas sun, or the bite of the Texas wind.

It was also common for pioneers to perceive their prairie-cross-ing alliance as a permanent community. It was not. Over the forty years of heaviest overland travel, virtually no wagon train stayed together after reaching its destination. Of the 124 companies that left Massachusetts in 1849, for instance, not one held together upon reaching the West Coast. These communities were created for one purpose: to travel a dangerous stretch of land. As they neared the Pacific, that bond began to unravel. And as it did, the prairie trav-elers were at last safe to chase their independent dreams.

Further Reading

Randolph B. Marcy. *The Prairie Traveler: A Hand-book for Overland Ex-peditions*. Published by U.S. War Department, 1859. Full text avail-able on the Web, at University of Kansas online collection of books (http://www.ukans.edu/carrie/kancoll/books/marcy/). Access date: April 2002.

Source

This chapter is based on "The Prairie Traveler," *The Alliance Analyst* (Feb-ruary 1996). The article was edited for this book.

PART FOUR

Building an Alliance Capability

Sustaining the Effort

25

Growth of Alliance Capabilities

James D. Bamford, David Ernst

In the 1980s and early 1990s, when the popularity of alliances began to rise, alliance practitioners were a lot like gentlemen Brits running the middle distance. The approach to success was decidedly unsystematic: training little, eating all wrong, drinking champagne one night, and winning the Olympic mile the following noontime. All talent. No regimen. Quite civilized. Then the entire world started to take the competition so very seriously. Winners were increasingly backed by countries with powerful sporting machineries: training centers, coaches, and ever more scientific methods of monitoring and enhancing performance. And that lithe, talented Brit started having a difficult go of it.

The same has happened in the alliance race. Today, the firms with the best internal alliance infrastructures are more likely to be standing among the winners. When *Forbes* magazine issued its first ranking of the forty most "magnetic" companies in the world in Spring 2001, many of the top firms had strong internal alliance capabilities—tools, systems, staff, and organizational structures that institutionalized alliance excellence and filled key management gaps. What should these alliance resources look like, and how should they be matched to a firm's business and strategy? Without clear answers, modern alliance practitioners will quickly fall behind in a race that is becoming more critical and complex by the day.

Rising Importance and Complexity

Until not too long ago, the typical global firm had to concern itself with just a few alliances that represented a small portion of its total value. And even these alliances often had similar objectives and structures. Fujitsu's major alliances were equity stakes in two Western computer companies, Amdahl and ICL. Colgate-Palmolive used alliances to gain local positions on its way to selling soap, shampoo, toothpaste, and other consumer products in emerging markets. And oil companies used joint ventures to enter new geographies and share exploration risk.

But such simplicity is fast disappearing. For many firms, alliances account for more than 20 percent of corporate value, whether measured as percent of assets, revenues, income, or market capitalization. Several oil majors had more than 25 percent of their assets in joint ventures by the late 1990s. Computer software maker Siebel Systems claims that more than half of its 2001 revenues were attained in association with alliance partners, and sees alliances as a central component of its business model in the future.

Most companies also have many more alliances than before, with many having fifty alliances or more. Public reports indicate that BP Amoco, Dow Chemical, Hearst, Johnson & Johnson, and Sony had more than a hundred alliances in their corporate portfolios by 2001. The most prolific alliance users had more than four hundred relationships. And the phenomenon is not limited to industry giants; many Internet start-ups created business models that depended on large numbers of alliances from the earliest stages of growth.

The complexity of alliances is also rising. Increasingly, alliances involve competitors or multiple partners, or stretch well beyond conventional industry boundaries. Alliances are also taking on all sorts of new structural variations—from nonexclusive product co-branding to joint ventures used as viable alternatives to outright divestitures. These changes demand that managers think about alliances in an entirely new strategic context. In the last few years, many traditional banks, logistics companies, and consumer goods manufacturers have entered into alliances with small and entrepreneurial firms to access new skills and markets. Likewise in the oil business, many majors have used alliances with technology and service companies to compete effectively in the exploration business. For instance, alliances have allowed firms to gain skills and share risk to explore highly challenging areas such as the deepwater Gulf of Mexico.

As companies' portfolios have grown in size, value, and complexity, managers are confronting a new set of challenges and opportunities. Rather than focusing attention and resources solely at the individual alliance level and managing each venture separately, there is now both the chance and the need to build corporation-wide alliance capabilities. In the most experienced firms, these capabilities may include a streamlined corporate alliance unit, an alliance mapping system, a deep and extensive database, and various tools, systems, and dedicated staff.

Internal alliance capabilities such as these have the potential to create substantial value and fundamentally alter the firm's alliance performance. Corporate alliance resources can help managers tap into the accumulated wisdom of peers and predecessors, and so improve overall alliance success. They can promote a more cohesive corporate alliance strategy, as well as increase the speed and effectiveness of alliance formation. And they can help prevent portfolio conflicts, whether between different alliances or between alliances and internal units.

Perhaps the most important benefit of an internal alliance capability is the potential to improve the management of alliances. One McKinsey study found that 50 percent of alliance failures resulted from poor management—the process of governing and operating existing alliances. Thus building an alliance capability has the potential to formalize alliance management processes, create valuable tools and communities for alliance managers, and transform alliance management from an art into something approaching a science.

Advanced Alliance Infrastructures

What are the key elements in the emerging alliance infrastructures of advanced firms? To answer this question, we investigated the experience of more than thirty companies through interviews and a roundtable meeting. We found that a number of corporate alliance resources were common to many advanced companies. These resources fall under four headings: staff, tools, organization, and systems, as shown in Exhibit 25.1.

Staff

Many companies appoint a chief alliance officer to oversee alliances and help build and maintain the corporate alliance infrastructure. In addition to the chief alliance officer (often a VP-level role), leading firms often dedicate other staff to help manage the alliance portfolio. A number of leading high-tech companies have created the position of alliance director: a role generally focused on coordinating the most important and complex corporate relationships. At one U.S. computer hardware company, alliance directors oversaw relationships with the firm's most important software, hardware, and system integrator partners—relationships that often contained more than ten separate operating alliances across the company. Such directors do not manage any of these operating alliances; instead they are responsible for maximizing benefits and minimizing conflicts across the activities and for ensuring that top management is focused on the total relationship.

Other staff often complement the alliance directors and the vice president. For example, one pharmaceutical company appointed alliance integration officers, who were responsible for helping new research partners integrate with the firm—working closely with partners during the first six to nine months of the relationship. Over time, the firm found that these integration officers had a significant impact on success rates, especially for alliances with young biotech partners. Other firms have put in place alliance screening officers to

EXHIBIT 25.1 Elements of an Advanced Corporate Alliance Infrastructure.

Staff	Tools	Organization	Systems
• Chief alliance officer (VP alliances)	• Alliance mapping system	• Corporate alliance unit	• Partner Web site
• Alliance chiefs	• Alliance categorization hierarchy	• Alliance strategy and governance council	• Alliance database
• Specialist alliance dealmakers	• Corporate alliance policies	• Defined alliance roles	• Electronic partner application
• Alliance database manager	• Deal making and integration methodology	• Defined alliance career path	
• Alliance audit staff	• Sample contracts	• Alliance training	
• Alliance integration officers	• Alliance management tools (for example, sample performance scorecards)	• Network of alliance practitioners	
• Alliance screening officer	• Case histories	• Partner forums	
• Alliance trainers	• External alliance resource library (books, consultants)		

sort through the volume of unsolicited deal requests, alliance database managers to track the company's deals, and alliance auditors to periodically evaluate venture performance.

Few firms will need all these specialized alliance positions. The number and kind of staff needed depends on the characteristics of the alliance portfolio and the firm's corporate culture. But it is clear that as alliances increase in volume, value, and complexity, all firms will need staff beyond the traditional business development deal-makers to bring the most out of an alliance portfolio.

Tools

Advanced alliance companies also have a rich collection of alliance tools—devices that help executives and managers make alliances work. The most basic and useful tool is a set of corporate alliance policies. Ideally no more than one or two pages long, these guidelines should capture the firm's philosophy toward alliances and explain what is and what is not expected in alliances. One company has a list of thirty-five alliance rules of thumb. At a second company each alliance is expected to generate $500 million in sales within two years; no more than 40 percent of a partner's business is allowed to overlap with the firm's own business, and both sides are expected to agree to a set of alliance goals and appoint a team to achieve them.

Another useful tool is a partner hierarchy—a framework that classifies alliances along a few relevant dimensions, such as importance to the firm. Often containing no more than three or four levels of partners, an alliance hierarchy allows company managers and partners to quickly size up the expected level of resource commitment to the alliance. At one software firm, for instance, an alliance categorized as "strategic" can expect a full-time alliance manager and technical training for some of its staff. Alliance mapping is another tool—that is, a snapshot of alliances across business units, products, technologies, and partner sets. Done well, it is a critical way to link overall strategy to alliances.

The most advanced firms also tend to have well-developed alliance process methodologies, especially relating to the recurring tasks of alliance structuring, negotiation, and launch. These methodologies included frameworks for partner screening or diagnosing cultural fit, methods for valuing parent contributions, and models of alliance performance scorecards. It is also often useful to collect documents from past alliances such as letters of intent, loaned-personnel agreements, and joint venture contracts, and to develop checklists for partner screening and negotiation.

Organization

Many experienced companies create organizational structures and routines to foster excellence across their alliance portfolio. The most basic of these structures is a corporate alliance unit—a functional office that contains perhaps five to ten managers, headed by a chief alliance officer. These units often have close links to corporate business development, though many computer companies put the alliance unit in the sales and marketing organization. No matter where it is located, a corporate alliance unit serves as an overall organizational home for alliances, a place where anyone concerned with alliance issues can go for assistance.

Beyond a corporate alliance unit, a number of firms have created a corporate alliance council—a virtual practitioners' forum for key alliance managers. One leading U.S. consumer-goods company set up a twenty-member alliance council composed of business unit heads and CEOs of major joint ventures. The council met several times a year with the goal of shaping corporate alliance strategies and sharing experiences and best practices. Other firms have experimented with broader-based networks of internal alliance practitioners.

In addition to these explicit structures, other organizational elements include well-defined alliance roles: a small set of distinct alliance positions, each with clear qualifications and responsibilities as well as some basic performance metrics. Many companies also find it valuable to create defined career paths for alliance managers and other alliance practitioners. When individuals understand where they can go after two or three years of successfully performing an alliance-related role, the firm has a higher chance of attracting top talent to alliances.

Systems

As alliances become more important and numerous, new management systems are needed to connect different people to different elements of the infrastructure. An alliance Web site is often at the heart of these systems. Typically containing all the tools discussed in this section as well as a database of active alliances, such a Web site can be a wonderful way to connect alliance practitioners scattered across the company to one another and to the codified expertise of the firm.

Some companies have taken this idea one step further, creating Web sites that partners can access. One U.S. computer software firm, for example, had devoted a team of fifteen people to build and manage its alliance Web site. The site could perform a number of valuable services, including screening candidate partners, providing basic information on the firm's approach to alliances, and allowing partners to communicate with one another.

Stages of Growth in Alliance Infrastructure

Not all companies need an extensive alliance infrastructure. How much and which elements to build depends on the nature of the firm's alliance portfolio and its alliance performance. As a general rule, when a company has more than thirty alliances representing 20 percent or more of its value, the company should consider making a real commitment to an advanced infrastructure.

We have found that firms tend to build infrastructure in stages— and that the movement from one stage to the next is often tied to a dramatic change in the business model or to negative performance. One U.S. company committed to building a far-reaching alliance infrastructure after the introduction of a new product that led to the transformation from a direct to indirect sales model. A leading U.S. electronics and office equipment company invested in corporate alliance capabilities after understanding that its main products needed to be linked into the wider office environment and hence that its business model depended on alliances with computer and software makers.

Failure may also be a catalyst. At one large U.S. financial services company, an internal audit discovered that three different business units had licensed the same product from one partner, costing the firm several million dollars. Top management concluded that the only way to minimize such problems in the future was to build resources to manage and oversee the portfolio as a whole. In each case, market realities created a choice: either manage that portfolio of alliances well, or lose.

Broadly speaking, the growth of an alliance infrastructure follows the stages shown in Figure 25.1. Catalysts that highlight the need for a deeper capability often help firms move from one stage to the next.

Firms in Level I of the growth path typically have few internal processes and a tendency to form alliances reactively. Where expertise exists, it tends to be confined to a limited number of individuals (usually dealmakers and lawyers) and focused around issues related to up-front structuring, such as valuation and negotiation.

A catalyst like a high-visibility alliance failure or a recognition that alliances are a key to executing strategy can then push a company to make an initial investment in corporate alliance resources, moving it up to Level II. Typical investments to advance in this way include the codification of basic processes and the development of basic tools such as a set of corporate alliance guidelines or alliance hierarchy. The new stage is often marked by more standard and repeatable approaches to alliance situations, greater portfolio coordination, and improving returns. Level II companies typically also

FIGURE 25.1 Alliance Capabilities: Three Levels.

Level 1: Most Companies	Level 2: Advanced	Level 3: Worldclass
• Few alliance processes • Limited number of alliance experts • True skills confined to certain elements of up-front deal making (for example, partner screening, valuation, negotiation) and to certain types of alliances (such as large bilateral JVs) • Alliances formed reactively	• Some standard alliance processes (especially around deal making) • Small community of alliance practitioners • True skills expand to new areas (for example, launch and governance) and a few new alliance types (such as customer-supplier alliances) • Most alliances still formed reactively or with unclear links to corporate strategy, but a few formed proactively	• Widespread codification of alliance processes, including those relating to alliance management • Large and well-connected community of alliance practitioners • True skills cover all aspects of the alliance lifecycle as well as all of company's • Most alliances formed proactively, with strong links to corporate strategy

have a moderate number of experienced alliance practitioners spread across several business units, and corporate-level support for legal, financial, tax, and technical issues.

A further catalyst may push a company to Level III. At one company, the catalyst was a company-wide survey showing that a large number of managers felt they needed internal training on alliances. Level III capabilities include standardized alliance procedures and policies, a firmwide alliance database, and a corporate body overseeing alliances. Perhaps most important, companies at Level III have a very clear view of what kinds of alliances should be pursued to leverage specific strengths, execute growth strategies, or fill capability gaps. By this stage, alliances have at last become an integral part of the strategy process. By the start of the 2000s, probably no more than fifty companies had reached Level III, though future business success was likely to depend more and more on such capabilities.

This framework is a simplification and not all companies will start at the beginning and pass from one level to the next. (For example, an alliance-dependent start-up must be built with Level III skills in place from the beginning.) Nonetheless, this framework allows executives to compare their internal alliance capabilities with others and so determine whether to invest in additional corporate alliance resources.

Future Champions

Today's world-class alliance organizations may not hold that title for long. As alliances rise in number, complexity, and value, companies will need to develop alliance infrastructures to perform tasks that few companies currently do well. These include better ways of linking alliances to strategy, greater efficiency and speed in alliance formation, and more comprehensive management of the alliance portfolio.

Linking Alliances to Strategy

Alliances need to directly support the overall strategic goals of the company. Yet all too often alliances take on a life of their own, at best contributing peripheral value to the firm. To better link alliances to strategy, firms should start with a clear vision of where alliances fit within the business model; a version of this vision or road map could be included in their annual report or business plan. Done well, this defines where alliances should (or should not) be used, as well as some basic venture structures and metrics.

Beyond this, firms may want to develop indicators that test the fit of the alliance with strategy. One leading pharmaceutical company tracks on an annual basis the percentage of alliances that were initiated from the company rather than resulting from unsolicited ideas from partners. The firm believes that self-initiated alliances are an indication that the alliances are well linked to corporate strategy; it seeks to push this number from 40 percent to 60–70 percent. Another mechanism to link alliances to strategy is a corporate audit process where alliances undergo periodic external reviews. Firms will also find it useful to require all alliances to define their mission on one sheet of paper. This simple statement of intent forces a level of clarity and allows others in the company to assess the value of the proposed alliance to the overall vision of the firm.

Speeding Up Alliance Formation

Increasingly, a firm's competitive advantage is tied to the speed with which it forms alliances. Although alliance formation speed depends on many factors, it is possible to use new technologies to accelerate the process. New information technologies offer a chance to develop online partner screening tools in which potential partners provide basic company and alliance information; the electronic alliance application can then be routed to the relevant company managers. This may not be appropriate everywhere, but it makes sense for many leading high-tech firms, including pharmaceutical companies and computer software and hardware makers.

Managing the Portfolio

Most important, future winners will monitor and manage the performance of their alliances as carefully and as effectively as they monitor and manage performance of businesses where they have full control. These companies will take steps to manage conflicts and promote synergies across their alliance portfolio.

As noted, not all companies will need an extensive alliance infrastructure. But for those with large numbers of alliances that contribute substantial value to the firm, it simply will no longer suffice to rely on the talent of skilled but unsupported amateurs.

Further Reading

James Bamford and David Ernst. "Managing an Alliance Portfolio," *McKinsey Quarterly*, 2002, 3, 29–39.

Robert E. Spekman, Lynn A. Isabella, and Thomas C. MacAvoy. *Alliance Competence: Maximizing the Value of Your Partnerships*. New York: Wiley, 2000. Chapter 9.

Source

This chapter is based on "Managing Alliances: Skills for the Modern Era" by James Bamford and David Ernst, *The Alliance Analyst* (March 1996). The article was edited and updated for this book.

26

Alliances Across the Corporation

Unisys

It was not a pretty picture, recalls Patricia Higgins, who was president of the communications market sector group at Unisys in 1995, describing the state of the company's alliance program at that time: "Our partners perceived our alliance policies as poorly defined. Expectations were unclear. We weren't leveraging our strengths. Our sales force was reactive and often inaccessible. Our business units were not partnering as a unified team to serve clients. And we were missing opportunities for our business, for our partners' businesses, and for our clients' businesses."

She immediately went to work to extract her group from such an ugly and unproductive existence. This was important work for Unisys: the company had forged 130 alliances in the previous five years, ranking it among the top twenty in alliance formation in the Fortune 500. And alliances promised to become even more important to the company in the future. With clients in over a hundred countries, limited financial resources, and the need to offer customers total product solutions, alliances seemed to be the only realistic way for Unisys to compete and to grow.

Models of Alliance Organization

Higgins set out to develop a new approach to alliances, a model that, in her words, "begins and ends with delighting the customer."

Unisys began by surveying its customers and partners, asking their opinion of Unisys products and services that were created or delivered through some form of interfirm collaboration. The responses isolated a major problem: Unisys was sending terribly distorted signals when alliances spanned several business units. The origin of the problem, Unisys management came to believe, was the absence of any single contact point for a given alliance. "The left hand had no idea what the right hand was up to," explained Higgins.

Over the years, different companies had tackled this problem in different ways. At one time or another, they each developed different organizations that struck a balance between central coordination at headquarters and local authority at business unit levels (see Figure 26.1).

At one extreme lay the corporate alliance group model, in which a staff organization at headquarters was charged with coordinating alliances across the corporation, setting policies, and providing tools to business units (Model 1). Many firms took this approach in the 1990s. One drawback of this model was that the corporate alliance group could lose touch with business realities at the local levels and might begin to impose rules that did not serve the immediate needs of the business units. On top of that, in an age of slimmer corporate bureaucracies, the fact that the group would be a pure cost center was a disadvantage.

One response to the cost-center problem was to build the alliance function into staff groups that already existed, so that no new bureaucracy was needed (Model 2). This was the model of one U.S. software firm, in which the corporate business development office took on the task of assembling and distributing the company's best practices with alliance management. A drawback of this approach, however, was that the group had other functions at the same time; in particular, a group like corporate development tended to be oriented toward acquisitions and deals and be less involved in ongoing management of business ventures.

At the other extreme of the centralization-decentralization spectrum in managing alliances across the corporation was complete

FIGURE 26.1 Coordinating Alliances Across the Corporation: Four Models.

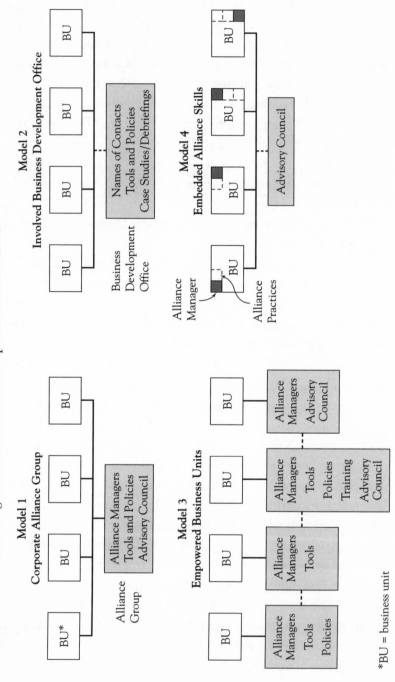

Model 1
Corporate Alliance Group

Model 2
Involved Business Development Office

Model 3
Empowered Business Units

Model 4
Embedded Alliance Skills

*BU = business unit

devolution of power to the business units (Model 3). At one point, Lotus Development had such a model. The idea here is that local units be empowered to design and manage their own alliances, perhaps with tools developed centrally but subject to little oversight from the center. The obvious drawback of this model is that it could lead to precisely the problem facing Unisys in 1995: alliances formed by different business units would not be coordinated with those of other units; at the worst, they might even be at cross-purposes to each other.

Unisys took a different tack, aiming at central coordination and consistency without adding to the bureaucracy. "Probably one of the worst things we can do would be to establish a whole host of alliance managers and support staff only to determine later we wanted to take them away," Higgins told her staff. "That could cause even more strain on an alliance." Higgins also kept the Unisys alliance organization embedded in its various business units—not off on its own in a staff department. The result (Model 4) tended to combine the best of both worlds—alliances across business units were coordinated centrally, but decision-making power on day-to-day issues lay squarely in the lap of local business units.

Design Principles for Crossing Business Units

The Unisys corporate partnering model was built around three core beliefs. The first was the idea that alliances that spanned multiple business units needed a designated relationship executive. Second, that executive should reside in the business unit with the greatest interest in that relationship. And third, cross-divisional communication was best kept informal.

Consider Unisys's alliances with Microsoft, IBM, and Novell, and others like them. These touched several Unisys business units, from Higgins's own communications sector group to groups focused on financial services and health care. These alliances were also likely to cover a range of value-chain activities from technology development and marketing to systems integration and customer support. Finally, they typically served clients in dozens of countries.

Such multidimensional complexity demanded coordination. "We not only established a relationship manager for each," explained Higgins, "but also defined selection criteria, as well as guidelines, policies, and practices for these partnerships."

The new model not only helped create better new alliances, it also transformed established relationships. Since the 1980s, Unisys had been allied with Oracle; over the years, the two partners had developed myriad agreements across multiple business divisions. "There was little coordination, absolutely no focus, and few opportunities to leverage our combined strengths," says Higgins.

Under the new model, the Oracle relationship was now managed out of Higgins's communications group, which worked closely with the software maker to develop new applications in emerging industries. As a result, revenue from the alliance grew by more than 200 percent in the first year that it was managed in this model, and Oracle recognized Unisys as its "Global Distinguished Partner of the Year."

Grassroots Movement

The beauty of the Unisys model lay in its grassroots nature and its flexibility. Every alliance at Unisys was launched from a business unit. That business unit, focused on filling the specific need of a client, would develop the initial alliance business plan, negotiate the agreement, and manage the relationship. With time, other Unisys businesses might see opportunities to work with that same partner. When they did, the company had a process whereby a corporation-wide alliance advisory council was asked for resources for a designated relationship executive.

"For a given alliance, the relationship executive might report directly to me, because I have such a high level of interest in the business," Higgins said. "But they might also have a dotted line responsibility into the advisory council. This gives us flexibility without getting us bogged down in bureaucracy." A preference for speed and nimbleness also shaped Higgins's own relationship to the advisory council. "I am not on the advisory council, nor should I be, in my personal view. My whole role is to grow my business."

Leadership from the Relationship Managers

The Unisys model put a lot of responsibility in the lap of the relationship managers: they developed and led the implementation of the strategic plan; they managed and grew the partnership; they enlisted the support of various parts of Unisys; they allocated resources, managed costs, formed cross-company teams, and coordinated alliance activities across businesses and continents. In theory, a great job, especially for an ambitious manager seeking frequent audience with the heads of business units.

It was therefore critical for Unisys to attract its best and brightest into these relationship manager positions. The job demanded that they not only know how to operate within a large corporation but also have some demonstrated success within it. This led to improved effectiveness, explained Higgins:

These relationship managers could command respect when requesting resources or support from various business units in order to solidify and enhance the relationship. It also sent a strong signal to the rest of the organization about just how important the alliance program is. If you do not put some of your best and brightest there, your organization will perceive that this is just a bureaucratic process set out to the side. The corporation has made a commitment to put talented people in these positions because they view the success of these alliances to be directly related to the success of Unisys.

For a young star, therefore, there were few better opportunities to gain wide exposure than to be a relationship manager. Unfortunately, few Unisys high-potentials wanted the job. "It was new," explained Higgins. "In large corporations, you often determine the direction of your career path by looking at others who have successfully moved up in the organization." The relationship manager post provided none of these reference points. So Higgins and other corporate officers had to step in and make a public appeal that promised young stars that the relationship manager route could be a new path for corporate success.

No Bureaucracy, Please

In the 1960s and 1970s companies like General Electric built massive—and, at the time, widely admired—planning organizations. By the 1980s, however, they came to see that it made little sense to have strategic planners tell business units what to do. Higgins was insistent that Unisys avoid falling in the same trap.

"There are some initiatives which, if you were to look at our announcement, would make you think there is a modest amount of bureaucracy," she said. "There is a formal communication process; there is an advisory board; there are regularly scheduled meetings which formally review and measure the alliances; and there are executives in charge of alliances." But the appearance was misleading. "The communication is far more informal than formal," she explained. "We put a formal process in place, but still believe that, at least for large corporations, the informal communication channels are probably the most effective."

One Unisys alliance actually ran aground because of a lack of informal, pick-up-the-phone communications. "We weren't talking to each other," said Higgins. "And it became almost a feeding frenzy: the tensions rose a bit, and then we avoided meeting again. It finally got to the point where it was totally out of perspective." A well-oiled informal communication channel should avoid such breakdowns.

Persistent Challenges

Even with a new and improved alliance program, Higgins's group continued to face some core challenges that were unlikely to go away. First, there were those within the company who didn't buy into the alliance partner model. It was the not-invented-here syndrome, explained Higgins: "There was a hesitancy to divulge to partners information that was traditionally kept close to the vest, and there was absolute paralysis when it came to packaging competitive technology as part of a Unisys solution. Other companies may experience this attitude as protectionism among managers who don't appreciate alliances as opportunities to extend globally, share risks, and establish a presence in new markets."

As part of a solution to this problem, Unisys developed a "target marketing model." This device asked managers and executives to articulate the compelling reason for the client to buy the solution. If an alliance was part of that, the model demanded an explanation for how the partner brought unique value. "Everything should be fact-based, measurable, and directed toward providing a better service to the customer," said Higgins.

The second core problem facing the new alliance program was the tricky matter of cooperating with competitors. "Many of the companies we were talking to about alliances were our direct competitors," said Higgins, adding, "Some of them bring some very, very good capabilities to the table. The market is moving too fast—I can't develop it all internally. Without these partnerships, I'll miss the mark and I won't serve my clients well. Unisys has transformed itself from just a technology company into a services company. Clients want the best possible solution. If I don't deliver that, my credibility is shot. So if the best solution means HP or Tandem technology, then that is what I am going to deliver to my client."

Higgins's solution to this problem: look at yourself first. "Be realistic about your company strengths—the strengths you really have, not the ones you wish you had," she noted. "Come to grips with where you excel and where you don't. Until you can do that, don't sit across a table from a competitor."

And then, once you are talking to a competitor, don't just dive into a deep, wide-ranging relationship. "We put a toe in the water first," said Higgins. "We look for a quick success or two—but no more than that. Test the water, feel if the values and the culture are not that similar and see how easy it is to work together and see how satisfied the client is." Even so, the tensions inherent in cooperating with rivals were unlikely to go away; instead, they were likely to become the daily fare of Unisys's new alliance program (see also Chapter Six).

Further Reading

Yves Doz and Gary Hamel. *Alliance Advantage*. Boston: Harvard Business School Press, 1998. Chapter 9.

Henry Mintzberg and Ludo Van der Heyden. "Organigraphs: Drawing How Companies Really Work," *Harvard Business Review*, Sept.-Oct. 1999, pp. 87–94.

Source

This chapter is based on "Back from the Brink," *The Alliance Analyst* (April 1996), which reported on a presentation made by Patricia Higgins at the Conference Board in New York. The article was edited for this book.

27

Training for Collaboration

As companies come to depend more on alliances, they confront the need for alliance training—whether to attend or develop educational programs on alliances. Since the mid-1990s, more and more business schools have been offering alliance courses to managers. At the same time, conference organizers and various associations have launched alliance programs and workshops. These offerings fill an important market niche, but many companies find them insufficient.

External alliance training has a number of drawbacks. It can be superficial, unable to explore alliance issues in meaningful detail. It can be irrelevant, unable to cover those specific situations and structures that matter most to an individual firm. And it can be hard to institutionalize the learning. In most cases, managers spend a few days hearing what some consultant or academic thinks about the different phases of alliance development, but not internalizing the framework.

Responding to these shortcomings, companies are investing in internal alliance training. These are not rent-a-professor programs where an outsider gives a generic course to a company audience. Rather, they are training programs built from the ground up inside companies. Motorola developed an alliance training course and put hundreds of executives through it; Sun and BellSouth developed workshops targeted to their top executives. Others developed alliance workshops to help train new joint venture managing directors and others with substantial contact with their networks of alliances. But these firms are still pioneers: a Booz-Allen & Hamilton study showed that less than 15 percent of companies have invested in internal alliance training. The Booz-Allen data also revealed that alliance training tends to be concentrated in the top hundred executives, and rarely spreads to the ranks of middle managers.

When should companies invest in internal alliance training? How should these training programs be structured? Who should lead them? And what factors separate successful alliance training initiatives from mediocre ones?

To answer these questions, we examine two companies: Bell-South and Dow Corning. Both have looked closely into internal alliance training programs, and both have created successful platforms for alliance learning.

Top-Down Learning: BellSouth

Since creating its Leadership Institute in the mid-1980s, Bell-South pushed hard on executive education. In the early 1990s it poured resources into training in service excellence. It brought customers face to face with BellSouth executives, created intricate simulation exercises, and ultimately honed a curriculum for thousands of company managers. After that, the Leadership Institute ran large-scale education efforts on marketing and the competitive marketplace.

In the late 1990s, Val Markos, director of the institute, decided to try his hand at alliance training. After all, alliances were becoming almost as important to the new BellSouth as corporate leadership and customer service. "Alliances were pervading our industry," said Markos. "Yet when we went out and interviewed the people in BellSouth who were working on joint ventures and alliances, it became very clear that the learning was bottled up, and that we were not succeeding in sharing it across the company."

The Pilot

Markos crafted an alliance education program geared to change this. He planned to keep the classes small. Twenty to twenty-five managers would be invited. To get a mix of perspectives, he planned to invite some from the field and some from corporate staff functions; internal faculty would keep the discussion germane and academics and consultants would provide outside views. To keep the pace varied, general presentations would be interspersed with small working groups. "Everyone in the class was, literally, considered faculty," said Markos.

The pilot session worked well. One manager with little prior exposure to alliances soaked up the information. The more alliance-savvy participants benefited from the vivid case studies and broader view of the external faculty. A manager who had previously worked strictly with third-party relationships explained, "One of the most helpful things was learning about the history of alliances in other businesses and hearing the perspective of outside consultants. When BellSouth courses are taught by BellSouth people, we just don't get the outside perspective we need."

Sounds great? Perhaps. Yet after three sessions, just when the machinery should have been warmed up, it was stalling. Markos brought the initiative to a halt. It wasn't working.

Going Off Track

"Somehow, we weren't quite getting the right people in the room," said Markos. "Out of the twenty-five, there usually would be a handful from procurement and the fifteen to twenty others were from places like marketing, international, or other divisions." In theory, such diversity should have created dynamism. In reality, it created two divergent populations: procurement and everyone else. These two groups were impossible to satisfy simultaneously. "Didn't matter which way we went—if we catered to one the other got bored rather quickly," said Markos. "Both groups had very established and detailed guidelines for doing their alliances, and we just couldn't seem to dig the discussion out of these specifics."

Markos adapted. He decided that the original net had been cast too widely, and probably should not have included the supplier-relations executives. "They should have had their own course," he explained later. Markos also decided to modify the guest list to include more senior people. If the vice president of strategy couldn't learn from the vice president of marketing or the chief financial officer, then there was little hope for cross-organizational learning in the trenches.

Going to the Top

Markos had high ambitions for a one-day course focused on corporate officers. He wanted the attendees to capture existing knowledge, address corporate issues identified in earlier sessions, and take action on these issues. "We pegged the individual learning," said Markos, "but we didn't really zoom in on solving problems. In a group of thirty, there wasn't agreement on actions to be taken or, in some cases, even on the issues." Still, virtually everyone who attended was pleased.

Everyone except Markos. He had wanted to generate some momentum—momentum to solve structural problems at BellSouth or, at least, momentum to reshape the alliance education effort. But talk of the Leadership Institute's role touched a nerve. The problem actually lay in the successful track record of the institute: It had always led massive culture-changing initiatives. So corporate executives were worried: "They are going to teach a thousand people how to do alliances? We don't need a thousand people running around looking for partners," was the thinking of some. So Markos backed off. He dropped the alliance initiative where it stood, and, following the suggestion of the corporate officers, developed a less panoramic course on win-win negotiations.

The BellSouth experience offers some lessons:

- *Cross-functional learning doesn't happen naturally.* Simply assembling a mixed crowd is no guarantee of integration. Yes, individuals across functional boundaries have much to learn from one another, but they also have incongruous interests.
- *Executive education shouldn't work alone.* Part of the resistance to Markos's plans stemmed from the fact that BellSouth's education department was seen as driving the alliance train. Strategic planners felt left out, or even displaced.
- *Content must be in sync with strategy.* No matter how dazzling the faculty, training still depends on the relevance of the material. An academic whose favorite alliance case is Nike's Asian supplier network may not prove useful to a telecom company.
- *Proper framing of the issues is important.* Markos wasn't being radical when he defined *alliance* as including sourcing agreements as well as equity joint ventures. But BellSouth managers did not share this definition and not enough was done in course content to convince them that they should.

These lessons are applicable to many types of training situations, but they were particularly relevant to the top-down approach that Markos pursued. From the start, he saw the role of the education as driving cultural change. That is a valid role and one that is valuable in many contexts. Other companies see alliance training as filling a more modest goal. Dow Corning was one company with a different model.

Bottom-Up Learning: Dow Corning

Dow Corning also needed to improve its alliance skills. In early 1995, two groups in the firm's main chemicals business conducted strategic capability assessments that identified alliance deal making and management as important but underdeveloped skill areas. Dow Corning had always done its share of joint ventures. But something was afoot in the chemical business. The pressures of globalization—in production and marketing—were intensifying. No longer a peripheral activity, joint ventures were becoming a core part of the business.

Dow Corning followed a different path from BellSouth's. Rather than use a high-profile alliance training workshop as "the lantern on the hill," Dow Corning took a lower-key approach that deemphasized training in the short term. It spent the first year developing best practices and connecting isolated pockets of expertise.

Rather than use executive education to drive the effort, Dow Corning turned to a group of strategic thinkers in new business development. To lead the initiative, Dow Corning chose Greg Whitaker, whose first move was to accumulate knowledge. He attended a number of alliance conferences and business school courses, and enlisted the help of an alliance consultant. He also turned inward, interviewing Dow Corning managers involved in alliances. Was there a recipe for success? Who could provide reliable expertise? "When we finished all that, we came to a very simple conclusion," Whitaker explained. "For us to upgrade our alliance capability, we first needed a process, a communications delivery system, and a support infrastructure. Then we could do the training."

Whitaker found that Dow Corning's alliance expertise, while strong, was scattered in many pockets. The legal, accounting, finance, and economics functions all had real skills, but they weren't connected. Whitaker's research made him see that Dow Corning was similar to many multinationals: "A manager seeking support on alliances will likely first wander into the legal or finance departments. It's just the way our culture tends to work. You've got to get the document and the numbers right. Sure, a lawyer can cite the chapter and verse of a good contract, but Americans often overlook the importance of things like strategic vision or how an alliance depends on human relationships."

Whitaker had a fix. First, to allow business units to see the whole alliance process, he needed to break apart the alliance value chain and accumulate expertise for each stage in one accessible place. Then, in time, he needed to provide specialty training for each of those alliance pockets and ensure that the process was institutionalized. Over the course of the following year, Whitaker's work had four components: the company intranet, senior management support, critical need focus, and individual consulting.

Use the Intranet

Whitaker had seen generic alliance process models developed by SRI, Booz-Allen & Hamilton, and others. Inspired, his team took the various stages of an alliance—planning, searching, negotiating, structuring, and managing—and customized them to match the chemical business of Dow Corning. Then the team began to build detailed tools and frameworks under each stage. "As it turned out, much of the information already existed," says Whitaker. "Once we started poking around, we found that, for example, someone in legal might already have a highly developed description for one piece of the alliance process, while someone in marketing might have another piece."

Once the information was gathered and culled, the model was made electronic. Whitaker's team developed an appendix containing a list of internal and external experts, as well as a selection of sample alliance worksheets. They put the "electronic outline" on a local area network and also made it available on disk, paper, and even in a PowerPoint presentation. In other words, Dow Corning reduced the need for training by creating an online and ever-ready alliance tutorial. But this did not render human interaction obsolete.

Get Senior Management Support

Within six months, the alliance process was fairly well formed. In the summer of 1996, Whitaker got the chance to demonstrate the alliance process to the company's operating committee, which allowed him to make sure that the new business development group's effort was on track with executive management's expectations. "My goal was to elevate awareness of the process and gain their support for the approach," Whitaker notes. He wasn't seeking additional resources; he simply wanted endorsement and some assurance of use.

Indeed, Whitaker was really looking out for the managers in the business units. He knew that mid-level managers could develop creative alliance ideas, but that they would go nowhere if senior management did not understand the process, the context, or the overall thinking. "The great thing about the electronic outline is that it allows a senior executive to ask some very, very pointed questions about an alliance," Whitaker says. "We are doing everything to guarantee the highest probability of success."

Focus Education on Critical Need

After all this, Dow Corning was ready to begin training. But unlike BellSouth, Dow Corning did not rush out to train line managers. At Dow Corning, the first effort would be to train support staff. Over a series of months, Whitaker gave tailored sessions to such groups as business development, legal, economic evaluation, and governmental affairs. In tone and substance, these were more presentations than training courses. And they were full of nicks and blemishes.

These sessions delivered two benefits. First, they advanced corporate thinking. "On many occasions, these groups saw that we had left out parts, or even omitted entire steps in the process," Whitaker explains. "They also uncovered whole new layers of internal alliance expertise which we had never known about. It was amazing." The second benefit, of course, was that Dow Corning was strengthening the alliance support net. The more these functions knew and thought about alliances, the greater the chance of success. Strength also came in connecting the expertise areas to one another. During his presentation to, say, legal, Whitaker made a point to talk about the capabilities of accounting, planning, and procurement.

Individual Consulting

Within a matter of months, the focused presentations were done. Whitaker and the new business development department returned to their familiar role as internal consultants. They are called in to provide support for specific alliances. "Right now, I am working on four projects," Whitaker said a year after starting the initiative. "It is the high-level strategic stuff—either helping someone think about a strategy involving alliances, or doing a postmortem on a deal that went wrong. Hopefully, in time, as this alliance process takes hold, there will be fewer and fewer postmortems."

In the future, Whitaker believes, the new business development group will not simply provide its accumulated wisdom to Dow Corning project teams. Ultimately, many of these processes will be offered to potential alliance partners. "One value often overlooked," Whitaker says, "is that we can bring to the table a process that allows all parties to answer the question, 'Is this relationship good for you and me?'"

And what about the alliance training course? According to Whitaker: "Once we get some of this fine-tuned and market-tested, we will get the company's employee development group involved. But we need to incubate it a little more before it becomes a larger training effort."

Alliance training is an important part of a collaborative core—an essential mechanism to raise alliance skill levels across the company. The experience of BellSouth and Dow Corning show that alliance training must be linked to a wider corporate alliance infrastructure. Companies should avoid having alliance training occur in an environment lacking in the other processes, tools, and systems to form and manage alliances. Second and related, alliance training should not be driven solely by corporate education units. It is important to draw in business unit leaders, joint venture managing directors, and other executives with experience in the field. Finally, corporate educators should pick the best elements from the top-down and bottom-up models described here.

Further Reading

John P. Kotter. *Leading Change*. Boston: Harvard Business School Press, 1996.

Source

This chapter is based on several articles in *The Alliance Analyst*, especially "New Track for Training, Parts I and II" (August 1996). The articles were combined, edited, and updated for this book.

Master Builders

28

Grandmasters at the Extremes

Many companies are starting to create institutionalized alliance capabilities for forming and managing alliances—processes and approaches designed to ensure that the company builds on its alliance experiences. But what should this capability look like, and how formal should it be? Does alliance strategy and management deserve to be a formal unit like strategic planning or corporate business development, with full-time staff, detailed processes, and a defined home in the organization? Or should an alliance capability be more informal, a looser structure and approach that creates corporate instincts and habits?

To find out, we interviewed executives at numerous leading companies. Our discussions began in 1994 and ran through 2001. From the start, we noticed that the alliance grandmasters had fundamentally different approaches to organizing their alliance capabilities. Some followed highly structured processes; others used relatively informal methods. What was puzzling is that both approaches seemed to work.

Corning was an example of the informal approach. Throughout its history, Corning relied on joint ventures to create many of its most successful new businesses, including Dow Corning, Owens Corning, and Siecor (Siemens Corning). More than 25 percent of its revenues were coming from alliances in the mid-1990s, and alliances remain an important part of its business today. But even fifty years after forming its first alliance, Corning continued to take an informal approach. For instance, it had not even documented its list of best practices or partner search guidelines. Instead, its alliance capability was all about instinct. Corning senior vice president of business development Peter Booth offered simple and down-home advice to determine whether a potential partner was suitable: "Go and sniff their hindquarters and see if they smell like us."

Other companies, such as Eli Lilly (Chapter Thirty-One), Lotus Development Corporation (Chapter Twenty-Nine), and Federal Express (Chapter Thirty) did follow explicit processes and had documented lists of best practices for their managers. One large U.S. computer hardware and electronics firm had a 400-page alliance binder that was updated constantly. It contained case histories, tool kits, and checklists. It had been sent to seven hundred managers, taught in a two-day class, and was available online for its managers to access. This company was also successful with its alliances, as were Eli Lilly, Lotus, and FedEx.

Why did these companies arrive at such different approaches? What approach is appropriate for your firm?

Informal Learning

"Let me tell you straight away," says Peter Booth of Corning, "that we don't do anything that is even remotely like what some other companies are doing or proposing to do." Corning had no corporate development staff focused on alliance management issues. It had no course taught by veteran alliance managers. In short, it had no institutional mechanism for alliance learning.

Yet the institution learned. To understand Corning's thinking, one had to follow how it entered alliances. The ball got rolling at the business unit level—not in a corporate development office—when a manager identified an opportunity. It was that manager's job to determine Corning's strategy: What was the product? Who were the customers? What were the economics of the business and how would the company make a profit? And most important, what were the capabilities that Corning lacked to make the business a success?

Sometimes Corning did not have all the pieces. It may have lacked the technology, financial resources, or market position required to put the product in customers' hands while the market was still ripe. "That manager—or group of managers—then must find a partner, or drop the idea," Booth explains. "If they decide to go ahead, they then just head down the hall and start asking people about alliances—they ask people who are known to have experience in the development of partner relationships what they think. And that begins the further education process."

This approach was effective because Corning had alliance wisdom running through its veins. At Corning, according to Booth, "there is a fairly common set of notions about alliances that the chairman holds, the president holds, the vice chairman holds, I hold, and our group of executive vice presidents holds. We all think alike about this subject." And that thinking is fairly simple. Alliances are for the long term. They are judged on their own merits and treated as free-standing and independent businesses. And above all, notes Booth, a company must do business only with people it trusts. These plus a few other pieces of back porch wisdom are about all that Corning sees in broader alliance principles (Exhibit 28.1).

Formal Processes

Before they embarked on building an alliance capability, some of the other pioneers that we interviewed were like many other large U.S. and European companies. They recognized alliances were increasingly important, particularly in fast-paced and unpredictable businesses. They recognized alliances were touching many more managers than ever before, managers who had little experience or skills in thinking about the intricacies of interfirm collaboration. For example, few inside these companies knew how to protect against technology leakage when creating an R&D alliance with a

EXHIBIT 28.1 Corning's Alliance Principles.

During the last eighty years, Corning has created and managed some of the most successful and enduring joint ventures, including Dow Corning, Owens Corning, Pittsburgh Corning, Samsung-Corning, and Siecor (Siemens-Corning). What are its keys to success? Underlining the firm's focus on building trust and large, independent businesses, a Corning senior executive offered the following alliance principles:

- Know your partner.
- Seek partners with compatible corporate cultures.
- Seek partners of similar size; the partners need to be more or less equally capable of funding the venture and absorbing the inevitable business downdraft.
- Ask both parents to make roughly equal contributions of skills, capabilities, and so on.
- Build alliances around sizable business opportunities—those that could be the basis for a company that will last for fifty or a hundred years.
- Choose opportunities that are sufficiently definable so that a management team can be put in charge and told to go do it.
- Structure alliances as real career opportunities for their managers.
- Design alliances in such a way as to prevent competition with either corporate parent.
- Allow the alliance management team to work without undue interference.
- Spend time with your partner's leadership team—become friendly on a social basis.
- Do business only with people you trust.

competitor. Fewer still knew how to structure exit mechanisms or how to assess the merits or price of an equity investment.

In response, our interviewees typically headed in various directions to improve their companies' alliance skills. At times, they attended alliance seminars taught by business school professors or consultants. At other times, they looked to their corporate business development groups for one-on-one consulting. But mostly, they simply ventured into the fire unprepared—assessing, forging, restructuring, and on occasion terminating deals with the wisdom of a good manager, but not with a real understanding of what their companies had done in the past, or what other businesses were doing in the present.

This approach typically worked well enough for a time. But there was usually a wake-up call at some point. In the case of one U.S. computer hardware firm, the corporate education and training unit sent out a broad questionnaire on training needs. Managers overwhelmingly ranked strategic alliances as the number one area where they needed more training. "That was the event that triggered the earthquake," according to a business development manager at the company. For other companies, the turning point was a failed major alliance, or the sudden realization that the company's alliance network was growing out of control.

Their usual response was to set out to systematically document and disseminate the corporate alliance wisdom. But right away, it became clear to most that alliance training and skill building that depended on external courses and ad hoc internal networks were seriously flawed. The practices had to be more specific to each company, and they had to be disseminated more widely than typically had been done.

Problem One: Creating Custom Information

"General alliance courses may give a lot more stories and anecdotes," noted one manager, "but what they generally lack is a lot of specific implementation detail." Indeed, a Harvard Business School professor who led such seminars admitted to these shortcomings. "How can these conferences ever get into implementation detail when there is just one executive from scores of different companies?" he asked. "They can look at broad strategic issues, gain a framework for understanding, but they are not going to tell a manager from company X what to do on Monday morning." Another executive at a major U.S. corporation and an occasional alliance conference attendee concurred: "It's frustrating. You go to a conference and get all excited because there are people like you. But then you come back to your company and it feels like you are one against the world."

One U.S. high-tech company saw a solution. In an initiative led by corporate business development, it created an in-house alliance course, given for two days twice a year and open to anybody in the company who wanted to come. The courses were run not by outside consultants or company training staff, but by the company's own senior managers—people who had put together and managed multiple alliances. The curriculum was built around the company's own case studies; the idea, said one executive, was to "walk them through the background, and define the potential issues. The goal is to draw out discussion." The course also looked at broader trends and policies, for instance explaining alliance best practices and discussing specific topics such as how to manage alliances with the Japanese.

In developing this rich course material, the business development group had to be more disciplined than in the past in analyzing alliances. After this, explained one manager, "We would hold a postmortem with all the involved parties after a new alliance was formed. We would look at the original objectives, the implementation, what went right and what went wrong in the formation process." Periodically, the business development group would also revisit existing alliances and evaluate their ongoing progress. The results were written up in a management briefing that went into the new corporate alliance database.

Most companies that build a formal alliance process do not rely just on their own experience. Eli Lilly used consultants to conduct a review of industry best practices, and then adapted the tools and techniques it found to its own needs. An executive from another company described how his company constructed its list of best practices: "We started with our own list, derived from conversations with our own folks. Then we added ideas gathered through bench-marking activities and from outside seminars." When this is done well, companies end up with a mix of practices tested by others that also fit in their company.

Problem Two: Expanding Access

Leading alliance companies differ in how they disseminate the alliance wisdom they assemble. A management education class is one avenue. But such classes are time- and people-intensive and tend to reach only a thin layer of company management. To cast a wider net, some companies create an alliance binder or Web site that becomes accessible to all middle managers. When online collaboration tools became readily available in the early 2000s, companies began to experiment with full-blown communities of practice for alliance management. This meant using the company intranet to provide information, enable meetings, take courses, and provide advice. Some companies also experimented with extending their online communities to partners, enabling managers from both companies to work together and share information on the intranet.

Conclusions from the Contrast

Corning clearly was at one end of a continuum—one that had many other high-tech companies on the other. Which end is better, and when should firms consider one approach or the other?

Beware of the Informal Corning Model

The Corning model may seem easy to replicate. After all, how hard can it be to sense if partners are trustworthy and have a corporate culture that "smells like us"? But beware. Corning has the instinctive, almost effortless, ease of Michael Jordan shooting free throws with his eyes closed. It is not the way to learn. It is, rather, one way to act once you have already learned to the level of a master. Admire, applaud, and gape in disbelief, but don't copy.

Test the Formal Model

You may think your ad hoc and informal approach is working well enough, so why change it? Maybe you shouldn't. To determine whether your company may need a more formal corporate alliance program, companies should look at a couple of different indicators.

One is your partners. A large U.S. pharmaceutical company recently went out and surveyed fifty of its biotech partners to understand how well the company formed and managed alliances compared to its competitors. It found out that it was strong in deal making but weak in ongoing management. As a result, it invested more resources in developing and disseminating alliance management tools and policies.

A second indicator is company managers. In many cases, firms will find that the current ad hoc approach to alliances is simply not preparing managers for the work ahead.

A third, and often even better, indicator is the nature of the company alliance portfolio. The more alliances that a company has, and the more important these alliances are to the business, the more the company needs to take the formal path. As a simple rule of thumb, if a portfolio contains more than thirty alliances and represents 20-plus percent of overall company value, the firm should consider a formal alliance capability.

Tailor Your Approach

In the end, most firms will choose a point somewhere between the two extremes. Understanding just where on this continuum to fall depends on many factors. As a simple diagnostic, companies should look at these parameters: number of alliances, value of alliances, variance in alliances, degree of corporate decentralization, and (perhaps most important) their own corporate culture.

But whether the formal approach would work in your company depends critically on your corporate culture and on the role of centralized processes and controls. For highly decentralized companies with an informal way of managing corporate knowledge, the organization will rebel at the formal approach. A focus on business units and managerial skills rather than formal processes may be more appropriate there—in other words, a model a few steps toward Corning's.

In the end, building an alliance capability is not unlike building any other general management capability, such as in project management, quality control, customer service, and so on. One way of thinking about the effort is as an exercise in knowledge management. How does your company manage its knowledge? All companies do that, explicitly or implicitly, regardless of whether they use the term. Once you figure that out, decide how alliance knowledge should be managed—chances are you will do it in a way somewhere between the two extremes.

Further Reading

Thomas H. Davenport and Lawrence Prusak. *Working Knowledge: How Organizations Manage What They Know*. Boston: Harvard Business School Press, 1998.

Margaret B. W. Graham and Alec T. Shuldiner. *Corning and the Craft of Innovation*. Boston: Harvard Business School Press, 2001. Chapter 5.

Source

This chapter is based on "Grandmasters at the Extremes," *The Alliance Analyst* (November 1994, reprinted in February 1997). The article has been edited and updated for this book.

29

Order Out of Chaos

Lotus Development

Entering the mid-1990s, Lotus Development had a poor reputation as an alliance partner. It had a dominant market position and proprietary products. "We were conquerors," Hemang Davé, Lotus's former head of alliances, explained in 1995. "Our attitude was that we had Lotus 1-2-3 and others needed us. We had terrible follow-up on partner requests, and so much personnel turnover that even a single alliance negotiation could, as the revolving door swung, be handled by multiple Lotus executives."

The problems stemmed in part from a lack of clarity around alliance strategy. "Alliances were almost always optimized around a press release," Davé recalled. "They were advanced by corporate dealmakers who never had enough time to understand the full potential value of any alliance. It was all about seeking hero value."

At best, the alliance strategy was uncoordinated. No single internal person or group had oversight for partnering activities. As a result, outside firms were occasionally granted exclusive agreements although it made little sense in Lotus's wider strategy. More commonly, outside firms received custom-made alliance contracts, although the level of managerial effort to write such contracts was completely inappropriate for the amount of business that relationship was likely to generate for Lotus.

Such chaos was not unique to Lotus and certainly does not reflect Lotus today. Many companies let their alliance network grow wild at the start, and only later intervene to bring order. The story of how Lotus did it is a good illustration of the challenges others will encounter and suggests how to overcome these challenges.

Falling into Chaos

Lotus's alliance with one large U.S. partner showed some of the trouble. The partner was a systems integrator and consultant, a firm that specialized in managing computer and telecommunications systems for large companies. In 1992, Lotus entered into a contract with it that made it a channel reseller of Notes, Lotus's hot new software.

The contract had two problems. First, the terms allowed the partner to undercut prices of other resellers, opening the gates for potentially massive conflict among Lotus's partner base. Second, the alliance focused on the one task Lotus seemed to need least: channel reselling. Lotus already had a huge group of resellers; what it required was the partner's expertise in consulting, systems integration, and applications development. "There are a couple of explanations of how we ended up with such an alliance," recalls Jim Adelson, director of business development at Lotus. "Lotus had a fragmented mentality, which probably encouraged us to not think through the wider implications of the pricing conflict. As for the focus on channel reselling, those were basically the types of alliances Lotus knew then how to do. We were just on autopilot."

The mistakes were not catastrophic. Other than this alliance (which was later successfully renegotiated), the problems hadn't contaminated most other parts of the company. As of 1992, Lotus was still internally driven, with alliances accounting for no more than 5 percent of total company revenue.

Explosion

But then Lotus Notes started to sizzle. Notes was fast becoming the standard for a new class of communications software that allowed groups of computer users to work together. By 1992, Lotus management realized that, if handled properly, Notes could become the industry standard, ending up on tens of millions of machines and earning hundreds of millions, if not billions, of dollars.

Lotus was utterly unprepared to realize this vision on its own. Unlike earlier Lotus products such as the best-selling 1-2-3 spreadsheet, Notes required all sorts of custom application development. It also demanded far more attention to customer planning, installation, integration, and after-sales service. "We just couldn't get Notes to market quickly enough, nor could we provide all the support Notes demanded," says Steve O'Neill, Lotus vice president of alliances from 1995 to 1996. "For every $1 of Notes business, there is probably $15 to $20 worth of ancillary business—everything from providing the hardware, training, support, right down the line. We simply couldn't provide that. We needed to find partners who could."

When Lotus CEO Jim Manzi and Bob Weiler, the SVP for sales, marketing, and support, realized this, they made a decision to transform the business model to one that depended on alliances, and to invest in an alliance infrastructure. No more hodgepodge approach to alliances. No more inconsistency. And no more alliances spanning uncontrolled across internal fiefdoms. Manzi went out and recruited Hemang Davé away from ComputerVision and gave him the charter to build an alliance organization. Davé became Lotus's first-ever vice president for strategic alliances. "I took the job on the condition that senior management would allow me to mortgage the short term for Lotus's long-term benefit," Davé recalls. "In fact, I am convinced that it ended up working so well that one of our partners, IBM, decided to pay a big premium to acquire us."

Fixing a Bad Deal

Davé was a master promoter and a diplomatic operator. He built a fifty-person alliance unit composed of some of the company's best and brightest talent. He established a tiering structure to ensure that nonstrategic alliances were never again mistaken for strategic ones. He persuaded Manzi and other senior executives that alliances could no longer be announced on a whim. And he opened multiple lines of communication and learning between senior management, alliance managers, and partners.

All of this was testament to Davé's ability to continually sell the concept of a collaborative capability. Yet for much of 1993, Davé was not building an overarching alliance infrastructure. Rather, he was busy putting out fires: "Step one was to roll up our sleeves and prevent from happening a couple of seriously bad alliances about to be signed. We also had to turn around alliances like the one with EDS, which offered us a lot but needed some adjusting. This allowed us to see what Lotus was all about, to see where the problems were, and to think about how we wanted to fix it. This approach built a lot of internal credibility for the alliance group. We were not preachers—we were the rescue team."

The real emergency was the IBM alliance. In 1991, Lotus had signed an agreement with the computer maker that gave IBM 33 percent of all Lotus Notes revenue, whether it generated the sale or not, in exchange for promoting the new software. This arrangement threatened the very viability of Notes. For Hemang Davé and other Lotus executives, much of 1993 was spent renegotiating with IBM. In the end, Lotus regained a large part of the Notes revenue in exchange for agreeing to develop software for IBM.

For Lotus executives, it was as if Davé, who led the renegotiation, had pulled a rabbit out of a hat. At last, the company had strong incentives to make Notes a success. On the heels of this win, senior management gave Davé the opportunity to build a wider alliance organization to support partners other than IBM. And they tipped the trough a bit to make sure he had ample resources. (Still later, of course, IBM acquired all of Lotus and Lotus became an important element in IBM's personal computer software business.)

Building the Framework

How did Lotus go about creating a collaborative core? "Lotus is not a very process-oriented place," Davé explains, "but we needed to organize these deals, create a common language and approach. We needed what I call a non-process process." Such sentiments were echoed by Davé's successor, Steve O'Neill: "We had all these disparate activities going on with major companies. We believed that if we organized and consolidated them we could turn it into a real strategic play."

A valuable ingredient in building the alliance organization was an independent strategy consultant, Dorothy Langer of Langer and Company in Boston, who first proposed the notion of a true partnering strategy to Davé over lunch in late 1993. Soon thereafter, Langer, Davé, and Adelson began to shape the new vision. To develop and refine their approach, they organized three different internal groups—a general forum, a task force, and a recurring workshop—and gave each a different role in building the processes, tools, and policies that were to underpin the collaborative core.

The Alliance Audit

The first step was to assemble a group of fifty or so Lotus executives and managers involved in alliances. The purpose was to tap into their deep and diverse experience so as to grasp the full range of alliance issues at Lotus and start to shape the overall direction of an alliance strategy and program. To kick things off, Langer presented a basic partnering framework that centered around five components: objectives, value, risks, obstacles, and boundary conditions. According to Langer: "If Lotus could articulate these with regard to its alliances, it would have a real strategy. They *are* the strategy."

Langer wanted them to transform her basic framework into something that was relevant to the Lotus situation. For example, she wanted the company to develop ten to twenty measurable objectives—such as revenue growth or market penetration—that it would seek through alliances. Lotus also needed to understand its value in alliances. "Your product is not your value," Langer explained to the managers. "If I need your product, I can go out and buy it." Langer wanted to know what Lotus would contribute to its alliances—brand recognition, momentum in the marketplace, an established customer base, or a crack development team.

She also wanted to understand the risks. "These are usually outside of the company's control," Langer explained. "Things like educating and abetting a competitor, losing staff to a partner, or creating a competitive reaction from a company like Microsoft." Finally, there needed to be an accounting of internal obstacles. Was, for instance, a key senior executive inherently hostile toward alliances?

"These lists were first conceived for the company as a whole," Langer notes. "Then, they would be used as a checklist for evaluating specific future alliances. So, for example, Lotus would look at a partner and ask 'What objectives of ours do they fulfill?' Of the twenty corporate-wide alliance goals, an individual partner might satisfy five or six."

This presentation was the first real worldwide discussion among Lotus alliance executives and managers. It provided feedback from a whole range of people within Lotus—technology developers, lawyers, marketers, and alliance managers. These were not just people from Davé's group. They came from the whole company, something which would later prove to be critical.

The Alliance Pyramid

Davé then created a task force. Made up of a dozen or so members from all over Lotus and assisted by Adelson and Langer, this group met every other week for nine months. The aim was to develop a coherent alliance strategy, including the tools and processes needed for success. One critical tool was the new Lotus alliance pyramid (Figure 29.1), which created a tiered structure for the company's partnerships. "What this did," recalls Davé, "was to let people know how much time and resources to devote to each one of these alliances." The Lotus alliances fell into this pyramid as follows:

- *Strategic*. These were long-term alliances that transformed the Lotus business model and touched multiple business functions. Such an alliance required substantial investment in technology development, as well as in retooling both companies' sales and support organizations. The firms expected the relationship to last for at least five to ten years. Lotus appointed a separate vice president to govern each of these relationships and make sure that it had the attention and support it needed to prosper.

- *Major*. These alliances were long-term and multifaceted, but did not change the Lotus business model. Major partners included hardware companies that bundled Notes with their computers and provided marketing, sales, and customer support, as well as system integrators. These partners received custom-written contracts and their own Lotus relationship managers. The latter formed a substantial portion of the staff of Davé's alliance unit.

FIGURE 29.1 How Lotus Organized Its 10,000+ Alliances, ca. 1995.

- *Project-Oriented.* These were alliances that were single-faceted, almost always in the pure technology realm. Just as a pharmaceutical company might align with a biotech firm, Lotus linked with a series of small entrepreneurial firms in the hope of generating product innovation.

- *Programmatic.* The final group of partners—and by far the largest in numbers—were the programmatic relationships. These were alliances that were managed as a group and entailed no customization. In 1995, Lotus had more than ten thousand programmatic alliances, the bulk of which were simple resellers. To govern and manage these relationships, Lotus created a separate unit known as the Lotus Business Partners Program and appointed a company vice president to oversee it.

Policies and Procedures

With the pyramid in place, the task force started to develop what Langer called corporate alliance "boundary conditions"—simple guidelines for how Lotus would approach alliances. "I suggested five never-to-be-violated rules," recalls Langer. "Things like: 'We will not share source code with a partner.' But the Lotus culture was just too free-wheeling to feel comfortable with 'never.' Instead of five iron laws, we created thirty-five 'rules of thumb.'"

One rule of thumb was to make sure that an alliance would account for at least 10 percent of both partners' revenue in the affected area. The reasoning was that such revenue levels led to commitment and helped ensure senior management attention.

Another rule of thumb was to be channel neutral. Lotus did not want to form alliances that simply moved business from one channel (that is, simple resellers) to another (that is, system integrators). Nor did it want one type of channel partner to be able to undercut another solely based on price.

A third rule of thumb was to build personal contacts that were broad enough to make the alliance not totally dependent on a single individual. Lotus was convinced that whereas alliances needed a champion and often an alliance manager, success depended on broader relationships. One reason was staff turnover, almost a given in the computer business. "But it goes beyond simply protecting against someone walking out the door," according to Adelson. "By relying on one individual, an alliance can be blocked from new and creative thinking. Also an alliance really suffers if that individual gets caught in a broader organizational restructuring." Someone who still has a job but whose power to act is reduced can no longer perform as alliance partners have been led to expect.

Spreading the Word

Davé then took the still-forming vision to Jim Manzi, who, according to Langer, "became totally committed to the partnering strategy." With Manzi's backing, Davé and Adelson then went out and gave their partnering presentation to virtually every senior executive in Lotus. "It was a way to establish a presence," notes Davé. "Sometimes we gave it individually to the vice president or senior vice president. Other times, they included their managers and others."

With the knowledge and commitment of senior management, the focus then turned to broader education. By early 1995, Langer and Adelson had developed and launched a customized training program. It was a one-day workshop given by Langer and aimed at delivering a coherent vision of alliances to the Lotus employees most involved in partnering. It was broad theory supported by Lotus-specific thinking, case studies, and rules of engagement. The plan was to put 250 to 300 Lotus employees through the workshop during 1995. (The IBM acquisition and concurrent reevaluation halted this effort midstream, with just over a hundred Lotus staffers participating in the workshop.)

An Organizational Home

The Lotus alliance program also included an alliance organization—a corporate home for many of the alliance staff, tools, systems, and processes. To oversimplify, the alliance group was located in the sales and marketing organization (Figure 29.2) and was led by a VP of alliances. It contained several directors and many relationship managers. At one level, the unit assumed the role of traditional business development, conceptualizing and initiating deals, and gathering, housing, and disseminating corporate wisdom on alliances. But it also had ongoing coordination and management responsibility for the alliances it formed.

According to Davé, the group's mission was clear: "We were to provide leadership, but we were not going to be the executors." This meant that resources gained as a result of an alliance were to be primarily allocated to the functional units that had the responsibility for delivery. So, for example, when Lotus signed a major expansion of the IBM alliance, the plan called for an additional staff of two hundred. Davé's group added a few heads of its own, but took the

FIGURE 29.2 Alliance Organization at Lotus, ca. 1995.

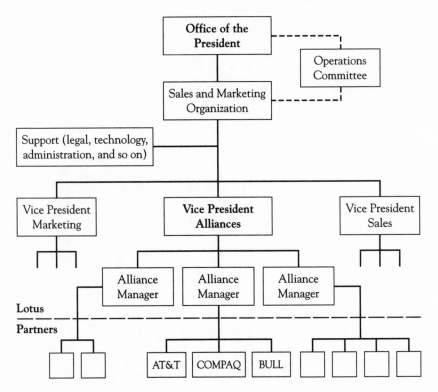

mass of the incremental funding and doled it out to sales, marketing, development, customer service, finance, and legal since each had new work associated with the enlarged alliance.

"We're a catalyst and a coordinator," reported Steve O'Neill. "And while all our major alliances span across multiple disciplines such as development, marketing and support, we don't necessarily do any of those functions ourselves. We don't write code, for example. We just make sure the tasks get done, and that the marketing department, for example, knows what the development department is doing."

As companies depend more on alliances, pressures grow to build a collaborative core—an institutional capability to form and manage alliances. Lotus Development did just this, creating the tools, processes, staff, and organizational structure needed to orchestrate its large portfolio of partnerships.

Further Reading

M. Bensaou. "Portfolios of Buyer-Supplier Relationships," *Sloan Management Review*, Summer 1999, pp. 35–44.

Carl Shapiro and Hal R. Varian. *Information Rules: A Strategic Guide to the Network Economy*. Boston: Harvard Business School Press, 1999. Chapters 8–9.

Source

This chapter is based on two articles in *The Alliance Analyst*, "Lotus Straightens House" and "Langer on Lotus" (December 1995). The articles have been combined and edited for this book.

30

From Art to Science

FedEx

David Payton was unsentimental about alliances. While other practitioners waxed poetic about trust, marriage, and the art of the alliance, Payton, Federal Express's managing director of strategic alliances, was terse. "There is no art to it," he claimed. "It is all science."

Indeed, Federal Express, one of the world's leading logistics companies, methodically built an impressive portfolio of alliances. The company's alliances fall into five categories: distribution, electronic marketing, technology, logistics, and co-locating.

This intense focus on alliances produced some systematic thinking on a number of issues, including choosing the right partner, matching the objectives of the alliance with the right structure, and prioritizing alliances. Speaking in 1998 from his experience in FedEx's Logistics and Electronic Commerce Division, Payton offered a peek inside the firm's quietly humming alliance machinery.

Finding the Partner

"Think of how long it takes to build a well-respected brand— and consider how quickly that brand will be tainted if you choose the wrong partner," Payton explained. Most companies have a method for choosing alliance partners, whether that method entails

canvassing the chairman's golfing pals or working through a detailed list of partner criteria. Federal Express was on the systematic side.

For FedEx, the first step was to determine what the company
needed from a partner. "You have to look at your strategic objectives
and base your choice of partner on a clearly defined, specific set of
needs that have to be filled," Payton noted. What knowledge, skills,
services, products, and technologies must the partner have? FedEx
made a list of those that were mandatory and those that were
optional. As the group of candidates was reduced to a handful, the
company considered corporate culture. Was the potential partner
the type to make investments for future growth, or was it completely
focused on the bottom line? Did the companies have a similar
approach to corporate management, R&D, leadership, and decision
making?

FedEx launched detailed research when only one good candidate remained. Exactly what did the partner bring to the alliance?
How would the market perceive the company and the alliance? How
would the alliance be perceived in the candidate partner company?
Payton learned the importance of these questions. One time, the
company spent months looking at a partner but didn't realize until
the negotiations that the partner planned to bring in contractors to
do the work.

FedEx also looked for any problems that the potential partner
had that might be transferred to FedEx. Did the partner have labor
relations troubles? Did it have a poor safety record?

Once the alliance team chose a partner, it took the deal before an alliance steering board composed of executives from all
over the company: marketing, IT, legal, sales, and operations.
The board members reviewed the deal on its proposed merits as
well as in light of their own needs. This meant that if the board
endorsed the alliance, its members were agreeing to commit resources to and champion the partner in their own functions and
units.

Structuring the Deal

As part of the process for evaluating an alliance, the FedEx alliance board also looked at the structure of the relationship. Although the characteristics and history of the individual deal clearly drove structure, the company also used some general guidelines to help make the choice. In particular, FedEx believed that the main goals of the alliance should have a strong bearing on the decision. For FedEx, alliances tended to have one of four main goals: cost or risk reduction, knowledge generation, market expansion, and new technology acquisition. Under each goal, the company developed a list of appropriate structures (Exhibit 30.1). For example, FedEx believed that the best structures for knowledge generation were joint development agreements and joint ventures.

EXHIBIT 30.1   Common Alliance Structures at FedEx, ca. 1997.

Cost or risk reduction
- Outsourcing
- Distribution agreement
- Licensing agreement
- Development agreement
- Joint venture

Knowledge generation
- Joint collaborative team
- Joint development
- Joint venture

Market expansion
- Distribution agreement
- Joint venture

New technology acquisition
- Licensing agreement
- Development agreement

The list was intended as a rough guide—not a set of steadfast managerial constraints. Likewise, some alliances had multiple goals, and managers had to make structural decisions under these more complex conditions. Also, managers sometimes found that the situation required them to use structures not prescribed in this list, for instance, using outsourcing agreements to enter certain overseas markets.

Prioritizing the Relationship

Determining the importance of the alliance was also essential to FedEx. According to Payton: "We have many more alliance opportunities than we have managers to pursue them. We have to have a way to prioritize." FedEx's solution was a mapping system. This tool plotted alliance opportunities along three dimensions: strategic value, resource requirements, and urgency (that is, how quickly the company needed to act on the opportunity). To keep things simple, each variable could only be labeled as high or low. The result was eight possible combinations, shown in Figure 30.1. Each was given a name and was associated with certain types of alliances.

This tool gave FedEx managers a quick sense of an alliance's value and requirements. For instance, licensing agreements with independent software vendors (who integrated FedEx software into their own programs) had low strategic value, low resource requirements, and low urgency. These alliances were worth doing, but they received little management attention and capital. At the other extreme, the alliances that were high in all three categories were what Payton referred to as "strategic inflection point" alliances—alliances so important as to fundamentally change the way the company works.

Approaching Science

FedEx's approach to alliances was not pure science, but in a field of warm truisms anything close was welcome. For example, FedEx's process for assessing potential partners was not revolutionary, but it

FIGURE 30.1   Alliance Mapping at FedEx, ca. 1997.

1. Ubiquity

Very common alliances that require little management. These are generally licensing agreements. Typical are alliances with independent software vendors to allow them to integrate FedEx software into their programs.

2. Marketplace
   position

Alliances that allow the company to move into a market before competitors. These are usually marketing agreements.

3. Resource
   drain

Nonstrategic work that needs to be performed. This is mostly outsourcing—such as fixing the Y2K bug in the firm's computers.

4. Operational
   necessity

Nonstrategic work that is more pressing than "resource drain." This includes outsourcing old services and products that have no growth potential but need to be maintained.

5. Expansion
   opportunity

Chances to distribute via a new channel or to deliver a new product. Typically, these are co-branding, co-locating, or distribution alliances.

6. Strategic
   alliances

Opportunities to advance the company's strategy quickly and cheaply.

7. Premium
   strategic
   alliances

Long-term investments that will be central to the company's strategy. They are generally joint ventures and joint development agreements.

8. Strategic
   inflection
   point

Deals that have the potential to fundamentally change the business. These are generally large joint ventures and acquistions.

Note: SV = Strategic value; U = Urgency; R = Resource requirements.

did spell out in clear logic and detail what the company needed in an alliance partner. It also had the benefit of forcing dealmakers to take each proposal before a broader audience—peers from elsewhere in the corporation who brought valuable perspectives. And the form listing alliance goals and structures was a useful starting point, although as Payton acknowledged, it was only that.

The mapping system was even more intriguing. The method appeared to have two main benefits: it forced executives to think about whether an alliance was worth doing and it gave senior management a sense of which alliances in a large portfolio of deals deserved the most attention and resources.

As a way of evaluating alliance opportunities, the mapping system made explicit what most executives understand implicitly—the need to know how an alliance fits strategically, how much it will cost, and how quickly it needs to get done. Perhaps the greatest value was found in the system's ability to classify the company's existing alliance portfolio. In this respect, the mapping system was a distant cousin of what some software companies like Lotus and others had done. These companies group their alliance portfolios into tiered pyramids, with a few crucial alliances at the top and the masses at the bottom. This allows senior executives to know which alliances they must focus on and which can be delegated to lower levels.

Ideally, what should a mapping system look like? The list will vary from company to company but a good system should do the following:

- Link value to resource requirements (including human resources, senior management time, and so on).
- Be easy to understand and used widely throughout the company.
- Have enough distinctions to be meaningful.
- Be flexible, allowing alliance partners to change categories as the alliance evolves.

FedEx's system seemed to meet these criteria, although it was unclear whether anyone beyond the dealmakers used it. True, it lacked the elegant simplicity of the pyramid model, but the pyramid model is a coarse screening device, suitable only for companies that have few different sorts of alliances. Lumping together licensing deals, joint ventures, and co-locating agreements in one tier, for example, may do nothing more than create confusion. FedEx slices its deals more finely, providing a more useful guide for executives.

FedEx's prescription is unlikely to suit all alliance practitioners. Most pharmaceutical firms, for instance, will undoubtedly have their own way of classifying the swarms of licensing agreements and research collaborations they form each year. Payton's unsentimental posture, however, is something even the most sophisticated practitioner would be wise to adopt.

Further Reading

Donald J. Bowersox. "The Strategic Benefits of Logistics Alliances," *Harvard Business Review*, July-Aug. 1990, pp. 2–8.

Source

This chapter is based on "The Cool Rationalist," *The Alliance Analyst* (June 1998). The article was edited for this book.

31

An Army of Diplomats

Eli Lilly

Nelson M. Sims, Roger G. Harrison, Anton Gueth

During eighteen months in 2000 and 2001, a team of executives at Eli Lilly & Co. focused on a single task: improving and institutionalizing the company's capabilities in creating value from its many alliances and partnerships, especially those with smaller biotech firms. Our mission was to invent the new culture and process we thought would be critical to the company's future. We were not revolutionaries working in a skunk works—we had a charter from the very top of the corporation.

All pharmaceutical companies want to get more new, innovative products to market as quickly and cost-efficiently as possible. To do that, they need new molecules and often new capabilities, skills, and sometimes simple capacity as well. To address some or all of these needs, virtually all major pharmaceutical companies, regardless of their overall business strategies, are increasingly relying on alliances. But although creating alliances may look like a relatively quick, cost-effective way to access new capabilities and keep the pipeline filled with new molecules, experience draws a different picture. Available data suggest that over half of all alliances fail to reach their intended outcome.

Some of that failure is normal, expected, and even valuable. Developing new medicines is a risky business, no matter how a company conducts it. We start off with far more good ideas, interesting concepts, and promising hypotheses than will ever result in validated targets for drug discovery, high-potential molecules, or novel drug delivery systems. The kind of natural winnowing that comes from testing our hypotheses and ideas and discovering what works and what doesn't is fundamental to the way we all learn.

That said, some failure in alliances has nothing to do with the risk inherent in hypothesis testing. Instead, the partners in the alliance simply couldn't figure out how to work together. Recognizing the difference between *technical* failure and *relationship* failure prompted a Lilly board member to ask the question that sparked the company's quest to improve the way it managed alliances: "If partnerships have been and will be increasingly important to Lilly's future, what is management doing to improve the organization's partnering capabilities?" In response, the special team came up with a system with which they soon ran all corporate alliances—the Lilly Alliance Management Process (LAMP).

While LAMP may sound bureaucratic, it was simply a road map used to streamline and simplify the process. Such systems exist to manage critical components of companies. And if Lilly was to be serious about a capability in alliances, it needed to systematize its approach—training managers, creating management structures, and assessing success according to predetermined criteria, all with the goal of making alliances work better.

Successful Alliances: First Principles

The team began by taking stock: reviewing current procedures, best practices, and the needs of existing alliance partners. To some extent, the review pointed out what the team already knew—that Lilly had been engaged in alliances and alliance management for a long time, at least since the 1920s when we began working with University of Toronto scientists Frederick G. Banting and Charles H. Best, who had isolated insulin and demonstrated its value in managing insulin-dependent diabetes. They had identified the molecule; Lilly had the capabilities to optimize its production and market it. The development of insulin was one of the great project management challenges of its day, with a very short timeline required in the agreement with the university. But it was astoundingly successful—for patients without treatment options for an otherwise fatal disease, and for the partners. By 1985, insulin had become a $400 million franchise for Lilly.

The next stage of the diabetes story was also partnership-based: Genentech Inc. cloned and then licensed to Lilly recombinant human insulin *(Humulin)*, which—along with its Lilly-modified analog molecule, *Humalog*—accounted for almost 100 percent of Lilly's total insulin sales in 2001. Nor had Lilly come up with its own oral anti-diabetic. It licensed it in through a co-promotion with Takeda Chemical Industries Ltd.: in 2001—after two years on the market—pioglitazone *(Actos)* was generating total U.S. revenues of over $600 million and was the fastest-growing drug in its class. Further alliances, such as Lilly's collaboration with Alkermes Inc. on inhaled insulin, were expected to build the franchise with new drug delivery technologies.

This history may have lulled the company into thinking it had greater alliance management capabilities than it actually had—at least until the Lilly board member asked the pointed question.

The initial review did reveal a basic pattern that alliances go through: a "find each other" phase (usually with the large pharmaceutical company finding the smaller company that has a molecule or technology of interest), a "negotiating phase" (which the big company often thinks of as the "get it" phase), and the actual alliance implementation or business partnership phase. Considerations about whether the partners could actually work well together were rarely considered explicitly, especially in phases one and two. And when they were considered in phase three, they were treated as secondary to the primary objective of moving the project forward on time and on budget.

The internal review of Lilly practices raised the suspicion that the company might have, in some cases, been lucky rather than proficient at alliance management. The successes clearly were more dependent on the individual talent and goodwill of people involved in alliances—from both sides—than on any kind of systematic management procedure. Nobody was following a particular process that focused on improving alliance results. Few were capturing information about failures and successes in a formal way and sharing what they learned throughout the organization.

The team's review of external best practices, provided by consultants from Accenture and by a survey of Lilly's actual partners, confirmed and elaborated what the internal review showed. The findings from an external survey (conducted by Pricewaterhouse-Coopers) were particularly telling. Alliances failed most frequently, said respondents, because of "cultural and process differences" between the partners. If these were addressed and accounted for, alliances were more likely to succeed. Technical issues actually ranked sixth in contributing to the success or failure of an alliance.

Indeed, badly managed relationships could erect barriers to scientific success on a given project. Perhaps more important, they would prevent the partners from working with each other again. In the long run, Lilly wanted its relationships to succeed so that partnerships could potentially work on other projects, and thereby increase the odds of scientific success. The company also wanted a reputation for partnering excellence that would allow it to be even more successful in gaining access to key partnership opportunities.

The survey work also confirmed what the internal analysis had suggested—that Lilly had some work to do if it were to become first-in-class at alliance management. The survey showed that Lilly was better than the average company in most attributes and categories that went into being a good partner: trustworthiness and credibility, organization and management, culture and values. But the survey also showed that the company needed to improve if it wished to be the leading firm in the industry on any of the attributes in these categories. In fact, Lilly was the number-one company in only two attributes: having a track record of successful partnerships and trustworthiness.

Based on the survey results and discussions with partners, the team identified several broad areas where they thought Lilly could improve its partnering capabilities. In effect, it needed to manage the alliance process just as rigorously as it managed product development activities.

Putting Principles into Practice

LAMP was the logical result of this work, as illustrated in Figure 31.1. The first new component was the Office of Alliance Management (OAM), which would be integrator, intermediary, and catalyst for best practice performance. If alliances were to work, there had to be an organization responsible for making them work.

The biggest responsibility for the OAM in any particular alliance would be to serve as the advocate for the collaboration itself, not for one side or the other. Its aim would be not simply to get the best results for Lilly but to get the best results for the partnership. This image of the organization as a kind of alliance ombudsman represented a major shift for Lilly, as it would for any organization, large or small, accustomed to concentrating on its own interests.

Indeed, because they were embarking on such a different path, the team also needed to make the roles and responsibilities of those involved in leadership of alliances clear to people inside and outside Lilly—and perhaps it was most important to reach those inside. Its analysis showed that lack of clarity for key leadership roles was one of the leading elements of alliance failure.

Roles of Key Alliance Executives

Every alliance was seen to have its own three-person management lead team responsible for the collaboration's success—an alliance champion, an alliance leader, and an alliance manager.

The *alliance champion*, usually a senior executive, was responsible for overall support and oversight of the alliance. Probably the most important responsibility of the champion was to facilitate or ensure communication between Lilly and its alliance partners by

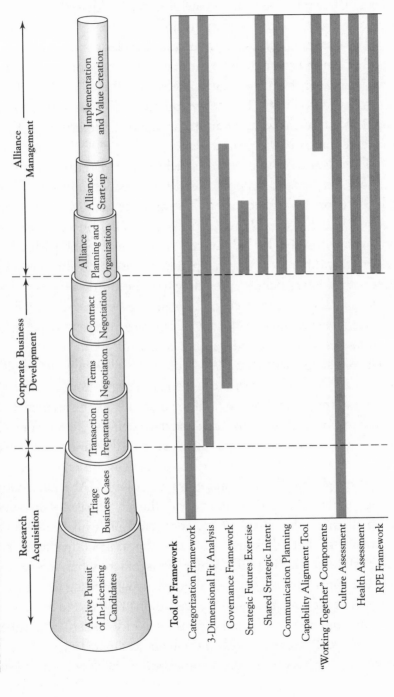

FIGURE 31.1 Process and Tools in the Lilly Alliance Management Process (LAMP), ca. 2001.

Source: Eli Lilly.

breaking down the normal bureaucratic barriers that can get in the way of a smooth working relationship.

The *alliance leader*, usually a technical leader, a project manager, or other senior person with an intimate knowledge of the area, was responsible for the day-to-day leadership of the alliance, and was ultimately accountable for the overall program. This meant ensuring that the teams were committed, capable, and united in their implementation of the project plan.

The *alliance manager* represented the OAM. This executive's primary duty was to support the alliance leader and serve as an advocate for the alliance itself. The alliance manager was essentially devoted to the alliance process and to business integration, and was responsible for helping the alliance leader and partners to resolve any differences that happened to arise. The alliance manager's other duties included providing training and development and serving as chief diagnostician in assessing the health of the alliance.

In a more general role, the alliance manager supported a portfolio of alliances, and so could capture and codify knowledge about alliance management that OAM could use in helping future alliances. Lilly deliberately recruited alliance managers from a wide variety of internal disciplines including corporate affairs, finance, and marketing, not only from research and development. As relationship integrators, their fundamental skills had to be listening to what was really being said and appreciating and influencing other people.

Although the alliance manager was part of the OAM, Lilly found it important for the manager to live with the functional area involved in an alliance. The alliance manager then could truly be seen as a partner within the business. As such, the alliance manager was responsible for alerting Lilly senior management when leadership problems arose. In one deal, an alliance manager recognized that a majority of the combined alliance team didn't understand the objectives and direction of the alliance: the alliance leader—a scientist otherwise well respected within the team as the technical chief— wasn't leading. Upon the recommendation of the alliance manager, the scientist became technical leader of the collaboration and a new overall alliance leader was appointed; the alliance's productivity improved markedly after this.

The responsibilities and degree of involvement of the OAM and the alliance manager varied from alliance to alliance. The alliance manager was always available for consultation and facilitation. But the manager was not always directly involved in day-to-day activities of the alliance. The alliance manager tended to be less involved with alliances with less strategic importance to Lilly and with lower management complexity; alliances that were both complex and of high strategic importance needed the heaviest commitment.

Alliance Managers During the Process

Initially, the OAM came in after the deal was completed, focused on making sure processes were thoroughly outlined following contract signatures. But the handoff from business development to alliance management proved to be too abrupt: Lilly's partners had to reorient themselves to an entire new group of individuals.

The OAM thus changed the process: an alliance manager began to visit the potential partner during Lilly's due diligence, trying to understand the partner's organization and culture. The goal was to identify ways to meld, not change, the two companies' cultures. During the contract negotiation itself, the alliance manager focused on governance principles. And once the deal was signed, the alliance manager coordinated the first interactions with the new members of the team and helped set the alliance's initial agenda.

Historically Lilly had appointed as alliance leader a project manager who focused on getting the alliance off to a fast start. Agendas for the initial alliance meetings revolved around tasks: they laid out project plans in great detail, assigned work responsibilities, and set expectations as to when the first deliverable milestones had to be met. It was not unusual for teams to be deep into technical discussions within hours of their first meeting.

Yet these alliances had sometimes performed poorly. The success of any alliance greatly depended on the strength of the relationships among individuals in both partners. The new kick-off meeting agendas developed by the OAM therefore started with social issues and focused on team building. The alliance manager and leader used widely published team exercises such as "Best Friend" and "Mission Possible" to get members from both companies to know each other, figure out ways of working together, and formulate and commit to a shared definition of the alliance objectives and goals.

Paradoxically, the alliance manager's initial involvement in an alliance often included persuading the partners that they needed to slow down and not take immediate action toward the alliance's technical goals. They first needed to put in place a solid foundation for their relationship and develop an understanding of what they were building together, how they would work together, and how they would respond to issues that undoubtedly would arise during the project.

The Tool Kit

To help them put such a foundation in place, the alliance managers used an extensive tool kit that Lilly developed. The kit documented processes, tools, frameworks, and approaches that the manager could use to support the alliance leader and the alliance itself at each phase of its development. Among other things, there were tools to clarify and gain consensus on the strategic intent of the alliance; to identify, align, and leverage the capabilities of both partners; to map and align the work processes of each partner so that they could more effectively work together; and to assess an alliance's health.

One of the tools was the Alliance Health Survey; the OAM used this to check the health of a given alliance on a regular basis. It sent a survey to all employees of the alliance from both companies; the Web-based questionnaire covered fourteen distinct dimensions that had been identified as key indicators for alliance success.

The results from two actual Lilly alliances are compared in Figure 31.2, which plots the feedback from both companies. Alliance A shows significant signs of stress, while Alliance B appears to be in good health, with each partner assessing the alliance similarly and favorably. The overall assessment of Alliance A is moderate at best (average favorable ratings 60–70 percent), with significant differences in the assessments of both partners. The collaboration clearly needed help.

This assessment tool allowed the alliance leader and manager in Alliance A to provide help where it was most needed—changing processes, using a "strategic futures" tool to realign the partners, and redeploying certain team members. Six months later, the collaboration was more productive and the team members reported a much healthier and robust working relationship that allowed them to address issues much more proactively.

Alliance B required no particular intervention. However, the results were shared with the combined team to reemphasize the importance of the quality of the relationship for the desired outcomes.

Institutionalizing the Lessons Learned

Yet another of the OAM's important tools, a database called *Partners*, aimed at a third component of the alliance management plan: to capture, codify, and systematically share what the OAM was learning about partnering skills. Lilly knew it wanted the OAM to be a learning organization, which also meant being a teaching organization. To achieve that, it needed to specify learning as someone's clear responsibility and develop a tool to support it.

In this case, the primary responsibility for capturing and sharing what the OAM learned belonged to the alliance manager. At each point in the process, the alliance manager used a repertoire of tools to help facilitate the partnership and reported the results of each use—including an evaluation of a tool's effectiveness in a given situation and a description of modifications that might improve its effectiveness.

FIGURE 31.2 LAMP Tool: Rating the Health of an Alliance (percentage of team members rating each dimension as favorable or very favorable).

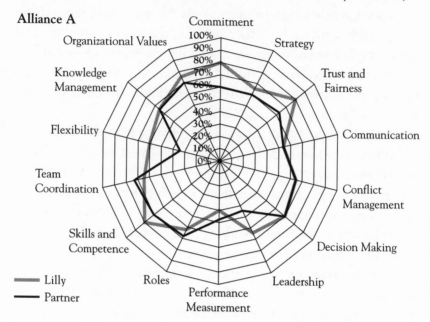

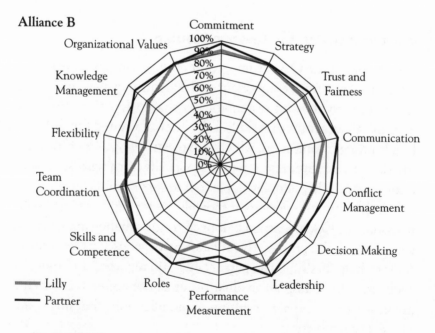

Source: Eli Lilly.

The *Partners* online database contained information about all of Lilly's 140 alliances, including a high-level overview, the collaboration contract, governance agreements and minutes, lessons learned, milestone and budget reporting, as well as all the existing tools and processes and online instruction on how to use them. It could be accessed by anyone responsible for, or involved with, an alliance.

The database facilitated training, helping those involved in alliances develop their skills in using the fundamental tools and processes. Training was part of the formal orientation sessions at the beginning of a new alliance. The OAM also provided help on an as-needed basis.

In its first year, the OAM trained nearly five hundred Lilly managers and research scientists. It also held its first "alliance summit," where external alliance experts and Lilly senior management reinforced the importance of alliances to an audience of almost a hundred key managers in Lilly and discussed best practices that they could help instill in the organization. The point these sessions reinforced over and over again: create an appropriate partnering culture for the company.

Much of the educational component provided by the OAM was designed for alliance leaders and alliance champions. The OAM shared with them the business case for alliances, so they clearly understood the importance of the alliance to Lilly. It made sure they understood the kinds of behaviors that were more likely to help a partnership succeed, which largely means treating the needs and interests of Lilly's partners with the same care as Lilly's own needs and interests.

The Return on Investment

Does the substantial investment that Lilly made in its alliance program yield a positive return on investment? Although indications were promising, it was too early for a definitive answer at the time this chapter was originally written. Most other pharmaceutical companies have no such process, so it was not possible to say that the Lilly process led to some of the difference in performance between Lilly and comparable companies.

The OAM and Lilly senior management certainly were convinced that they were making Lilly a more partner-friendly organization. At the level of individual partners, their annual Alliance Health Surveys showed that the new management processes were working. Survey respondents told Lilly that it had materially improved its ability to recognize and resolve difficulties in a partnership, and that it did so at an earlier stage, before they could become barriers to success. The qualitative evidence was also compelling. For instance, the company's alliance partners more and more frequently called the OAM to ask its counsel on the best way to work with Lilly; they clearly viewed the OAM as an honest broker.

Lilly's team believed that this kind of brand management—promoting the idea that Lilly cared about its partnerships—would in the end win them more key partners. Economically, they believed, the deals were going to be much the same: valuable new products and technologies would command relatively similar deal prices. The fact that more and more of the most sought-after products were effectively auctioned among potential partners would ensure that. But Lilly bet that its edge would be nonfinancial: it hoped to stand out in its ability to make an alliance successful.

Further Reading

David Champion. "Mastering the Value Chain: An Interview with Mark Levin of Millennium Pharmaceuticals," *Harvard Business Review*, June 2001, pp. 108–115.

David J. Teece. "Profiting from Technological Innovation: Implications for Integration, Collaboration, Licensing and Public Policy," *Research Policy*, 1986, *15*, 285–305.

Source

This chapter is based on "Managing Alliances at Lilly," *In Vivo*, 2001, *19*(6). Used here with permission of *In Vivo*'s publisher, Windhover Information Inc. of Norwalk, Conn.

About the Authors

James D. Bamford is an alliance consultant in Washington, D.C. His client work focuses on a broad range of alliance issues, including alliance strategy, governance and organizational design, alliance restructuring, and portfolio performance diagnostic. Bamford was co-founder and editor of *The Alliance Analyst*, the leading management strategy publication on alliances. He has also worked as a researcher at Harvard Business School and as a management consultant for an affiliate of Booz-Allen & Hamilton in Asia. He holds degrees from Tufts University, the London School of Economics, and Harvard University.

Benjamin Gomes-Casseres is a professor at Brandeis University's Graduate School of International Economics and Finance and principal of Alliance Strategy Consulting in Lexington, Massachusetts. He wrote *The Alliance Revolution: The New Shape of Business Rivalry* (Harvard University Press, 1996), edited two other books, and authored over twenty articles and chapters on alliances and international business; his work has been cited in the *New York Times*, the *Wall Street Journal*, and other business periodicals. A frequent speaker at industry conferences, he has been a consultant and executive trainer at leading companies, including Motorola, Sun Microsystems, Bell-South, Abbott Laboratories, DuPont, and DaimlerChrysler. He has taught executive courses on alliance strategy at Brandeis, Harvard, and on the Web. His Web site, AllianceStrategy.com, has been cited by *Forbes* Best-of-the-Web, and offers educational and managerial resources for alliance management. Prior to Brandeis, Gomes-Casseres was a professor at the Harvard Business School (1985–1995). Before that, he was an economist at the World Bank. He also holds degrees from Harvard, Princeton, and Brandeis Universities.

Michael S. Robinson is an alliance consultant in Sydney, Australia. He was co-founder and publisher of *The Alliance Analyst*—the leading management strategy publication on alliances. He has conducted joint research on alliances with management consulting firms including McKinsey, Boston Consulting Group, and Accenture. Robinson has also launched a number of publications including Taiwan's first English-language magazine on business and finance. Previously he worked as a management consultant for an affiliate of Booz-Allen & Hamilton in Asia, and a business development officer for a global insurance company. He holds degrees from The Wharton School and the University of Sydney.

Contributing Authors

Ashwin Adarkar is a principal in McKinsey & Company's Los Angeles office. He is a leader of the firm's west coast financial services practice. He also helped establish the firm's practice in India. Prior to joining McKinsey, Adarkar worked with Goldman, Sachs & Co. He holds M.B.A., M.S., and B.A. degrees from Stanford University. He has published in the *McKinsey Quarterly* and several business publications.

Asif Adil is managing director of Adil & Associates, a financial and management advisory firm. Previously, he was the chief financial officer of Lumenis, Inc., a medical technology company, and a partner at McKinsey & Company. During his twelve years at McKinsey, he worked in India, the Middle East, and the United States, and served as a leader of the firm's global alliance practice and its North American pharmaceutical and consumer practices.

David Ernst is a principal at McKinsey & Company and the leader of the firm's global alliance practice. He has served several hundred industrial and consumer companies on alliance-related engagements involving corporate strategy, alliance transaction, and post-deal management issues. His research and perspectives on alliances, acquisitions, and other topics have been published in over forty-five articles in the *Harvard Business Review*, the *Wall Street Journal*, the *Financial Times*, the *McKinsey Quarterly*, and other publications. He is coauthor with Joel Bleeke of *Collaborating to Compete*. Ernst was a member of *The Alliance Analyst's* advisory board, and a frequent contributor to that publication.

Stephen I. Glover is a partner in the Washington, D.C.-based law firm Gibson, Dunn & Crutcher and a member of the firm's Corporate Transactions Practice Group. He has an extensive practice representing public and private companies, including investment banks and venture capital firms, in complex mergers and acquisitions, joint ventures, and debt offerings. Glover is the author or coauthor of more than fifty articles and several books, including *Financial Institutions Acquisitions and Alliances*. He earned his law degree at Harvard and his undergraduate degree from Amherst College.

Anton Gueth is director of alliance management at Eli Lilly & Company. The alliance group he leads enhances Lilly's partnering capabilities by implementing processes and tools designed to build relationships that maximize value for both sides. Gueth earned a master's degree in agricultural economics from Justus-Liebig University in Giessen, Germany, and a master's in public affairs from Indiana University.

Roger G. Harrison joined Antares Pharma Inc. as CEO and a member of its Board of Directors in March 2001. Since 1984, Harrison held various leadership positions at Eli Lilly & Company, most recently as director of alliance management, where he helped to focus on the value of corporate alliances as part of the company's core business strategy. He has a continued interest in drug delivery technologies, including assessment and implementation of drug delivery programs. He has authored twelve publications and contributed to four books, and he holds nine patents. Harrison earned a Ph.D. in organic chemistry and a B.Sc. in chemistry from Leeds University in the United Kingdom; he conducted postdoctoral research work at Zurich University in Switzerland.

Bruce Kogut is the Felix Zandman Professor at the Wharton School, University of Pennsylvania. He has been a visiting researcher at the Ecole Polytechnique, INSEAD, Stockholm School of Economics, Humboldt University, and the Wissenschaftszentrum Center, Berlin. He has published extensively on alliances, privatization, and international competition. MIT Press recently published his edited book on the global Internet economy. Peter Cornelius of the World Economic Forum and he are publishing an edited book on global corporate governance with Oxford University Press.

Francine G. Pillemer is a partner with CMI Concord Group and an instructor in psychology, Department of Psychiatry, Harvard Medical School. Her advisory work focuses on the negotiation and relationship management issues that occur during consolidation and staff integration efforts. She has taught negotiation throughout the world and appeared in various multimedia products with her colleague Roger Fisher, co-author of *Getting to Yes* and founder of the Harvard Negotiation Project. She holds an undergraduate degree from the University of Michigan and master's and doctoral degrees from Harvard University in counseling and consulting psychology.

Stephen G. Racioppo is managing partner, new business models, for Accenture's global Financial Services practice. He has consulted on global financial markets for more than twenty-seven years and has written and lectured throughout the world on alliances, globalization, multisourcing, and IT transformation. Racioppo is frequently cited in the *Wall Street Journal, Fortune, Institutional Investor,* and numerous other publications. He serves on several corporate and civic boards and has a bachelor's degree from Rensselaer Polytechnic Institute.

Charles Roussel is a lead partner with Accenture, where he runs the firm's global Consumer Electronics segment. His areas of expertise include marketing strategy, strategic alliances, and corporate restructuring. He founded the firm's Mergers, Acquisitions, and Alliances Center of Excellence, and served as global director of thought leadership. Prior to joining Accenture in 1988, Roussel worked for the Yankee Group and for AT&T. He holds an MBA from the University of Chicago and an undergraduate degree from Bentley College.

Nelson M. Sims currently serves on the boards of directors of several biotech and health care companies. Sims retired from Eli Lilly & Company in 2001 following a twenty-eight-year career that included U.S. and international executive assignments. His senior positions at Lilly included vice president of sales and marketing for Hybritech Inc., president of Eli Lilly Canada Inc., and executive director of alliance management. Sims was the founding executive of Lilly's corporate strategic alliance management initiative.

Gene Slowinski is director of strategic alliance research at the Graduate School of Management, Rutgers University, and managing partner of the Alliance Management Group of Gladstone, New Jersey, a consulting firm devoted to the formation and management of strategic alliances, mergers, and acquisitions. For the last twenty years Slowinski has consulted and conducted research on the formation and management of alliances. His clients include Glaxo-SmithKline, Merck, Lucent Technologies, Motorola, Johnson & Johnson, ExxonMobil, AT&T, Becton Dickinson, Procter & Gamble, Battelle, and many other Fortune 500 firms.

Paresh Vaish is a senior principal at McKinsey & Company's office in Mumbai, India. He has been with the firm since 1986 and has advised clients on corporate strategy, operational improvement, and organizational change. Vaish leads McKinsey's Indian operations practice and has worked extensively with clients in the automotive sector. Prior to McKinsey, he was employed by Intel Corporation and has worked as a software engineer. He holds degrees from Dartmouth College and Harvard Business School.

Laura J. Visioni is a senior associate at Vantage Partners LLC, a consulting firm that specializes in helping Global 1000 companies improve how they negotiate, build, and manage their most critical relationships with customers, suppliers, and partners. A founding member of the firm, Visioni has consulted across industries to companies seeking to improve alliance performance, and has led Vantage Partners' ongoing research and reporting on alliance and partner relationship management. She is a graduate of Johns Hopkins University.

Jeff Weiss is a founding partner of Vantage Partners LLC. Weiss's practice focuses on improving the negotiation and management of partner relationships, with an emphasis on alliances, joint ventures, and outsourcing deals. Prior to Vantage, he held positions at Conflict Management Inc., Conflict Management Group, and the Harvard Negotiation Project. Weiss is a graduate of Dartmouth College and Harvard Law School, and is the author of a number of articles about negotiation, conflict management, and relationship management.

Index